MW00795717

ROMAN HELMETS

ROMAN HELMETS

HILARY & JOHN TRAVIS

AMBERLEY

First published 2014

Amberley Publishing
The Hill, Stroud
Gloucestershire, GL5 4EP

www.amberleybooks.com

British Library Cataloguing in Publication Data.
A catalogue record for this book is available from the British Library.

ISBN 978-1-4456-3842-3 (hardback)
ISBN 978-1-4456-3847-8 (ebook)

Typeset in 10pt on 12pt Sabon.
Typesetting and Origination by Amberley Publishing.
Printed in Great Britain.

CONTENTS

LIST OF TABLES

LIST OF ILLUSTRATIONS

LIST OF COLOUR PLATES

ACKNOWLEDGEMENTS

This book has been the result of a team effort with my husband, J. R. Travis, who has provided most of the photography and illustrations, along with the provision of on-tap supplies of coffee and brain-inspiring nibbles.

I should also like to express my special thanks to Marcus Vlpivs Nerva (Martin McAree) and other members of Legion Ireland Roman Group for their invaluable assistance in providing photographs of their equipment; and to D. Flockton Photography, for providing photographs of members of Deva V.V.

For the most part, however, this book was produced as a means to keep me out of mischief and to save me from terminal boredom during an infinitely forgettable year of serious illness, many weeks of which were spent as a reluctant guest of several local hospitals. I should therefore like to dedicate this book to the doctors and nursing staff at Southport District General Hospital and at Liverpool Heart and Chest Hospital, without whom I would not have been here to complete the following work.

I should also like to thank our many friends within the re-enactment community for their well wishes and support during my illness, particularly the Poor Knights of St Dysmas, who made welcome and pampered an invalid at their camp for a few escapist medieval weekends.

I

INTRODUCTION

BACKGROUND TO THE RESEARCH

The conventional public view of the Roman army comes from a number of sources: art, early filmography (the history according to Hollywood) and romantic literature. The academic viewpoint differs from these popular views, based on more solid, tangible evidence: ancient literature, sculptures, wall paintings and archaeological finds. In more recent years this has produced more reliable, evidence-based views of the Roman military, as portrayed in museums and by living history re-enactments.

The original study arose out a perceived weakness in current research into Roman military equipment. The conventional view still focussed primarily on the legionary soldier of the Imperial period, following the stereotypical image of uniformity, as seen depicted on Trajan's column, with all legionaries equipped in segmented iron cuirass (*lorica segmentata*) and auxiliaries in mail (*lorica hamata*) or scale (*lorica squamata*).

However, reality was somewhat different, with information on design, construction, developmental progression and use of equipment by the Roman military offered from a variety of sources – literary, sculptural and archaeological. These suggest that there was a range of equipment in use, often contemporaneously, serving a variety of military functions. In addition, these basic functional types further exhibit developmental changes over time as they adapt to changing fighting styles, enemy weaponry and external cultural influences.

As the Roman army existed for over a millennium, the basic components of their defensive armour assemblage would have been subject to continuous improvement and adaptation to whatever were their current conditions and requirements. As the Romans did not exclusively invent and develop armour, each piece of equipment would have had a 'history' beyond that of the Roman army, and consequently it was necessary to view the pre-Roman origins as part of the 'bigger picture'.

By establishing, therefore, the basic chronology of the origins of the Roman army and of its equipment, following this through time to view developments and innovations in equipment design, in comparison to 'current' events and the changing political and organisational climate, it is possible to theorise on possible reasons for the introduction of many design changes. The term 'changes' here perhaps is more appropriate than 'innovation', as not all 'changes' were necessarily improvements. The chronological changes noted in the panoply were then also echoed in the changing social structure of the army, with expansion of the boundaries of eligibility for military service and the transition from independently funded 'volunteers' to a modern, 'paid' professional army.

The range of equipment studied in this series of three books, restricted to defensive armour alone (body armour, shield and helmet), was also a deliberate choice, based on those items deemed most important in equipping the earliest Roman armies. It also permitted the discussion of the most commonly used materials (bronze, iron, leather and wood) and would therefore include aspects of virtually all of the activities of the military workshop, or *fabrica*.

Where my previous books have dealt with the body armour and shields used by the Roman military (legionary, auxiliary and cavalry), this book will complete the panoply of defensive equipment by taking a more in-depth view of the Roman helmet, discussing its origins (whether 'home-grown', or as a nostalgic 'homage' to classical Hellenic histories, or if drawn from the influences of Gallic/Celtic adversaries) and subsequent developmental progression in shape and function in answer to needs arising and technological advances.

However, when considering current research into Roman helmets it was noted that two different methods of helmet typology are currently in use, causing considerable confusion in the identification of Roman helmet types. The British system of helmet categorisation was devised by H. Russell-Robinson, based on his perception of developmental progression and features which he thought may indicate the geographical origin of the craftsmen involved in their manufacture, identifying some features as 'Gallic' and others as 'Italic'.

The Continental system, in contrast, uses a system based on the names of finds locations. It is far simpler to use, with less headings (which explains its popularity), although this benefit is also its weakest aspect, in that it is too generalised to best show developmental progression. With these dual systems in use, confusion abounds, compounded with the difficulty now in obtaining copies of the Russell-Robinson work for comparison (his definitive 1975 work having been out of print for many years). For this reason it was decided that the inclusion of a comparison between these typologies would be beneficial. A full gazetteer of all known Roman helmets, to indicate for each entry both 'Continental' and Russell-Robinson typologies, was therefore also included.

This list was further augmented by the inclusion of a large number of helmets from private collections. However, many of these did not fit neatly into the Russell-Robinson categorisations, which then would have required an even more unwieldy number of additional categories. This highlights the wide variety of helmets available, suggesting that, rather than viewing helmets as closely fitting into categories, we should perhaps be looking at the general trends in the development of main features over time, with minor differences indicative of a wide range of different workshops in operation and expressing the individuality of the craftsmen working within them.

THE STUDY OF ROMAN MILITARY EQUIPMENT

The study of the past is as old as the past itself, with the Roman 'historians' of our 'classical' literature reflecting on their own ancient origins. As our literary sources exist now as written reflections, this gives the impression that their primary interests were the political and social interactions of individuals rather than visual imagery. However, even in the Roman period, imagery was used on wall paintings (as seen at Pompeii) depicting images from mythology and presumably also from more ancient histories. This imagery would, however, have been based on contemporary styles of architecture, clothing and weaponry, with the exception of some 'classical' Greek-style idealised armour for representations of deities. This tendency to make use of contemporary styles of dress for subjects from the distant past can still be seen to exist in more recent periods, where the artists (or their intended audience) were perhaps unable to comprehend the passage of time.

Up to the seventeenth century, for example, figures in the past, including those of the Roman period, were portrayed artistically dressed in a style contemporary with the artist. An example of this is the portrait of William the Conqueror, commissioned by the Vatican in 1522 on the reopening of his tomb, where he is depicted in a sixteenth-century costume (half a millennium after his death), a copy of which still exists at St Etienne (Wood, 1981, 243, plate 29). Similarly from the sixteenth century, engravings by Andreas Alciati (*Emblemata*, 1581) depict Roman soldiers dressed in costumes of that period, but in a style which suggests a time of culture and grace, in much the same way that the Romans themselves appear to have viewed the culture of classical Greece in their own artistic representations (Feugère, 2002, 19).

However, during the eighteenth and nineteenth centuries, following the discoveries in Herculaneum and Pompeii and the introduction of 'Neoclassicism', artists began to portray the Roman soldier in more authentic dress, basing their views on images from ceremonial sculptures such as Trajan's Column. This can be seen in the engravings by Saint Sauveur in

1787, by Rich in his *Dictionary of Roman Antiquities* in 1861 (Feugère, 2002, 20), and even in the twentieth century in the work of Couissin (1926), although these still depict an image of artificially genteel culture and not one of battle-hardened professional soldiers who, in their time, had conquered half of the known world.

A more enlightened attempt at authenticity, using both sculptural and archaeological evidence, can be credited to Jacques Louis David (1748–1825) who painted a series of scenes with a Roman theme, including *The Oath of the Horatii*, which was inspired by Corneille's tragedy *Horace*. As an example of Neoclassicism, his painting depicts a dramatic instant within a setting of Roman-style architecture. The clothing was based on imagery from wall paintings, as found at Pompeii, and the armour on sculptural representations, such as those seen on Trajan's Column, so that his depictions were as close as he felt possible to current (for his time) archaeological and sculptural evidence, although in a somewhat theatrical style. Other paintings in the series include *The Lictors Bringing Brutus the Bodies of His Sons* (1789) and *The Rape of the Sabines* (1799), painted from Livy's *Early History of Rome*, although these are of limited use in depicting military equipment, the former containing no armour and the latter depicting naked warriors armed with just helmets and weapons. Based on a study of available archaeological evidence, their purpose was not to depict historical events but rather to echo contemporary events of the French Revolution, the artist himself being a member of the Convention, voting for the death of the French king (Lucie-Smith, 1971, 175–6).

Despite the work being carried out at Herculaneum and Pompeii, and at the forts along Hadrian's Wall, the early historians and antiquarians continued to use, as their main source of references for their image of the Roman soldier, images from grave stones, coins, small bronze and terracotta figurines, the Column of Marcus Aurelius and Trajan's Column. Of these, Trajan's Column was seen as the definitive image of the Roman army.

The development of what we would recognise today as 'real' archaeology commenced in the later nineteenth century (as opposed to the work of early antiquarian 'collectors'), with systematic and organised excavation of sites (such as those along the German *Limes* from 1892 onwards). The publication of these excavations has led to a greater knowledge base upon which to build increasingly more plausible reconstructions.

Our current knowledge of the Roman military and its equipment is still nevertheless of an organic nature, constantly changing and updating with new finds, developing an expanding bank of available information, particularly over the past century. There have been many merit-worthy and pioneering works, attempting to draw together the information current at the time, such as the work of Couissin. With the discovery of a large quantity of military equipment at Carnuntum in 1899 (von Groller, 1901a; 1901b) and still more remains from Newstead in 1905–09 (Curle, 1911), it was possible to compare actual finds to the sculptural representations on Trajan's Column, and it was von Groller's conjectural reconstruction of this material which then formed the basis for Couissin's artwork. However, von Groller's interpretation was purely desk-based, untested in practical terms, as have been many subsequent reassessments by historians.

It was another half-century before this material was finally studied by someone with an extensive knowledge of the manufacture of armour, H. Russell-Robinson, Keeper of Arms at the Tower of London. In 1953 he was able to apply his knowledge of medieval and oriental armour to the Newstead and Carnuntum body armour material to produce an initial and plausible reconstruction, which was on display for many years at the Grosvenor Museum at Chester. With the discovery of the Corbridge Hoard in 1964, comprising the well-preserved remains of up to sixteen different cuirasses, some partially assembled, we gained a sizeable and significant level of necessary information. This then allowed Russell-Robinson, in 1975, to build the most credible and complete reconstruction of (what is generally considered to be) the standard Roman legionary body armour (*lorica segmentata*), which is difficult to improve upon (Russell-Robinson, 1975), assisted by pre-reconstruction concept drawings by the historical artist/illustrator Peter Connolly (1975). Of greater relevance to this volume, in his *The Armour of Imperial Rome* (1975), Russell-Robinson also devoted a substantial part of his work to the subject of Roman helmets (legionary, auxiliary and cavalry), with descriptions, illustrations and photographs of many of the known examples, listing these under his own developmental categories.

Since that time, Connolly, in his own published works (1975, 1977, 1978, 1981, 2000), graphically represented a vast range of military equipment, including helmets (used by not only Roman but also Greek, Celtic, Carthaginian and early pan-Italic peoples, such as Samnite, Lucanian, Apulian and Etruscan/Villanovan), attempting to show each item's current archaeological state and its component construction, and to visualise its original use in combat context (pictorially bringing the subject to life in a format appealing to younger readers). However, in the case of the Corbridge material, at least, this imagery was flawed by factors outside his control – reliance on published illustrations and lack of access to the original material.

The study of Roman military equipment, however, was not the sole reserve of Russell-Robinson, nor did it end with him. It was also not confined to the study of material found in Britain, nor to English-speaking scholars. There has been a great deal of valuable work completed by historians and archaeologists worldwide before and since the 1970s. Major contributions include Bishop & Coulston (in addition to their invaluable individual works), whose *Roman Military Equipment from the Punic Wars to the Fall of Rome* (1993, and updated 2006) draws together information from across all time periods, from the Republic to Late Empire. Similarly, the works of Feugère, again spanning all time periods (2002); Junkelmann, for time and motion studies with reconstructed material (1986); Stephenson and Dixon, dealing with later-Empire and cavalry equipment (1999 & 2003); James, for the study of military equipment remains from Dura Europos (2004); and Stiebel and Magness, for the study of artefacts from Masada (2007).

Invaluable in the promotion of this field of study since the mid-1980s have been the annual Roman Military Equipment Conferences (ROMECs). These have provided a forum for sharing current information and ideas between scholars worldwide, cutting through the linguistic and cultural barriers which would otherwise distance their work. Their contributions are then disseminated to an even wider audience by publication of the ROMEC proceedings. This work then continues, on a daily basis, through instant interchanges of ideas on internet 'chat' forums such as RAT (Roman Army Talk), and Facebook, where questions can be raised and contributions made by both academics and amateurs alike.

However, as discussed, the work of many of these authors, while undoubtedly invaluable, is for the most part desk-based, including some 3D CGI imagery, with little or no interaction with the more 'amateur' manufacturers of reconstructed equipment, whereas the re-enactment contingent, through unquestioning reliance on the published material, continue to perpetuate and even exacerbate inaccuracies through copying other copies. Similarly, a demarcation can be seen between the works of the archaeologists and the historians, whose interest lies in the literal interpretation of the classical sources. This can then lead to differences of opinion between the solid evidence and the written descriptions, based on what is the current 'accepted' correct interpretation. These interpretations then vary through the decades dependent on the current political climate, social biases and aspirations to 'political correctness', and even between the cultural backgrounds and personal biases of contemporary writers, so that the accepted 'history' of Rome of even a decade ago can merit avid disagreement today.

II

THE SOURCES OF EVIDENCE

Although this study will primarily focus on the helmets of the Roman army of the Imperial period, it is also necessary to consider events and equipment of earlier periods in order to understand its origins, developmental sequences and the reasons for change. The literary sources therefore, despite any minor variation in interpretation of events, provide us with the basis for this study, with historical writings that build a basic chronology of events, which can help to explain the social and organisational structure of the army of the Republic, and later of the Imperial period. This then helps us to view the epigraphic, sculptural and archaeological evidence in clearer context.

LITERARY SOURCES

The literary works of numerous ancient authors have survived to the present day. These then form our 'primary' sources of information concerning the Greek and Roman world, civilian and military, mostly from a near-contemporary viewpoint (although, as outlined, some are not 'primary' but very much 'secondary' sources, describing events in their own 'ancient' history). As individuals, their writing styles and subject matter varied immensely, as did the level of their military knowledge. Some authors clearly had only the most rudimentary knowledge of military affairs and military equipment, in common with many of us today. Others, in contrast, came from military backgrounds, with first-hand experience of Roman army life, tactics, organisational structure and equipment.

The writings of the ancient authors cover a myriad of subjects, with only occasional glimpses of relevant information, but many describe the materials, technology and industrial/trade infrastructure available. Some sources help by building the historical context, describing the early inter-Italic wars, expansionist activities, later wider-reaching international wars (such as the Punic or Hannibalic Wars) and the inevitable home-grown Social War, allowing us glimpses of the adoption of new battle formations (from phalanx to manipular and cohort formations) and associated development of new armour and weaponry. They also describe political events, showing the emergence of the embryonic Republic, the development of its political assemblies and their links to military organisation. They show how these changed over time, through necessity, to encompass the inclusion of non-Roman, Italic allies, and extending military recruitment to the lower classes. This then allows us an insight into the changing nature of the Roman army, with the changing aims and aspirations of the soldiers, and their reasons for fighting.

Some of the events described may therefore have driven later changes in the organisational structures of the armies, or may have been instrumental in developmental changes in armour, weapon types or battle formation, perhaps following less than successful military conflicts (or, conversely, successful use of innovations), or possibly in answer to changing enemy weapons and fighting styles, as with Tacitus' description of the invasion of Moesia by heavily armoured Sarmatian cataphract horsemen (*Hist.*, 1.79).

Homer, in the *Iliad*, describes how Diomedes pulled on his head 'a bull's-hide helmet with no ridge or plume', and later in the same chapter describes how Odysseus puts on a helmet made of boars' tusks (similar to those seen in Figs 8 and 9), which he describes as 'a helmet that was first a cap of hide with bands of leather criss-crossed, and on these a boar's white teeth were thickly set, disposed with cunning on all sides. A felt lining padded the cap.' (*Iliad* 10.260–71)

Polybius (*c.* 200–118 BC) is one of the primary sources for the early to mid-Republican period, and is generally considered to be a reliable and knowledgeable source for the period from the first Punic War with Carthage in 264 BC, through the Hannibalic War of 218–202 BC, down to 146 BC. Polybius provides details of the level of available manpower raised by the annual levy at the Campus Martius, describing the methods of recruitment. He also describes the desired physical qualities of those eligible (able-bodied, aged seventeen to forty-six) and their personal attributes (Polybius, 6.19–42; 31.29.1). From his own experience Polybius described the manipular battle formation (6.19–26), and his close association with Scipio in Spain during the Hannibalic War permitted him first-hand opportunity to witness the latter's first use of the new cohort formation (11.23.1; 11.33.1). He also recorded the equipment used by legionary forces at that time, describing the rich members of the military alone as having access to mail (*hamata*), with the poorer *assidui* using the older-style pectoral plates (*cardiophylax*), the state providing equipment where necessary, for which the individual would make reimbursement from their paid allowance, or *stipendium* (6.39.15).

In addition, Polybius describes (6.23–4) how the *hastari* and the *triarii* were equipped with a bronze helmet, which he later describes as having 'as an ornament a plume of three purple or black feathers standing upright about a foot and a half in height', which he stated had the effect 'to make each man look about twice his real height', with the intention to intimidate an opponent and strike 'terror into the enemy'.

Some of the same information was also provided by Livy (59 BC – AD 17), although, as he was writing a century after the events, Polybius is in all probability the more reliable source of the two. Livy had no political or military experience, Rich (2007, 18) describing his details of military equipment as 'questionable', although accepting the probability of some testimony being acceptable, possibly where he does not diverge too greatly from other sources. One must therefore be cautious when using him as an accurate secondary source for specific dates, calculations and quantities. On the other hand, as a primary source who lived through the majority of Caesar's campaigns, the rule of Augustus and transition into the early Empire, he can provide first-hand accounts of events affecting the population of Rome, what they saw and felt, and any personal repercussions (although from his own potentially biased viewpoint).

This divergence is highlighted in the two authors' descriptions of the 'Spanish' short sword, or *gladius*, adopted by the Roman legionary (Polybius, 6.23.6). Livy describes its use by the Roman cavalry in the slaughter of Macedonians in 200 BC, producing beheadings and 'hideous other wounds' (31.34.4). However, the *gladius* being a short, stabbing sword suited to close-formation fighting (as in legionary manipular or cohortal battle line-up), it would be an unlikely choice for horsemen. Cavalry more usually would prefer a longer-bladed weapon, producing slashing injuries. The wounds described by Livy above would be more consistent with those produced by another 'Spanish' sword in use at that time, the *falcatta*, which has a long, heavy, curved blade. From experiments carried out by the author using a reproduction weapon, the blade was found to become almost weightless at the apex of its swing, its weight gaining momentum on the downward sweep, producing sufficient power to remove heads or limbs. The possible misunderstanding of the 'Spanish' sword by Livy therefore highlights his lack of familiarity with military equipment compared to Polybius' more extensive first-hand experience.

Unlike Livy, some sources had substantial first-hand military experience. As with Polybius, Sallust (who wrote works describing the second Catilinarian conspiracy in Rome in 63 BC, and the Jugurthine War in Numidia in 112 to 105 BC) and Julius Caesar (in describing his Gallic Wars) were able not only to accurately describe the equipment used but also to explain its manner of use. For example, Caesar (*Bell. Gall.*, 2.21.5), Tacitus (*Hist.*, 2.22, 2.42, 4.29) and later Ammianus (6.12.44, 20.11.8, 26.6.16) all describe the use of shields, both defensively and offensively, specifically in how to use them to stop arrows, and working cooperatively with fellow combatants; how to build a *testudo*; and how to build a shield wall. Other authors wrote military manuals and pamphlets, some of which have survived, even if in fragmentary form, the most notable of these being Xenophon, a serving cavalry officer who wrote a book (*Cavalry Commander*, *c.* 357 BC) describing the duties of a cavalryman, horsemanship and tactics. Other notable authors include Sextus Julius Frontinus (AD 30–104), who held the office of governor, writing a booklet, *Strategemata* (in four books), and Hyginus Gromaticus (of the third century AD), who wrote a manual on the fortification of camps, and on the participation of *nationes* (ethnic troop units).

Sallust (86–35 BC), is not only a valuable source for the historical events of the Jugurthine War, and the involvement of Gaius Marius, but had also served as one of Caesar's officers during the Civil War (Sallust, *Jug.*, 85.11–12; Rosenstein, 2007, 139). As an officer and supporter of Caesar, his reports of the latter's ancestor Marius' part in the Jugurthine War show his personal bias towards the *populares* movement, depicting Marius as the plebeian saviour of Rome (an exaggerated view which is not supported by many modern classical scholars).

Plutarch (AD 45–120) lived during the reigns of Trajan and Hadrian, but wrote of 'historical' rather than current events, describing many similar events to those found in the writings of Sallust, Caesar and Livy. Although focussing his works on the lives of famous statesmen and heroes, particularly their person attributes and motivations, he also documented events that may have been instrumental in developmental changes to military organisation, armour and weaponry. For example, he described the life not only of Marius, and his 'reforms' to the army and its weaponry (Plutarch, *Marius*, 1–46), but also the lives of subsequent influential persons, including Sulla, Crassus, Pompey and Caesar, who collectively contributed to and participated in the fall of the Republic.

As a valuable supplement to Livy, Dionysius of Halicarnassus, in his *Roman Antiquities*, wrote a detailed history starting with the foundation of Rome, covering the period down to *c.* 443 BC, using as his main source the official Roman Annals, which no longer survive (Rich, 2007, 7; Howartson, 1997, 192).

Although the writings of some authors focussed on important events and personas from their past, others wrote of more contemporary events and military campaigns. For example, Josephus (*Bell. Iud.*) reported on the Jewish Revolt of AD 66 from the viewpoint of the non-Roman, 'losing' side, providing valuable first-hand descriptions of military organisation, battle formation, siege warfare and the armour and weapons used by those involved (although by the time of writing he had transferred his allegiance and was perhaps also writing from a more 'Roman' viewpoint).

While we can find much in the writings of authors such as Josephus as being plausible and relatively reliable, others were perhaps not as accurate as one would have hoped. For example, the author Vegetius (writing around AD 430 to 435) wrote on military methods (*epitoma rei militaris*). However, although these read as though describing actual practices, often the author was portraying an 'ideal' situation which he would have wished for, possibly reflecting his imagined view of past glorious times. Therefore, while he describes each fort striving to self-sufficiency, the reality perhaps may have been one of less efficient performance.

Similarly, the collective works known as the *Scriptores Historiae Augusta* are not what they would at first appear. They are purported to have been written in the late third or early fourth centuries by a single author, describing events during the period AD 117–284, but with a gap around AD 244–253. However, they are now believed to be the work of a single author writing in the fourth century, who, for some reason, chose to conceal his true identity, perhaps for the purposes of making veiled political or religious comments (possibly 'anti-Christian'). Much of the work, particularly in the later periods, is considered to be highly fictional (Birley, 1976, 7–22). Howartson (1997, 274) suggests, as a preferred and more reliable alternative, the works of Herodian of Syria, writing in Greek around AD 230 on the subject of Roman emperors and military campaigns (in eight books), starting with Marcus Aurelius in AD 180 and finishing with Gordian III in AD 238.

Within this framework we therefore have many authors, providing a wide-ranging collection of information. Some describe the best materials to use for different processes, as with Pliny on fossil fuels and the best wood to use for charcoal or for use in shields (Pliny, *Hist. Nat.*, 16.77), and, similarly, Polybius on their construction (Polybius, 6.23.2–7). For descriptions of military actions and political events formative in organisational or equipment reforms, we have, for the earlier period, the writings of authors such as Pausanias (1.7.2), Polybius (6.19.2), Plutarch, Sallust and Caesar himself (Caesar, *Bell. Gall.)*, while for the Imperial period we have Cassius Dio, Tacitus, Josephus and Ammianus. For evidence on military life from the first-hand experiences of active serving members we have Sallust, Caesar, Josephus and Ammianus, with advice on training and recruitment from Vegetius.

SCULPTURAL EVIDENCE

Sculpture and artistic representations in wall paintings and mosaics are in a sense the Roman equivalent of photography. They provide an image record over time, from the early Republic to the Late Empire. Wall paintings and mosaics, however, are usually civilian in context and their contribution to our knowledge of military issues is limited, although they are an important resource for visual representations of gladiatorial equipment and combat methods, as discussed in greater detail in the later chapter.

As historians, we are always advised to have regard to potential bias within written histories, in that they are always written by the winning side, the vanquished, by necessity, being depicted with the extreme qualities of weakness, stupidity and malevolence in order to better promote the victor. Sculptural/artistic representations are to be viewed in the same light. As historical documents, their content may not accurately represent reality, but nevertheless they are still a valuable resource for historical sequencing, chronology and equipment, provided that their nature is understood. In the case of gladiatorial imagery on sculptures and frescos (which almost exclusively originate from Pompeii, and so are therefore limited to a specific time window, around the eruption of AD 69), these are unlikely to show any particular political bias, although they may be unrepresentative in the level of actual body protection used, the artist (or commissioner of the artwork) not wishing to unduly obscure the physical attributes of the subject.

Sculpture falls into two main types, ceremonial and funerary, both having strengths and weaknesses in their usefulness as evidence. It is therefore necessary to consider the reasons why each was originally made, and who made it.

Ceremonial sculpture is generally high in artistic quality, made for public relations purposes, to promote the achievement of an individual, or his regime, not entirely unlike the propaganda artwork of the recent past. It uses conventions of dramatic poses to form images of power and success, and the convention of large triumphal figures, crushing smaller, weaker (barbaric?) opponents through the use of superior force. It is therefore unsurprising that the majority of these monumental sculptures were erected during the Imperial period, the leadership depicted on each clearly feeling a need to promote its success to the people and its strength to any potential enemies.

As grave *stelae* are generally produced by military sculptors, often by masons within the same unit whose main duties are usually in connection with building walls, forts and other structures, they do not necessarily exhibit any great artistic talent. They are, however, more likely to give an accurate depiction of military equipment, with which they have first-hand experience, although sculptural depictions of helmets are not always clear, in that they are sometimes reduced in size, particularly in the case of helmet cheek pieces, so as not to obscure faces. In addition, on many grave *stelae* the individuals depicted are deliberately shown wearing no helmets at all, in order to show the features of the deceased.

However, sculptures can be useful to show features of items made from materials less likely to survive in the archaeological record, such as crests, and these visual representations may suggest possible crest materials (long, flowing horsehair plumes or high-standing individual feathers or feathered crests, for example). They may also indicate how certain features were used, for example in the sculpted head of King Pyrrhus of Epirus, Naples, which shows the method of closure of cheek pieces, whereby a slotted leather strap is pushed over a protruding stud on the bottom edge, near to the chin (Fig. 1; Russell-Robinson 1975, 15, fig. 10). This then suggested a similar method to that used on Montefortino-type cheek pieces with similar studs.

Fig. 1. Sculpted head of King Pyrrhus of Epirus, from Naples. His helmet shows a similar method of cheek-piece closure as was used on Montefortino helmets (from Russell-Robinson, 1975). (Artwork by J. R. Travis)

There are a number of important ceremonial sculptures which are of boundless value to the study of Roman military actions and equipment. The most notable of these is Trajan's Column. Trajan's Column is one of the best-known examples of Roman monumental sculpture and is widely used for its well-defined images of Roman military personnel, legionary and auxiliary. The column follows a convention of one man representing an entire unit of men, the design on each shield shown being used to depict a particular unit. As with some funerary *stelae*, Trajan's Column depicts some soldiers not wearing their helmets but carrying them slung against chests, which may indicate the use of carrying handles/loops found on helmet neck guards (Le Bohec, 1988, fig. 14.1–114).

Dedicated in AD 113, the column was erected within Trajan's monumental Forum complex at Rome (built between AD 106 and 113), inside a courtyard flanked by the Basilica Ulpia to the south side, the Greek and Latin libraries on the east and west (the Bibliotheca Ulpia) and Temple of the Divine Trajan on the north (Davies, 1997, 43; Osborne, 1970, 1155). It bears a pictorial documentation and commemoration of Trajan's victory in the two Dacian wars. It displays symbolically the men who fought and died on both sides (Rossi, 1971, 14), and Richmond (1982, 1) believed that it depicted the 'best illustrations of the army' (undoubtedly one of the most notable pictorial representations of the Roman army, used as a 'primary' source by scholars for centuries, with many suggested 'reconstructions' in academic and fine-art works based on its imagery). However, more recent opinions now agree that this image of the Roman army should be viewed with caution. While the artistic quality of the sculpture is superb, the representations of the figures depicted are highly stylised, and the equipment shown is of dubious accuracy.

Debate also surrounds the work of authors discussing the features and merits of the Column. Numerous works exist describing the Column, methods of its construction, reasons for its existence, and interpretation of featured events and equipment used, including Cichorius (1896), who produced a record of high-quality photographic images of the entire Column (from casts made in the 1860s by Napoleon III) still used by many modern authors (including Lepper & Frere, 1988; Fig. 2). However, in more recent years, caveats have been voiced. For example, Bishop and Coulston, among others, dispute the reliability of the depictions of equipment, which, although supposedly showing a 'snapshot' of the military in the Trajanic period, does not reflect the hard evidence of actual equipment found in the archaeological record (Bishop & Coulston, 2006, 35, 254–9).

Similarly, interpretations by authors such as Rossi (1971) of the stylistic conventions employed have been seen by some authors as outdated. For example, Rossi (1971, 14) suggested that the artist had utilised a convention separating visually the civilian legionary from the non-civilian auxiliary, by depicting all of the former in short tunic and bare legs, wearing *lorica segmentata* and carrying rectangular shield and *pilum*.

Fig. 2. Scene from Trajan's Column showing 'legionaries' in *lorica segmentata*, 'auxiliaries' in mail (*hamata*) and archers in scale (*squamata*). (From Cichorius, 1896, *Die Reliefs der Traianssäule*, LXXXVI).

This led to an assumption that *segmentata* was confined to legionaries alone – a view that has been challenged in recent years by increased archaeological finds of *segmentata* remains in non-legionary contexts. It is also possible that its use may have been influenced more by function within a unit/legion than by rank or citizen status. It must also be considered that by the Trajanic period *segmentata* had already been in use for a considerable period, with the images on the column representing later developed forms, and also possibly therefore later period identity of usage.

However, other contemporary sculptural representations suggest mail still being worn by some legionary troops at this time. For example, legionaries are depicted in *hamata* in the metopes of the *Tropaeum Traiani* at Adamklissi (Figs 3 & 4; Russell-Robinson, 1975, 170–71). Richmond suggested that these had been specifically provided with *hamata* to arm them against the Dacian falx (Richmond, 1967, 34–5; Russell-Robinson, 1975, 170).

The auxiliaries on the column, in contrast, were depicted either in mail, short trousers (*bracchae*) and with oval shield, or in regional/ethnic costume, as with the Syrian archers. Rossi also proposed the convention of using a single figure to represent a whole unit of men (not supported by Lepper & Frere, among others), the individual units being identified by their different shield designs.

The artistic conventions used on the Column are therefore arguably of greater significance than the study of the armour itself. At first glance the representations of the equipment carried by the men appear to be of equally high quality, but closer examination of the specific armour types, such as helmets and *lorica segmentata*, suggests that these are not as realistic as they at first appear. They do not seem to resemble any real types which have ever been found. Helmets are unusually small and the buckle fastenings on the *segmentata* girdle plates would not be feasible. In some instances the figures are bare-headed, their helmets removed and slung from their chests (potentially evidencing a possible use for the rear hooks fitted to the neck guards), although once more, shrunken to the size of a 'hamburger' bun, to avoid obscuring the subject.

In recent years many historians have favoured the design conventions proposed by Lepper and Frere (1988), who suggested a convention somewhat similar to the film maker's 'storyboard', with 'close-ups' to focus on incidents of important action. Richmond (1982, 2)

Fig. 3. Legionary from metopes of the *Tropaeum Traiani* at Adamklissi (metope 20), fighting Dacians with long, curved falx weapons. (Artwork by J. R. Travis)

Fig. 4. Legionary from metopes of the *Tropaeum Traiani* at Adamklissi (metope 21), fighting Dacians, wearing *squamata*, reinforced helmet and laminated arm defence on sword arm, and short greaves. (Artwork by J. R. Travis)

viewed the column as a 'picture book' of individual episodes showing the everyday activities of the army. These were then converted into a unified running sequence of interlocking scenes, produced by 'working up' the wartime sketchbooks of artists travelling with the army, whom he compared to the nineteenth-century journalist-artists (forerunners to modern TV and newspaper war correspondents). Each scene of the column could then have been based on sketches made during the campaign, which would allow for more precise details of buildings, costume, accoutrements and physiognomy of participants (Romans, auxiliaries, Dacians and allies) to be shown. In his view, any 'mistakes' would have been due to the stonecutter's interpretation of these drawings (Richmond, 1982, 5).

The work of Lepper and Frere, recognised as a major study of the column, reproduces the Cichorius plates, although disappointingly reduced in scale for reasons of economy and so greatly diminishing the value of their efforts. Their work discusses the reasons behind the campaign, but is, for the main part, a 'travelogue' attempting to relate the scenes depicted to the journey to Dacia undertaken by the army. However, they give little attention to the actual equipment used, most of which refers to the mule train rather than the troops themselves (1988, 266–9), and which strongly references the work of Russell-Robinson (1975).

Ultimately, any discussion of the military equipment shown on the column should consider the probability that the accurate depiction of the Roman army was not its primary function, a war memorial to the two Dacian campaigns (the first consisting a series of expeditions leading up to the second campaign of organised conquest) being probably only a secondary consideration (Davies, 1997, 46–65).

Representations of armour, shields and other military equipment can also be seen on other sculptural sources, some from earlier and some from later periods, which can be combined with the images from Trajan's Column to give a greater understanding of typology

Fig. 5. Altar of Ahenobarbus, featuring soldiers in *lorica hamata* with Celtic-style 'cape' shoulder protection, wearing close-fitting Attic-style helmets with long, flowing horsehair plumes and carrying oval shields with long vertical *spina*. (Photograph by Marie-Lan Nguyen/Wikimedia Commons)

and developmental progression. The Altar of Domitius Ahenobarbus (Fig. 5), dating from the second half of the first century BC, contains images of Roman officers (in Attic-style helmets with long, flowing horsehair plumes) and legionaries (in Montefortino-type helmets) wearing the long *lorica hamata* with shoulder doubling of the late Republican period (Russell-Robinson, 1975, pls 463–4). They can be seen to carry the longer, curved oval shield in use by legionary troops at that time (as described by Polybius, 1.22.5, 6.23.3), similar in form to that found at Fayum (Kimmig, 1940), with an oval *umbo* (boss) and long *spina* (central rib).

Other similar stylised images exist on ceremonial monumental structures. These include sculptures of Roman legionaries and cavalrymen from the Aemilius Paulus monument at Delphi of around 168 BC (Russell-Robinson, 1975, 165, plate 460); the Great Trajanic Frieze (contemporary with Trajan's Column) incorporated into the later Arch of Constantine in the Forum Romanorum (Russell-Robinson, 1975,

Fig. 6. Schematic of a scene from the Aurelian Column showing legionaries carrying shields with a range of shapes, their helmets bearing small, high-standing crests. (Artwork by J. R. Travis)

182, plate 494); on the columns of Antoninus Pius (Russell-Robinson, 1975, 184, plate 497); and Marcus Aurelius (Fig. 6; Russell-Robinson, 1975, 185, plate 498–9); and on the Arch of Severus (Russell-Robinson, 1975, 183, fig. 189). The pedestal relief from Kaestrich fort at Mainz (Fig. 7) also depicts figures representing both auxiliary and legionary soldiers, the auxiliary soldier appearing to wear a helmet of Coolus type, with rounded bowl and no crest knob; another, described as a 'returning soldier', may possibly also be an auxiliary, wearing another helmet of Coolus type, but this time with crest knob; whereas the pair described as 'fighting legionaries' appear to wear an early form of Weisenau/Imperial iron helmet, the bowls stepped down at the occiput; the cheek pieces cusped for eyes and ears; but instead of 'eyebrow' embossing to the forehead, they are decorated with large fish or dolphins (perhaps designating them as marines).

However, caution must be exercised in using these images as definitive of Roman military equipment. As with the other grave *stelae* and monumental sculptural reliefs, methods were employed that may mislead. In addition to the scale of equipment being reduced to fit the available space and not to obscure the bearer, the images on Trajan's Column for example, represent a snapshot in time dating only to the period of the Dacian wars. They cannot therefore allow any insight into equipment of earlier or later periods, nor can they show any developmental progression. The quality of the work is undoubtedly excellent, being carried out by skilled artists, although it is unlikely that they possessed any great knowledge of military equipment, other than ceremonial or processional, as would have been seen in the capital city of Rome by any other citizen. They may have only ever seen the army in ceremonial uniforms, during triumphal marches, and possibly then only from a distance. They may not have had first-hand knowledge of specific equipment of units, so while their depictions of Roman soldiers may have looked convincing to the artist and the general public of Rome, they may not have accurately reflected reality. Furthermore, as ceremonial armour, even in modern times, has always drawn more from archaic models, the equipment depicted on Roman monumental sculptures often followed the artistic convention of using equipment representative of earlier 'classical' periods.

Fig. 7. Figures from pedestal relief from Kaestrich fort at Mainz: (a) auxiliary soldier; (b) returning soldier; (c) fighting legionaries; (d) marching legionaries. (Artwork by J. R. Travis)

By contrast, grave *stelae* can provide detail on shield shape and decoration in relation to known military unit, function and dating context. The artistic quality of grave *stelae* is usually not as high as on monumental sculptures, but this is compensated by the level of technical knowledge of the funerary mason. Because of their very nature, *stelae* will have been produced at relatively short notice, soon after the demise of the subject. They are not usually the highly decorated, well-planned, expensive works described above. They would probably have been produced by a stonemason attached to a unit, probably himself a soldier, whose main job would have been the production of numerous building blocks for construction projects – forts, gateways, aqueducts, and perhaps even Hadrian's Wall. While some were accomplished stonemasons, they were not necessarily 'artists' in the sculptural sense. These 'stone cutters' are described by Tarruntenus Paternus as being among the list of men within the legion known as '*immunes*', exempted from 'more onerous duties' (*Digesta: Corpus Iuris Civilis*, L.6.7; Campbell, 2000, 30).

They would have had first-hand, comprehensive knowledge of the equipment which they were trying to depict. Their accuracy is therefore on a level almost with a photograph. However, there are still some conventions at play which must be considered. Three main basic conventions can be seen in designs of funerary *stelae*. The deceased may be shown standing, facing forward; he may be seated, flanked by aspects depicting a banquet; or, if he belonged to a cavalry unit, he may be depicted on horseback, possibly trampling an enemy underfoot, perhaps followed by a smaller figure representing his groom. This latter convention is a symbolic image, as with the monumental sculptures, promoting the concept of Roman superiority. Noted cavalry *stela* include those of Longinus, AD 43–61, from Colchester (Russell-Robinson, 1975, 106, plate 306); Flavinus of the *Ala Petriana*, from Corbridge (Russell-Robinson, 1975, 106, plate 307); and that of the recently discovered cavalryman from Lancaster. It is also of note that, where armour is shown, *stela* depict almost universally the use of mail rather than *segmentata*, which again calls into question its exclusive use by legionary troops. If *segmentata* had been in such widespread use, as is suggested by the images from Trajan's Column, one would have anticipated a far higher incidence of its appearance in these funerary *stelae*.

In order to fit the image neatly into the given space, large objects like spears (*hasta*), javelins (*pilum*), shields or standards were often shrunk down considerably. Other features, like mail, as seen on monumental works, being difficult to reproduce in stone, may have been painted on, with the stone surface left smooth (leading many now to speculate on existence of leather armour). Objects, such as shields, would not be depicted fully in 3D, as the sculpture would not require that level of depth; they would be flattened, not possessing the true curvature of the original. Soldiers can be shown without helmets, so as not as to obscure the facial features, and to make the subject recognisable. In later periods armour may not be worn at all, the subject being depicted wearing his off-duty stand-down kit of tunic, belt and sword (or may be seen wearing a military cloak, or *sagum*, similarly obscuring equipment), which is of minimal use when studying the equipment.

EPIGRAPHIC EVIDENCE

Epigraphic evidence bridges the divide between literary and sculptural sources, although its value is limited. It can, however, provide clues as to identity, religious beliefs and the ethnic origin of the personnel at a fort, as well as which unit built a new fort, gateway or stretch of wall. There have been a number of items of Roman equipment found inscribed with their owner's name (sometimes also providing the name of his legion and commanding officer). In the Republican period, armour was bought by the individual soldier before the campaign. If not lost, or damaged beyond repair, it would be brought home with him and, if not buried with him, may have been handed down to his successors. This is evidenced by the high incidence (around 49 per cent) of Iberian finds of Montefortino helmets dating from the Hannibalic or Punic Wars found in funerary contexts (Quesada Sanz, 1977, 153). It is also seen in the considerable age of the helmets in the Les Sorres shipwreck, which must have been heirlooms up to four hundred years old by the time they were consigned for recycling (Izquierdo & Solias Aris, 2000, 1.11).

With the new 'professional' soldier of the Imperial period, equipment was issued on recruitment, leased for the duration of service and paid for by deductions from pay. Tacitus tells how soldiers had to 'pay for their clothing, weapons and tents' (*Ann.*, 1.17). On retirement, or death, this equipment could be taken home by the individual, possibly accounting for occasional finds of military equipment in civilian contexts. More probably it would have been handed back, traded in to supplement the pension (to which he had been contributing for many years). A soldier's equipment was valuable to him. Therefore, as a form of investment, many augmented their basic kit with the addition of decorative belt plates and more ornate swords, daggers and shield bosses, etc. Some items of equipment, being more expensive or more relevant to personal safety, would rank higher in importance and are the items more likely to be marked with the owner's name for safekeeping. This could take the form of a simple engraving of the owner's name, and/or his centurion. Other items may be more elaborately decorated, as with the shield boss from a member of the *legio VIII* found at Durham, England (Bidwell, 2001, 10, fig. 5A). These inscriptions can help to identify the original owner, his legion and perhaps his rank and ethnic origin, possibly providing dating evidence where loss can be identified with specific campaigns (as with the inscribed mail hook from Kalkriese). Some items have been found which bear more than one name inscribed on them, indicating that equipment was often handed on to other recruits, a process not dissimilar to that in modern armies (Bishop, 1985, 9). With the assistance of these multiple inscriptions it is possible to build up an individual history for one specific item of equipment.

As armour is, by design, made to withstand substantial abuse, it can, and often does, remain in use for prolonged periods. With modern weapons, technology tends to cause premature obsolescence. However, in the case of traditional armour, as worn ceremonially by military units such as the Life Guards and the Horse Guards, helmets and cuirasses may have been in use for centuries. I have purposefully made use of the living memories of J. R. Travis ('Bob'), a retired member of the British Life Guard Cavalry, as they are one of the few remaining military units who still make use of traditional armour assemblages, as the closest comparative to the Roman cavalry still extant. His recollections included as a new recruit having to learn the history of each individual component part of his armour (his helmet, sword, cuirass and even boots), some pieces having seen action dating back to the Battle of Waterloo in 1815. The British Army were not unique in their use of cuirass armour at that time, and much of the armour still used in the twentieth century was taken from Napoleon's *cuirassiers* and *carabiniers* after the battle for reuse by the British (including the cuirass used by Bob Travis), with some presented to the unit by Napoleon III, so use of the Life Guard's equipment for analogies would effectively be the same as use of their French or German equivalent (J. R. Travis Snr, pers. comm., December 1999).

ARCHAEOLOGICAL EVIDENCE

Caution should be exercised in placing too much reliance on epigraphic sources for dating, in the absence of other evidence of context. For example, epigraphy would not be an appropriate method to 'date' artefacts which appear for sale on the international market without find location or dating context that can be corroborated in any other way. Many of these 'finds' may originate from illicit excavations, perhaps aided by metal detectors, their new owners unable or unwilling to offer information on origin because of the risk of prosecution and financial loss. Their archaeological value is therefore almost zero. This then becomes all the more suspicious when inscriptions of previous Roman owners' names appear during 'cleaning' and 'conservation work', permitting retrospective epigraphic 'dating', as with the supposed Roman 'hybrid mail shoulder plates' which have been the focus for much recent debate. On closer inspection (which is not always possible, where the objects are in private collections), some such inscriptions on artefacts have unsurprisingly been exposed as forgeries, which then devalues further what may have been an interesting and important find.

In reviewing the archaeological evidence for items of military equipment we have to consider the nature of the finds, where they were found, what they were made of, and how they came to be 'lost'. Artefacts make their way into the archaeological record through a number of processes. They may be 'lost' accidentally, through an act of random carelessness, or through some catastrophic event. They may have been deliberately discarded for some reason (perhaps because an item was of no value and had reached the end of its useful life, or perhaps the opposite case, of a valuable item discarded as part of a votive offering). This may then have relevance for 'dating' of the artefact or implications for wear evidence. Some articles are therefore more likely to reach the archaeological record than others, and are more likely to appear through some methods than others.

High-value, high-status items are unlikely to be discarded deliberately at the end of their usefulness. If damaged in some way it is likely that they would be repaired, and when the original owner parted with them it would be either through sale, theft or death of the owner. Small items, even of high value, may be 'lost' accidentally (although the owner would normally take greater care not to do so) or through some catastrophic event. If this 'event' were the result of an attack on the owner, it is expected that such a valuable item would then become 'booty', hence the majority of finds from battle sites, such as Kalkriese, consist of low-value fragments dislodged from the main piece of armour (hinges, buckles, mail hooks, etc.), with larger pieces only being found from locations from which looting was not possible (as, for example, at Kalkriese, where artefacts, including the cavalry face mask, were found under a collapsed earthwork; Fig. 81; Bunz & Spickermann, 2006).

It is possible that a high-status item may be stashed away at times of impending danger, with its owner unable to retrieve it later. This may even be a 'stolen' item, stashed for later but with its retrieval thwarted, as was suggested for the 'Sword of Tiberius' (Bishop & Coulston, 1993, 73, fig. 38.2) and the Vindolanda 'standard' (Birley, 1977, plate 14). Some high-value items were never 'lost', but were deposited with no intention of future retrieval. This would be the case with items 'offered' ceremonially or buried with a deceased owner. This is more likely to be the case with items retrieved from 'native' contexts, perhaps graves of auxiliary troops or of enemy forces (plundered 'booty'). Frequently, in the case of helmets and swords, these can exhibit signs of deliberate damage, to 'kill' the artefact, as seen with some of the Montefortino helmets from Iberian grave contexts (Quesada Sanz, 1977).

Occasionally, personal items that would have been considered relatively valuable to their owner (helmets, shields, swords, etc.) are found undamaged in water contexts (river or coastal). These may not have been deposited through any particularly ritualistic/religious action, but could have been 'accidental' losses as a result of a catastrophic event. In particular this category would feature the Durham shield boss of *legio VIII Augusta*, found as a result of perceived coastal shipwreck, and several finds of helmets possibly 'lost' during less than successful river crossings of the Rhine, and the River Po at Cremona. The latter have been associated with cautious confidence to the military action of AD 69 (Russell-Robinson, 1975), although ritualistic deposition can still not be ruled out.

By far the greatest number of items which find their way into the archaeological record are 'rubbish' – by that meaning low-value, old, worn out, broken, often without any potential for repair or reuse (Bishop, 1985, 9). They are not always complete items, sometimes being just broken-off scraps, but although they would have been 'low value' to their owners, they can be invaluable as indications of wear damage. Caution has to be exercised here, however, not to lend too much weight to any apparent high-frequency occurrence of some items. Large numbers of an item may not necessarily imply its widespread use in preference to a known alternative, but may simply represent a less effective item which was more easily broken or more easily lost (as may be the case with the later *lorica segmentata* tie rings; Thomas, 2003, 109–13).

It follows that most items have had a 'history' before their loss. They are unlikely to have been lost on the first day of manufacture, and in fact the opposite is almost always the case, items exhibiting signs of prolonged use, wear and possible combat damage. As with today, where modern Horse Guards wear cuirasses dating back several hundred years, Roman equipment passed through many hands during its useful life. Men would rarely take their kit with them on retirement. Having 'bought' it on lease through deductions from pay, they could then cash in their kit when they left, passing it on to new recruits. This can be seen evidenced in items bearing the names of more than one owner.

Some of the more personal items of kit could also have been taken home by veterans on retirement, as can be seen in occasional finds in non-military contexts, for example in graves and votive contexts. As grave goods are not often found in burials of ethnically Roman citizens, these are more usually indicative of auxiliary/provincial people, or may even represent equipment looted from their original owner (Quesada Sanz, 1977, 153).

Most finds of military equipment, however, do come from military sites. This is in part due to the nature of how the Roman army occupied a site, their use and reuse of materials, the logistics of manufacture and distribution of men and arms. Accepting that most armour would change hands throughout its period of use, and that troops moved around the Empire on campaigns and individuals possibly moved between units, the individual pieces of armour may be well travelled from their place of origin/manufacture to their eventual loss/disposal/deposition.

Although the Romans were no paragons of virtue when it came to polluting their environment with industrial processes, they were quite efficient at recycling used materials (as evidenced on leather shield covers from Vindonissa, Valkenburg and Roomburgh, some with reused panels displaying stitching holes from earlier *tabulae ansatae*; van Driel-Murray, 1985, 43–54; 1989, 18–19; 1999, 45–54). Because of the effort expended in the production of even the smallest object, from raw material to end product, every effort would be made to prolong its useable life and to make use of residual parts at its termination, hence the caches of finds such as the Corbridge Hoard (where sections of multiple sets of pre-used *lorica* had been stored for repair and future reuse), and large pieces of tent panels, cut from the original object for reworking into patches or smaller items (as can be seen in the museum at Ribchester).

Despite this, some items were eventually discarded, finding their way into ditch infill with other non-recyclable waste. This process would be accelerated at times where the military were actively closing down a site and relocating. In these instances, even objects that were not necessarily irretrievably broken could be discarded. It is clear that when a military site was being decommissioned, everything was assessed for its future usefulness, value and portability. Bulky, lower-value items are particularly likely to be discarded at this time, whether broken or not. Anything which could be taken away for reuse would be packed up and taken with them, even to the extent of dismantling timber buildings. Whatever remained, whether un-reusable, broken, old or worn out, would be burned and buried to prevent its use by an enemy. This is evidenced in the demolition fires at a number of sites, including Doncaster, Yorkshire (Buckland, 1978, 247), and in the quantity of finds from defensive ditches of forts such as Newstead, Scotland (a site which has produced a number of well-preserved cavalry sports helmets and face masks; Curle, 1911, 56, 161, Figs 82, 84, 87).

Although it is inevitable that some rubbish would make its way into a fort's defensive ditches, if left, these ditches would quickly become blocked and cease to serve their primary function. It is logical to assume that these ditches would therefore have been rigorously maintained. This would then support the view that these items would have entered these ditches towards, or at the end of, the fort's period of military occupation.

Another feature of Roman military policy on decommissioning a site was to sabotage the water supply, rendering it useless to enemy forces. It appears to have therefore been a practice to deposit rubbish in the fort's wells, with the intention to both block and pollute them, and this may also include organic items, such as dead animals.

The practice of cleaning out a site when decommissioning it has therefore given us a large quantity of artefacts from a variety of contexts. These have the additional bonus of being in deposits which aid in dating fort wells and ditches – either dating the artefact where the decommission date is otherwise documented, or in dating the closure of the fort where found in context with other dating evidence (coins, pottery, etc.). This then leads to the other issue relating to finds – differential survival. What we are able to find from excavation is influenced by a number of factors: the material from which the artefact is made; the likelihood of that material surviving in the conditions where it was deposited; the possibility of the site being damaged or redeveloped in later periods; the probability of items being deposited in the first place (whether large/small, high-/low-status, easily broken, easily recyclable, worth stealing/looting). Objects retrieved from ditches may therefore possibly be either small, accidental losses (of high or low value and not necessarily broken) or deliberately disposed of. These would then be the sort of objects of no further use or value. They may be made of organic materials, such as wood, leather, textiles or bone (as seen in the many finds of leather scraps and worn-out leather objects from many fort sites, such as those at Ribchester and Vindolanda), or metallic, such as iron or copper/brass.

The waterlogged, anaerobic conditions within a ditch would provide a high possibility of survival for organic material, although this could be further influenced by the acidic/alkaline properties of the surrounding fill matrix. Metallic objects, on the other hand, may fare less well, particularly the iron objects, although at some sites, where soil conditions are favourable, copper/brass objects can survive surprisingly well, as can be seen at Vindolanda, near Hadrian's Wall.

It is therefore apparent, with the exception of a few objects deposited by genuine 'accidental loss' and subsequently rediscovered by equally random and accidental means (as with the river deposits), that the majority of artefacts are retrieved from predictable contexts, such as fort ditches. This would suggest a further level of bias in the archaeological record – influence by choice of sites excavated. This factor must also be considered in civilian as well as military contexts. In the past there appears to have been a deliberate thought pattern at play in the choice of excavation locations. To some extent this would have been influenced by the visible nature of certain site types. High-status residences are more easily pinpointed by aerial photography than are smaller, low-status buildings, with a larger footprint and more substantial walls. In similar fashion, forts are often visible, not only in aerial photographs but also to the naked eye. Where these forts are situated within a later developed urban context, the shape of the defences and often the internal road system can still be identified in the present-day town road plan. However, on a number of sites in rural contexts the fort has been built in a defensive hilltop position, and in these cases often has not seen any subsequent redevelopment, with substantial walls, ditches and even internal roads and buildings visible. The visible nature of certain site types has therefore permitted more selective excavation.

Mindful of the increased probability of artefact survival in some parts of these sites, it would be tempting, if funding or time is not available, to 'cherry pick' these specific locations. It is possible, however, that these are precisely the areas that are necessary to define the boundaries of the site, with the added bonus of supplying dating evidence for period of occupation. However, in the case of high-status civilian sites, it does appear that preference is exercised in favour of the potentially 'richer' family rooms, rather than the lower-status servant's quarters, workrooms and outbuildings, which is a shame as these are precisely the locations where most of the everyday activities took place.

Similarly, in forts, where it has not been possible to excavate the full site, often only the defining ditches, bathhouses and officers' quarters have been investigated. It may be that the remainder of these sites have been left unexcavated as a deliberate measure for the highly commendable reasons of protecting the underlying archaeology (as all excavation inevitably leads to destruction of the site itself), or maybe left for a later date when improved excavation methods would render up greater information than currently possible. In these cases we may in future be able to build a more accurate picture of the functions of these internal buildings where the majority of everyday activities took place.

In the case of sites investigated under time restraints as rescue excavations prior to subsequent redevelopment (as was the case with the Roman industrial site at Templeborough, near Sheffield, Yorkshire), these opportunities are now lost to us. In fairness, the excavations at Templeborough by Thomas May in 1916 and 1917 were actually re-excavations of a site previously stripped and damaged by nineteenth-century antiquarians, which is precisely the argument in favour of leaving a site unexcavated. However, as the entire site was then comprehensively bulldozed in preparation for the twentieth-century steel workings – to well below all archaeological levels – leaving the site until later was not an option available, and we can only be grateful for whatever information was retrieved from what was clearly a major industrial complex of considerable importance to the Roman iron/steel and weapon production and distribution infrastructure (May, 1922; Travis, 2008). Similarly, at Corbridge (Red House), a further 'rescue excavation', in preparation for a major road development, uncovered some lower-status, non-residential, internal buildings of the earlier fort, providing an insight into storage, cart garaging and possible '*fabrica*' workshops (Hanson *et al.*, 1979, fig. 2). In order to gain a clearer image of the Roman military industrial and weapon production infrastructure, these are precisely the type of buildings that need to be examined.

It is to be hoped that more such sites could be excavated in the future, particularly in those areas with potential for redevelopment (that is, not in the relative 'safety' of the Hadrian's Wall 'tourist' corridor, and not in the inaccessible hilltop locations, such as Hard Knott in Cumbria), and preferably without waiting until they should become 'threatened' sites. It may be, however, that further development in the study of Roman armour lies in less densely populated parts of the world than in Britain, such as in the arid eastern regions, where preservation of material may be better and where remains may not be damaged or threatened by overlying later construction layers, or in re-evaluation of excavated material from these regions, as for example at sites such as Dura Europos and Masada (the 1964–5 excavations of the latter being the subject of a recent final report; Stiebel & Magness, 2007, 1–94).

ARCHAEOLOGICAL EVIDENCE OF HELMETS

The helmet is arguably one of the most important pieces of individual military equipment. Russell-Robinson (1975, 13) suggested that the origins of 'Roman' helmets can be found dating back to the Bronze Age, with examples of similarly shaped cheek pieces from Knossos dating to *c.* 1400 BC. It is possible that some form of head protection may even predate this, although made from less durable materials. It is not possible to say with certainty how widespread its use was during these early periods, but it is reasonable to deduce that it would have been rare, being mainly for status rather than defence, although the scarcity of archaeological finds cannot be taken as representative of the level of popularity. The helmet was clearly an expensive object of personal equipment, because of the labour-intensive process to produce the metal and the workmanship involved. Probably only on rare occasions would it have been buried with its owner. At the end of its usefulness, in the majority of cases, it would no doubt have been melted down and reused.

Archaeological evidence of helmets is plentiful as many helmets have been found (over 270 examples of known Roman-style helmets listed in this study), and in some respects this number is surprisingly high. In view of the apparent cost of the workmanship invested in a helmet, along with its obvious value to the owner for personal protection, one would have thought that the owner would have taken greater care to avoid its loss. Survival of any artefact depends on where it was deposited and the material used in its construction, some soil conditions not being conducive to good preservation of metallic artefacts. Many helmets found are made of bronze or copper-alloy, although the high percentage of bronze compared to iron finds may not be representative, as iron does not always survive so well and iron helmets can be heavily corroded and very fragmentary. Some helmets have been found in river contexts, possibly as a result of accidental losses during known campaigns, which, although unlucky for its original owner, offers potentially accurate dating for use and loss. However, as helmets are resilient, made to withstand substantial damage, they often remained in use for long periods, and many are known to have been inscribed with the names of multiple owners. They could therefore be relatively old when lost, even in these datable contexts. Other helmets have been found in grave contexts, although not always in 'Roman' graves. Many of these finds appear to have been deliberately damaged, in order to 'kill' the piece. This could be evidence of mercenary, auxiliary or non-Roman troops who had returned home on retirement, or could represent equipment looted by enemy forces and retained as booty.

Analysis of the find sites can help to show the spread of a style geographically (suggesting cultural influences) and chronologically where contexts can be dated. This analysis may then suggest origins for typological variations and possible manufacturing sites, as stylistic similarities may suggest possible factory locations or common cultural influences.

III

EARLY HELMET DEVELOPMENT

Reaching back to mankind's earliest existence, there have always been disputes. Man has always felt the need to beat his neighbour over the head with some heavy, sharp or pointed object. At the same time he has always felt the desire to display his greater wealth and possessions (often resulting in his neighbour then expressing a similar need to beat him over the head with a heavy, sharp or pointed object in return). It is therefore the most natural thing in the world to invent ways and means to minimise the damage caused during such an encounter, particularly to protect that most important part of the body – the head.

Helmets of some form have probably always existed, fashioned from whatever was the most durable material available at the time. However, that material, although durable, may have been perishable and, not being able to withstand the ravages of time, would not exist in the archaeological record (perhaps boiled and hardened leather, '*cuir bouillée*', or rawhide, or even – as in the case of the Dendra helmet found near Mycenae – boars tusks laced on leather thongs; Fig. 8; Warry, 1980, 12). The earliest known helmet is Sumerian, dating to 3500 BC. Known as 'the Golden Wig' of Mes-kalam-dug, and found at 'Ur-of-the-Chaldees', it was made of beaten and engraved gold with a wadded linen lining, probably secured under the chin by a leather strap (Woolley, 1976, 235–6). Based on the archaeological evidence, it may appear that helmets may have originated in the Near East, although that could be due more to preferential preservation of finds in those locations.

With the technological advances of the Bronze Age, however, the potential for metallic armour arrived. Initially, the production of even a small amount of copper involved considerable resources (with plate armour requiring larger amounts than helmets), so it is logical that the first appearance of metallic armour was in the form of a badly crushed copper (or copper alloy) helmet, dating to around 2500 BC. The helmet was one of six buried with their owners (along with the remains of another fifty-four individuals), in a royal burial pit at Ur in Mesopotamia (Fagan, 2004, 184). Contemporary with this archaeological evidence, the 'Vulture *stele*' (depicting a victory of King Eannatum of Lagesh, the *stele* is so named because of the vultures seen devouring the bodies of the vanquished) offers sculptural representations of a phalanx-like formation of armoured soldiers carrying spears and large rectangular shields, wearing close-fitting helmets covering the head down to the neck, fighting in apparent 'shield wall' formation (Fig. 10; Fagan, 2004, 185). However, it is not possible to tell what material these helmets are made from. They may be copper or bronze, like the examples from Ur, although they could also be made from some other material, such as hardened leather.

We cannot be sure what influences the development of these helmets in the Near East had on those in the West. However, based on the archaeological evidence, the Western equivalents do appear to follow a separate tradition. For example, a millennium later (dating to around 1500–1400 BC), the helmet from Dendra is not fully fashioned in bronze (only the cheek pieces), with the bowl formed of laced boars tusks. However, the functionality of this entire panoply has been questioned, the lack of flexibility in the cuirass suggesting that it may be more ceremonial than practical. The helmet similarly may be more for display purposes than for actual physical protection. The deep bronze cheek pieces however, do display some similarities to later Greek Corinthian and Illyrian helmets, and much later Roman examples, suggesting a continuance of stylistic influence (Fig. 8). The earliest helmets from mainland Greece, dating to 1200 BC, appear to be made of leather reinforced by boar's tusks, similar to the example from Dendra, but without any metallic parts (Fig. 9).

Fig. 8. The Vulture *stela* (*c.* 2500 BC). (Artwork by J. R. Travis, from Fagan, 2004, 185)

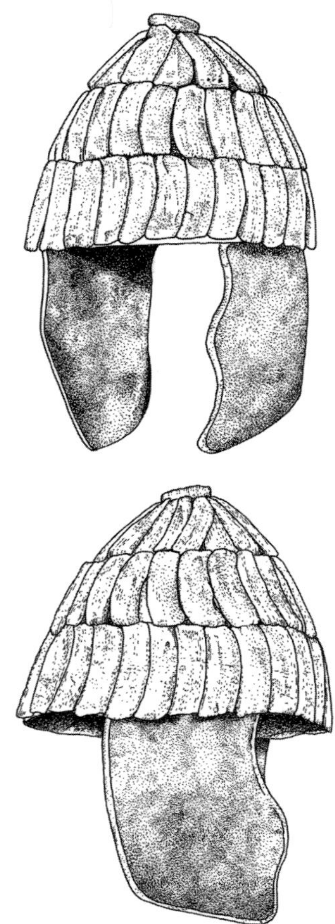

Fig. 9. Boar's tusk helmet similar to that from the Dendra Panoply, *c.* 1400 BC. (Artwork by J. R. Travis)

In the eighth century BC the use of bronze helmets still appeared to be relatively rare, the helmets primarily used as status symbols, handed down from father to son, although usage increased during the sixth century BC. By around 750 BC the development of the early 'hoplite'-style helmets can be seen, as in the helmet in the Argos panoply, a forerunner of the Illyrian style, with deep, integral cheek pieces and high crest (Warry, 1980, 13). However, throughout the areas of Italic influence, cruder styles of head protection were still in use, in the form of simple 'pot' helmets (Figs 11–14). Even as late as the fifth century BC, outside of Greek and Italic areas, simple helmet forms continued, for example with the scale-constructed helmets of the nomadic Scythian people of the central Hungarian plain and the northern steppes, although these used the stronger, more 'modern' material, iron (Fig. 18).

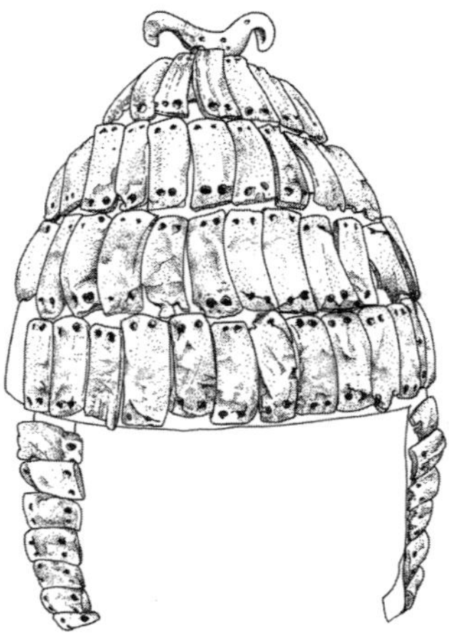

Fig. 10. Boar's tusk helmet from the Dendra Panoply, *c.* 1400 BC, found near Mycenae. (Artwork by J. R. Travis, from Warry, 1980, 12)

Fig. 11. A selection of 'pot' helmets, showing the variety of construction designs. (Artwork by J. R. Travis)

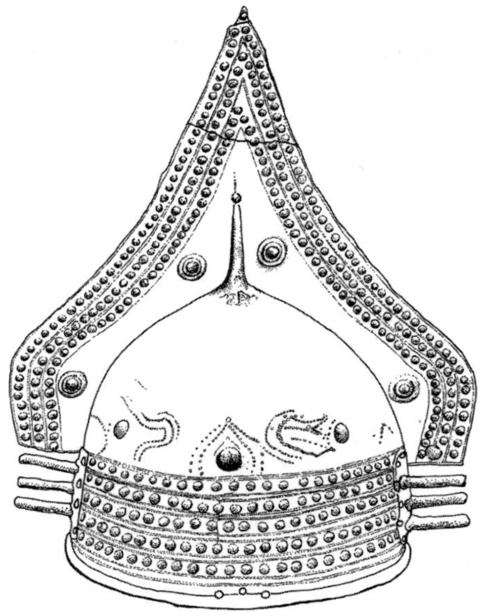

Fig. 12. Villanovan/Etruscan bronze crested helmet, 775–750 BC, from Vulci, Etruria, possibly made at Tarquinia. Made of two hammered sheets riveted together with the edges crimped; decorated with repousée bosses, concentric circles, helmets and birds' heads. The helmet shows central European influence, as does the water bird motif. Now in the British Museum (GR1968.6–27.1). (Artwork by J. R. Travis)

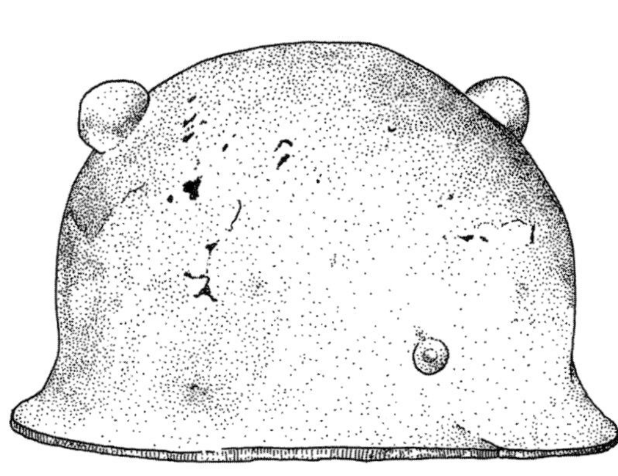

Fig. 13. Picene bronze 'pot' helmet (once crested), 600 BC, found near Ancona. It is a type of helmet known from Picenum, Umbria and Etruria. Knobs on the bowl were intended to help deflect blows. Now in the British Museum (GR1911.4–18.4). (Artwork by J. R. Travis)

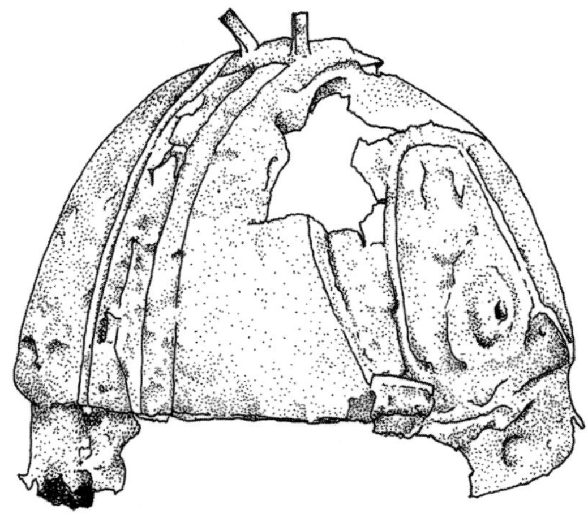

Fig. 14. Picene bronze crested 'pot' helmet, 550–500 BC, from Aufidus (Ofanto), Cannae. The bowl was once fitted with a horsehair crest and lead-filled bosses set on iron discs. Now in the British Museum (GR1772.3–3.4 – Bronze 2730). (Artwork by J. R. Travis)

Fig. 15. Bronze 'Negau' helmet. Central Italian, dating to 400–300 BC, probably from Vulci. Now in the British Museum (GR1878.10–19.302). (Artwork by J. R. Travis)

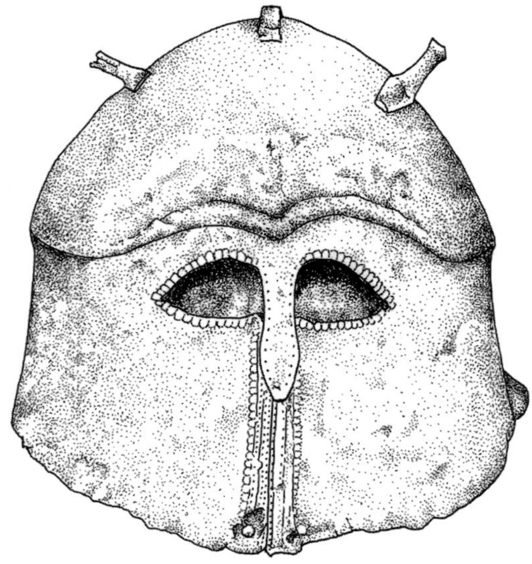

Fig. 16. Apulo-Corinthian bronze helmet, south Italian, 400–350 BC, from Ruvo, Apulia. The helmet has a cut-out 'face', with an integral nose guard, overlapping the wide cheek guards, which meet and join at the centre front, completely enclosing the face. The bowl was further decorated with incised boar motifs, and was once fitted with both crest and side plumes. Now in the British Museum (GR1856.12.664). (Artwork by J. R. Travis)

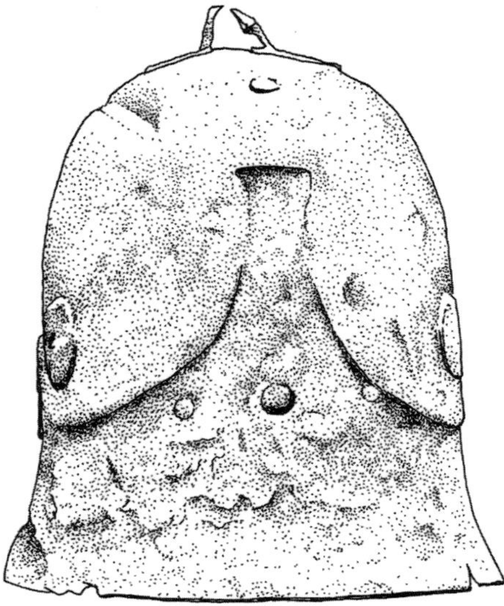

Fig. 17. Lucanian 'bell-krater' bronze helmet (the shape derived from the Chalcidian style of helmet), south Italian, 350–250 BC, said to be from near Bolzano. The helmet would have originally been crested and had cheek pieces. Now in the British Museum (GR1937.11–17.1). (Artwork by J. R. Travis)

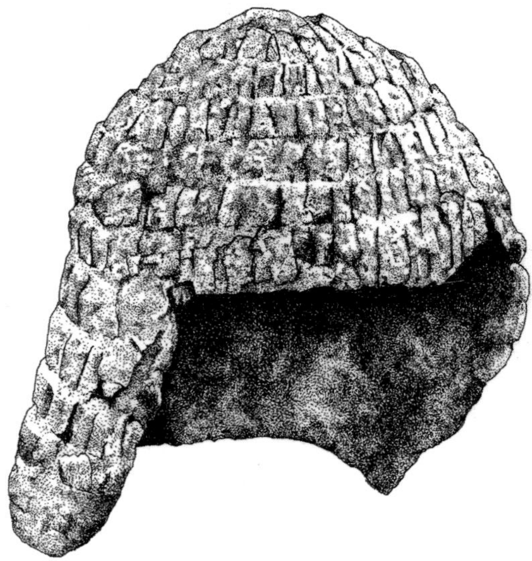

Fig. 18. Scythian helmet from fifth century BC formed of iron plates. (Artwork by J. R. Travis, from Fagan, 2004, 46)

Here it is probably also worth noting the 'disc-and-stud' helmets in use by lower-status Italic warriors (Fig. 21). One such helmet, dating to the seventh century BC, was found from the Necropoli Sotto La Rocca-Lippi, La Tomba Principesca N.85 (in Bologna, Museo Civico Archeologico). It was made of wickerwork, with a domed cap, reinforced by the application of bronze discs of varying sizes placed all over the bowl. The gaps between these discs were then filled with tightly packed small bronze studs (Fields, 2011, 16). The remains of what must have been a similar 'disc-and-stud' helmet were found in Sepolcreto Benacci, tomb 494, dating to the eighth century BC. This consisted of four bronze discs with a central stud, each raised on two washers of different sizes, to create a stepped effect (*ibid*). A similar pattern of helmet can also be seen worn by five of the warrior figures on the *Certosa Situla* (Fig. 20).

By the fifth century BC, both the 'Corinthian' and 'Illyrian' styles of helmet were in use by Greek hoplites (Figs 19, a-d; 22–26). Both of these were close-fitting helmets, formed from a single piece of bronze by beating over a ball-ended stake. The differences between the two styles were that the 'Corinthian' style covers most of the face, with nasal protection and cheeks that wrap around towards the mouth, whereas the 'Illyrian' was more open in the face. It had long cheek pieces, but these did not wrap around the face and it lacked the nasal protection. These were higher-value and higher-status helmets, however, the less wealthy using a cheaper, 'mass-produced' helmet, the 'Pylos' type (Warry, 1980, 44, fig. 8). This was a simple bell/conical shape, with a waisted ridge, flaring out close to the base. It had no cheek pieces, attaching to the head by leather strap ties. This may have been the forerunner of the later 'Negau' bell helmet used by the lower ranks of Samnite and Etruscan forces in the fourth century BC (Warry, 1980, 103; Figs 15 & 28), and possibly even the Celtic (and eventual Roman) Montefortino, and is also similar to those worn on the *Certosa Situla* (Zotti, 2006; Fig. 20).

As time progressed, both Corinthian and Illyrian styles developed along similar lines, with the introduction of a cranial ridge to increase internal ventilation and at the same time to produce a 'crush' zone to absorb blows. The sides of the helmets were cut away, exposing the ears slightly but improving hearing for the wearer. Cheek pieces were also elongated still

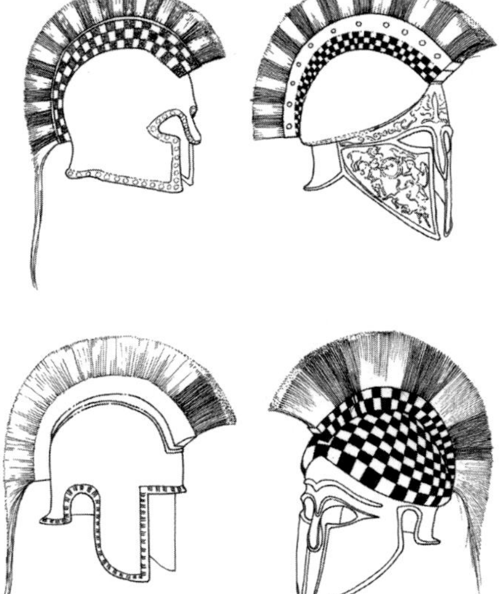

Fig. 19. Early Greek hoplite helmets (after Anglim *et al.*, 2002, 18): (a) simple Corinthian; (b) classic Corinthian; (c) later Illyrian; (d) later Corinthian. (Artwork by J. R. Travis)

Fig. 20. Warriors carrying a variety of shields (round, oval and sub-rectangular) as depicted on the *Certosa Situla*. (Artwork by J. R. Travis, from Zotti, 2006)

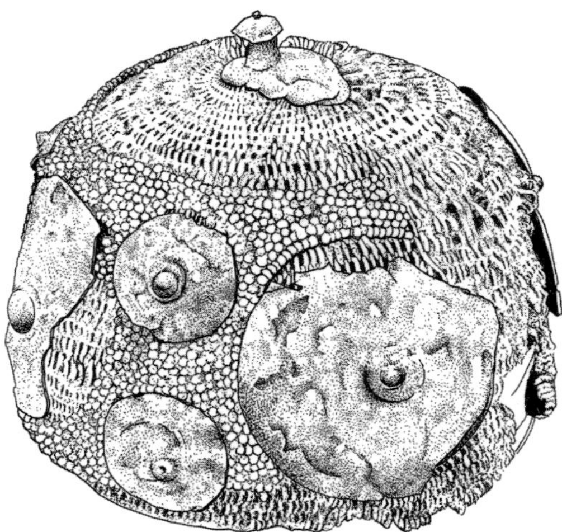

Fig. 21. Disc-and-stud helmet, dating to the seventh century BC, from the Necropoli Sotto La Rocca-Lippi La Tomba Principesca N. 85 (in Bologna, Museo Civico Archeologico). The bowl is made of domed wickerwork, reinforced with bronze discs of varying sizes; the gaps between the discs then filled with tightly packed small bronze studs. (Artwork by J. R. Travis)

Fig. 22. Statuette of an ancient Greek hoplite or heavy foot soldier, from the Berlin Museum around 1900. (Artwork by J. R. Travis)

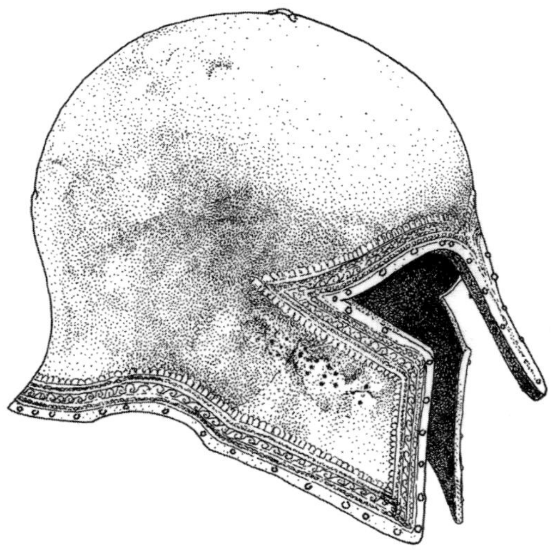

Fig. 23. Simple Corinthian bronze helmet, Greek (possibly Corinthian), *c.* 650–570BC. Found at the Sanctuary of Zeus at Dodona in north-west Greece, although an inscription on the right cheek guard ('OLUMP') suggests that it may have been originally intended to be offered at Olympia. Now in the British Museum (GR1904.10–10.2). (Artwork by J. R. Travis)

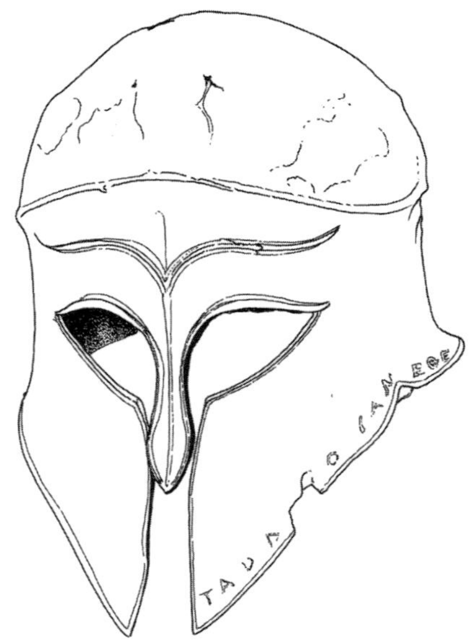

Fig. 24. Classic Corinthian bronze helmet, Greek, *c.* 460BC, from Olympia, with an inscription stating that the Argives dedicated it to Zeus as spoil in battle with Corinthians. Now in the British Museum (GR1824.4–7.32). (Artwork by J. R. Travis).

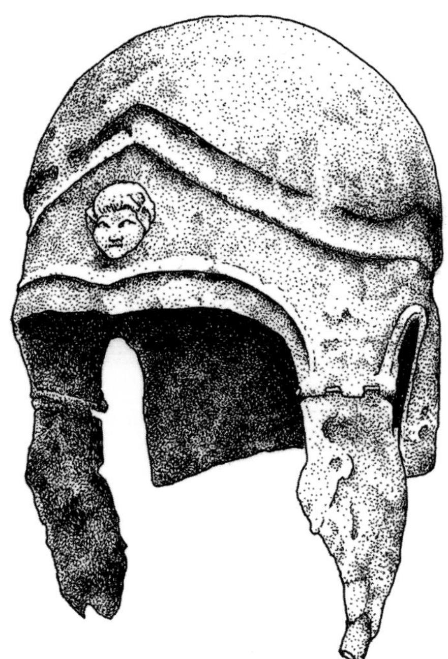

Fig. 25. Attic bronze helmet, Greek, fifth century BC, possibly from Athens, ornamented with a silver satyr's head. The cheek pieces are the correct type but may not belong to the same helmet. Now in the British Museum (GR1883.12–8.3). (Artwork by J. R. Travis)

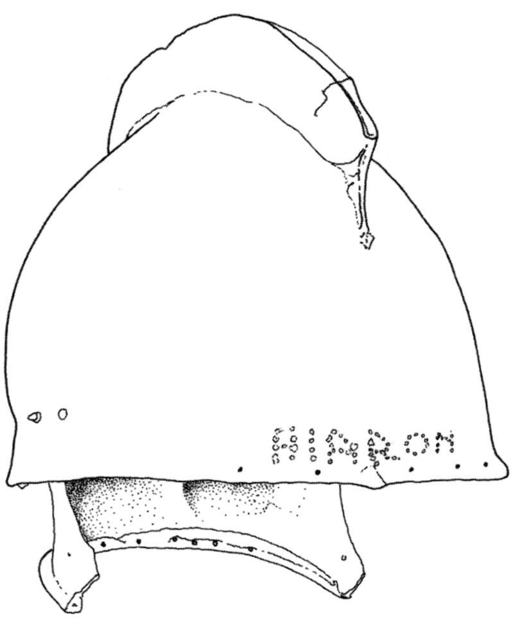

Fig. 26. Thracian-type bronze helmet, Greek, 450–400 BC, from Lake Copais, Boeotia. An inscription punched above the rim ('HIARON', meaning 'sacred') suggests it had been a votive offering in the sanctuary. Now in the British Museum (GR1927.10–11.1). (Artwork by J. R. Travis)

further to protect the mouth and throat, in the Corinthian style wrapping further around towards the mouth or in the 'Apulo-Corinthian' types fully enclosing the face (Fig. 16). A further, more open variant of the Corinthian style of helmet was the 'Chalcidian', which was later to develop into the 'Attic' style used by the Romans into the Imperial period. This had the cranial ridge, small nasal protection (although this tended to disappear through time as it impeded vision), long, rounded cheek pieces and cut-away ears for improved hearing (Warry, 1980, 44; Figs 27–29).

An additional feature of this combination of the close-fitting helmet with the extra-long cheek pieces was that its central balance point was further forward (most of the weight being at the front), which enabled the wearer to push the helmet up on to the top of his head when not in use. This allowed for greater ventilation and visibility, the extended cheek pieces acting as a visor to shield the eyes. This method of wearing the helmet pushed back can be seen depicted sculpturally in the busts of both Themistocles and Pericles (Warry, 1980, 28 & 40). A corruption of this feature can be seen continuing into the Roman period, in the Etrusco-Corinthian style of helmets worn by officer and cavalry, whereby the helmet is provided with a 'face' on the upper visor part of the helmet (Figs 30a, 95). However, these helmets were also fitted with additional cheek pieces, indicating that, in these cases, the helmet was intended to be worn in this fashion at all times (Russell-Robinson, 1975, 137, pls 413–416).

One marked difference between these Greek predecessors and their later Roman counterparts lies in the style of crests and manner of attachment. The Greek style of crest was made of horsehair set in a solid wooden base, similar to a brush, fixed directly to the helmet along the crown and being allowed to flow freely down the back. Spartan warriors, however, are depicted with transverse crests, similar to those on later Roman centurions' helmets (Warry, 1980, 52). It was unlikely that any attempt was made to colour the hair (unlike the bowl of the helmet, which was often elaborately decorated), so these crests would probably utilise the natural shades available, from white through browns to black (Warry, 1980, 44). In contrast, later Roman crests would be raised from the body of the helmet on a shaft fitting, a feature that appears to originate in the Italian variations of these Greek styles by the Etruscans and Samnites (Figs 28–30; Warry, 1980, 109).

Following the reforms of the Athenian general Iphicrates in the fourth century BC, the 'Thracian' type of helmet was introduced, although the form did not come from Thrace; the name derives from the shape (Anglim *et al.*, 2002, 30; Fig. 27d). In this style the helmet rises in a backward-sloping, conical shape, with the top part curving forward, resembling the hats worn by Thracian peltasts (and also similar to later Phrygian-style caps). The Thracian peltast wore a soft fox-skin cap, pointed at the top, with very long earflaps that could be tied out of the way at the back of the head. He may also have worn a simple metal skullcap underneath. The 'Thracian'-style helmet echoed the shape of this cap in its bowl. It could be worn without cheek pieces, but could similarly have very long, pointed cheek pieces. In one style these cheek pieces joined at the chin and were decorated to look like a beard, producing a 'face helmet' similar to later Roman cavalry styles (Fig. 27).

From the sixth century BC, the development in helmet styles can be traced spreading east from Greece across Europe, with the Greek designs being taken up in the northern regions of Italy first. The helmets in use by the Etruscans included the more open Corinthian variant, the 'Chalcidian', adopted from the Greeks, combining it with their own style of long crest attached to the centre of the helmet. At the same time, they also embraced the local Italian fashion for a bell-shaped, conical helmet, the 'Negau', optionally combined with a raised lengthwise or transverse crest. Although Warry (1980, 109) attributes this style of helmet to an Italian origin, it does bear marked similarities to the Greek 'Pylos' type. Like its Greek counterpart, it could be simply tied with leather thongs, or could be combined with large cheek pieces, in one variant embossed to resemble a mask, as with the Greek 'Thracian' described above (Fig. 28; Warry, 1980, 109).

The Samnites were similarly influenced by Greek colonies in the southern parts of the Italian peninsula, using both the 'Attic' style (derived from the 'Chalcidian') and one combining features of the Attic and the Thracian, the 'Thraco-Attic', with hinged cheeks and curved peak. These could be combined with the Samnite's own style of upright feathers, wings and raised crests (Fig. 29; Warry, 1980, 106). Some combinations of these feathered 'Attic' helmets can be seen depicted in use by Samnite cavalry on a fourth-century BC tomb at Paestum. Another regional helmet type (for example as used by the Lucanians) which may have had developmental influences on later forms was the 'bell krater', with its central crest and embossed decoration with swirling volutes (Fig. 17).

The Greco-Etruscan-style hoplite method of fighting was introduced, according to tradition, as part of reforms to the Roman military system by the sixth king, Servius Tullius, with manpower also being divided into five classes based on a property test (Livy, 1.43; Burns, 2003, 62–3; Goldsworthy, 2003, 25; Table 10). Each class carried a different level of equipment, each adding items as wealth permitted, in order of perceived importance and affordability. Putting aside the most basic piece of equipment carried by the poorest class, being purely offensive and with minimal cost to carrier (sling and stones), the defensive equipment was added in the order of shield, then helmet, greaves, then cuirass. The choice of the shield as the next piece of equipment of choice was possibly due to the associated cost, in that it would cost its owner considerably less than a well-made helmet. However, despite its obvious cost, at a time when a soldier's equipment was self-funded, it is notable that the helmet is the next item of choice, before the comparatively cheaper greaves or cuirass, being included by the entire top three of these classes.

By the third century BC, higher-status Romans, like their Etruscan and Samnite neighbours and rivals, were using Attic-style helmets, which also may be combined with feathers and raised crests (Fig. 30–32). This close-fitting shape of helmet, with a cranial ridge for ventilation

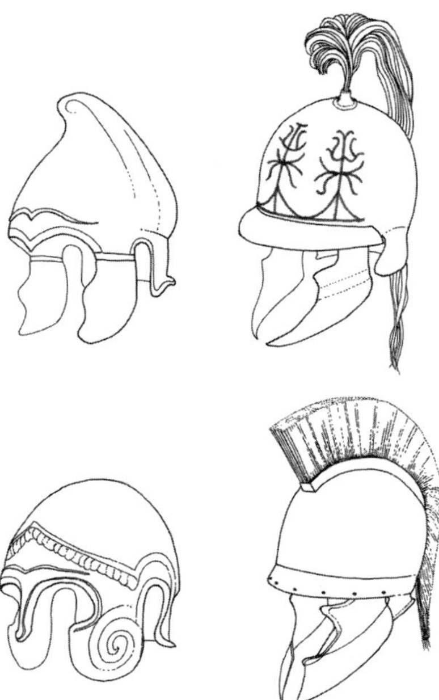

Fig. 27. Later Greek hoplite helmets (after Anglim *et al.*, 2005, 30): (a) Thraco-Attic; (b) Thracian; (c) Chalcidian; (d) Thracian with cranial ridge strengthening. (Artwork by J. R. Travis)

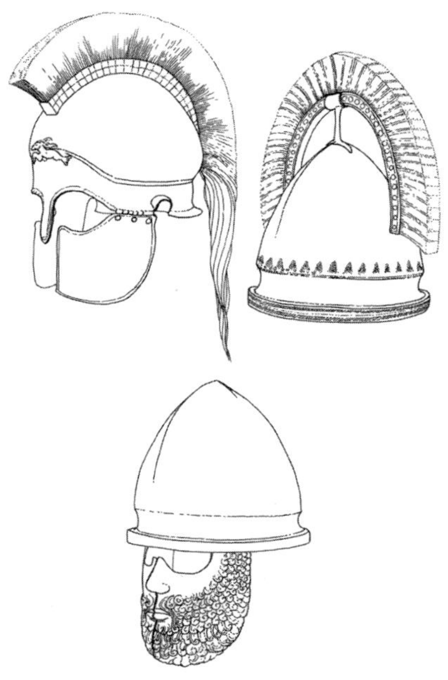

Fig. 28. Etruscan helmets: (a) Chalcidian (fifth century); (b) Negau (*c.* 500–200 BC); (c) Negau 'face mask' type (from Warry, 1980, 109). (Artwork by J. R. Travis)

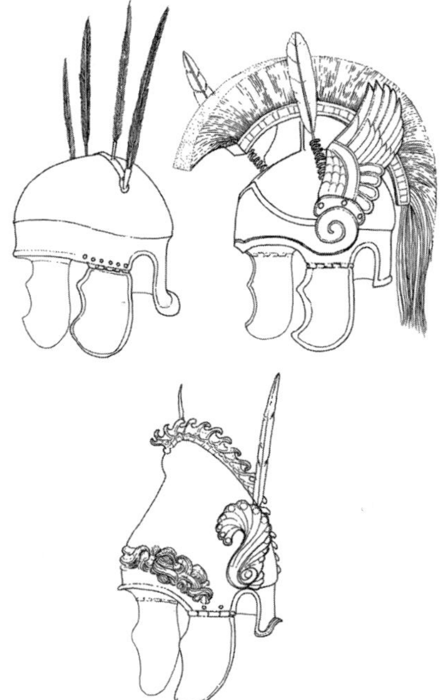

Fig. 29. Samnite helmets: (a) Attic (*c.* 400 BC); (b) Attic (southern Italic form); (c) Thraco-Attic (from Warry, 1980, 109). (Artwork by J. R. Travis)

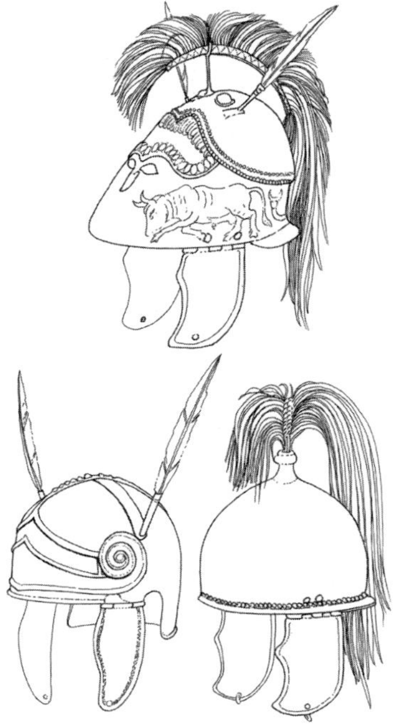

Fig. 30. Roman helmets: (a) Etrusco-Corinthian; (b) Attic; (c) Montefortino (from Warry, 1980, 109). (Artwork by J. R. Travis)

and cut away at the ears for improved hearing, was retained for officer and cavalry helmets throughout the Republican and Imperial periods. Often it was highly decorated, as in cavalry parade helmets. In use for high-status officers and parade helmets, the 'Etrusco-Corinthian' was a corruption of the earlier 'Corinthian style', mimicking the Greek fashion for pushing the helmet on to the top of the head by sloping the bowl backwards and decorating the visor with a 'face' on top (Warry, 1980, 109). This style may also be decorated by feathers and/or a raised crest, or by elaborate applied decoration as on that dating to the first century AD from Autun (Russell-Robinson, 1975, 137, pls 413–16; Fig. 95).

These Greco-Etruscan-style helmets continued in use into the first century BC, and possibly even into the Early Imperial period, as retro-styled parade armour and for sculptural representations. However, by the late fifth to early fourth century BC, they were generally superseded by the Celtic-style conical Montefortino helmets, fitted with either a button or plume holder, and with the appearance of some iron helmets in the cisalpine region in the fourth century BC (Figs 33–35). The Montefortino helmet appears to have been brought to Italy by invading Gallic tribes, being adopted first by the Etruscans and later becoming popular with both Roman and Carthaginian forces. The Carthaginians were known to have equipped their mercenary troops prior to and during campaigns. It is therefore not always clear whether helmets, when found, belonged to Roman or enemy forces. However, a helmet can be seen with apparent strong similarities to later Montefortino helmets, worn by a terracotta bust of a warrior made in Cyprus around 600 BC, found at the sanctuary of Apollo at Phrangissa, Tamassos (British Museum, GR1910.6–20.3). As such, the development of the Montefortino may not necessarily lie with a Celtic origin, but may have

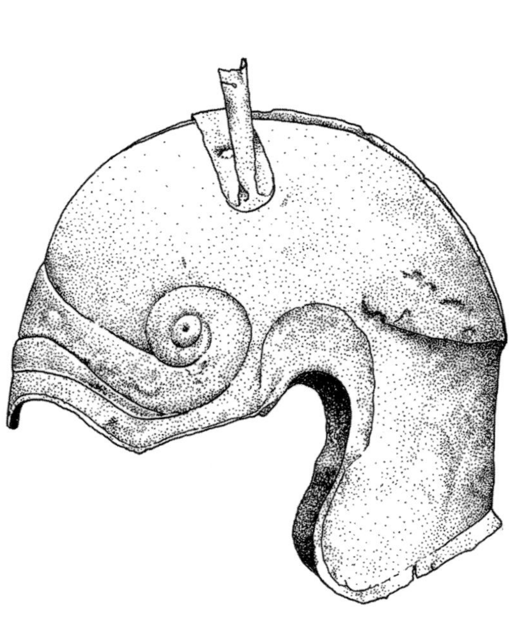

Fig. 31. Samnite-Attic bronze helmet. It was originally provided with cheek pieces and was plumed as a 'bell krater', as seen on Paestan tomb paintings. Now in the British Museum (GR1842.7–28711). (Artwork by J. R. Travis)

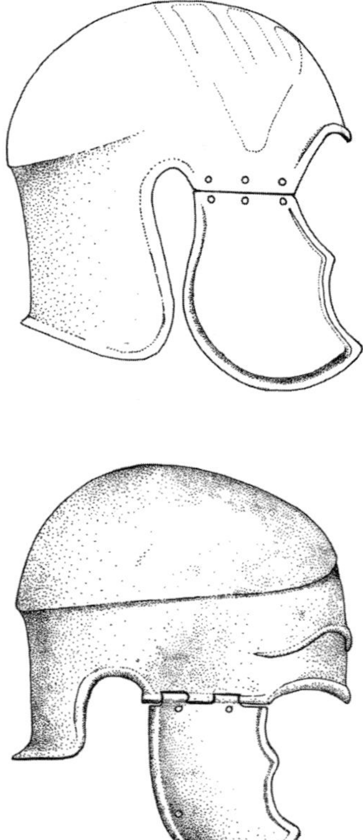

Fig. 32. Late Attic bronze helmets of fourth to third century BC. (Artwork by J. R. Travis, from Russell-Robinson, 1975)

been acquired by them from elsewhere, perhaps Cyprus/central Mediterranean. Alternately, the Cyprus example may have also originated from Celtic influence, or they may both have a common origin, or may even represent a totally separate development of an almost identical style (however unlikely).

This Montefortino 'jockey cap'-type helmet eventually became standard lower-rank issue to the first Republican legionaries, although officers continued to wear the retro-classic Greek-style Attic, Italo-Corinthian helmets. In this early to middle Republican period, men were still recruited from those satisfying the property test, able to provide their own equipment. They probably brought their equipment with them from their home regions on recruitment, suggesting small-scale supply, with equipment being the work of local armourers. At the end of each campaign, the survivors would return home, taking their equipment with them on discharge. This equipment may then have been passed on to a family member for future use, or may have been buried with its owner, the majority of helmets in Republican period being found in civilian contexts.

From dating contexts of finds and study of apparent stylistic developments, two apparent breaks in the continuity of manufacture have been identified. These seem to correspond with the Marian reforms at the end of the Republican period and those of Augustus at the start of the Imperial period. These reforms brought about changes in the structure of the armies and also an increase in manpower (Cary & Scullard, 1979, 219). The nature of the individuals recruited into the armies was radically changed by these reforms. Geographical boundaries were expanded to include men from outlying regions, and the property requirement was lowered to include poorer classes, to increase the potential recruitment base. Many of those made eligible for service by these reforms were not able to afford to finance their own equipment. It was therefore necessary to equip large bodies of additional men in a hurry at state expense. It appears that this need may have been met by a degree of mass production, from 'factories', possibly state owned. Equipment produced at this time appears to be reduced in quality of manufacture, materials and finishing, with less decoration and evidence of innovation in techniques used to speed up production (applied rather than integral knobs and crests, spinning rather than beating to form the bowl, etc.).

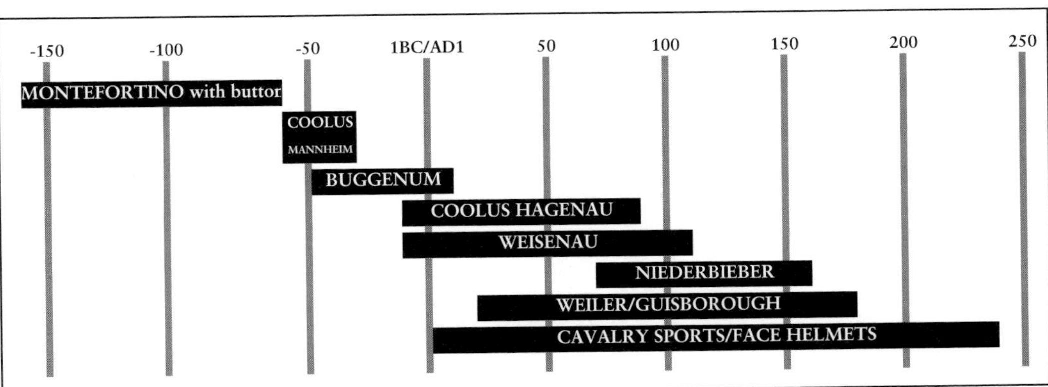

Table 1. Chronology of helmets of Republican and Imperial periods, using P. Couissin typology.

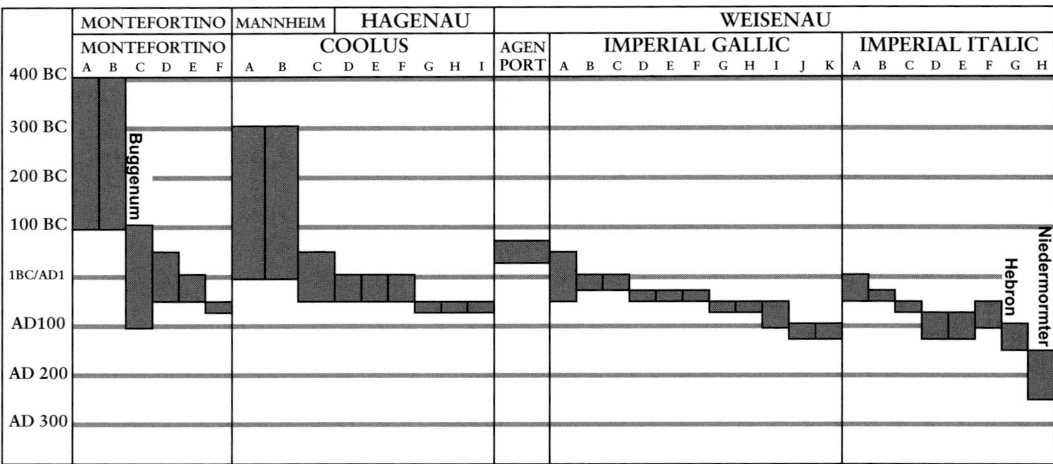

Table 2. Chronology of helmets of Republican and Imperial periods, comparing H. Russell-Robinson and P. Couissin typologies.

IV

BRONZE HELMETS OF THE EARLY REPUBLICAN PERIOD

DEVELOPMENTAL SEQUENCE – CONTINENTAL SYSTEM AND RUSSELL-ROBINSON SYSTEM

Two systems categorising helmet types, from this period onwards, are currently in use simultaneously. The Continental system was developed by P. Couissin in 1926, using the name of the find's location. For example, for bronze helmets we have the 'Montefortino', 'Buggenum', 'Coolus Mannheim' and 'Coolus Hagenau', and for iron helmets the 'Weisenau', 'Niederbieber' and 'Weiler/Guisborough'. The Continental 'Weisenau' is a term applied to all iron infantry helmets appearing from the mid-first-century BC Augustan period, through to the first and second century AD. This system is still widely used on the Continent, although, being greatly simplified, this can be both an advantage and disadvantage, at times being too general to allow identification or to suggest developmental progression. Furthermore, the naming after find spots can lead to confusion, with some sites of lengthy occupation perhaps providing numerous finds of greatly different styles.

To attempt to show ancestry and developmental progression, in 1975 H. Russell-Robinson developed his own classification of helmets based on visible features. Under his system the bronze helmets were grouped as the 'Montefortino' (Figs 33–35), and 'Coolus' (Figs 36–37), with the iron helmets under the earlier 'Agen/Port' (Fig. 39), leading to the later 'Imperial' issue. Within these headings he then identified many subgroups, attempting to identify the chronological development of component features while also incorporating apparent cultural influences. In addition, he identified differences within 'Weisenau'-type helmets to suggest 'Italic' or 'Gallic' influences and possible regions of manufacture, developing his own categories of 'Imperial Gallic' (Figs 42–47), and 'Imperial Italic' (Figs 48–52).

MONTEFORTINO – TYPES A TO F

The Montefortino is a simple bronze 'pot' helmet, topped by a button-shaped crest knob or plume holder, described by Russell-Robinson as resembling a 'jockey cap' (1975, 13). It was the longest-serving of all Roman-style helmets, remaining in use, in one form or another, from the fourth/late third century BC, from the Punic Wars, throughout the Republican period, and into the early Empire of the first century AD. It is not exclusively a 'Roman' style of helmet, being used by neighbouring and even opposing cultures, including the Carthaginians. It was a style believed by Russell-Robinson to have originated with the Celtic peoples and to have been brought to Italy by Gallic tribes during invasions of the late fifth and early fourth century BC (Russell-Robinson, 1975, 13), although Russell-Robinson also makes comparisons with conical helmets used in Minoan and Mycenaean Greece from around 1400 BC, suggesting an earlier or common origin (Russell-Robinson, 1975, 13). Feugère reports these 'Celtic-style' helmets then being produced by the Etruscans of northern Italy by the fourth century BC, the style diffusing southwards, being issued to the first Republican legions in the fourth to third centuries BC (Feugère, 2002, 70). However, the Etruscan people were also known to have followed a local fashion using the 'Negau', a conical, 'bell-shaped' helmet (Warry, 1980, 109). Later, the Celts also adopted this style of helmet, indicating a bidirectional influence rather than a clear-cut diffusion through Celtic penetration.

In his study of Montefortino-type helmet finds in Iberia, Quesada Sanz also contests the attribution of the origin of all examples with crest knob and angled neck guard to Celtic invasions, seeing them as Celto-Italic, Italic-Celto or Etrusco-Italic developments, rather than Gaulish, citing work of the German scholar, P Stary (1979). He maintained that the Spanish Celts in the Iberian peninsula were not part of the La Tène culture of Europe but adopted some imported elements into their own, the Montefortino helmet among these, developing into this their own decorative style. These features can be seen on several helmets of the Galician type, indicating local indigenous production during the second half of the first century BC (Quesada Sanz, 1997, 162). These are very distinctive, with heavy cable and incised decoration and long, pointed, decorated knobs (Quesada Sanz, 1997, 157). Whereas the adoption of the Montefortino helmet type into Italy can be seen during the fourth century BC, becoming standard issue to the first Roman legions, in Iberia this appears to occur much later into the mid-third century BC (Quesada Sanz, 1997, 153).

Of the sixty-one examples of Iberian Montefortino helmets studied by Quesada Sanz, almost half (49 per cent) came from indigenous, often funerary contexts, dating to the end of the third, through to the second century BC (Quesada Sanz, 1997, 155). These he believed to have been of Italic origin, used in either the Hannibalic/Punic Wars by soldiers of both Roman and Carthaginian sides or dating from the early Roman conquest (Quesada Sanz, 1997, 162). However, helmets do not appear to feature widely in grave contexts, for which Quesada Sanz offered two possible reasons. He proposed either that the majority of helmets at that time could have been made of organic materials, or that their use was not universal, featuring more as imported status/wealth symbols. However, he pointed out that some rich burials are found without helmets, where others are found in apparent low-status burials. He suggested that these may represent the property of returning Carthaginian mercenary or allied forces, included into burials as booty, or as Carthaginian 'issue' (Quesada Sanz, 1997, 163), citing Polybius and Livy, both of whom report that Hannibal issued looted Roman weapons to his troops after battles at Trasimene and Cannae (Polybius 3.87.3; 3.114.1; 18.28.9; Livy, 28.46.4). Several helmets were also found from Villaricos in Almeria, the location of an important coastal recruiting centre for Punic mercenaries.

These early Montefortino helmets, where used by the original Celtic cultures, consist of just the basic conical bowl, with decorative or plain crest knob and small neck guard, but without cheek pieces, being secured to the head by simple straps. The introduction of cheek pieces appears to be attributable to the Romans, incorporating long-standing features from pre-existing helmet types, although these, as suggested by Russell-Robinson, may be traced back to Bronze Age Minoan/Mycenaean cultures, or even earlier (Russell-Robinson, 1975, 13).

In his study of Iberian helmets, Quesada Sanz noted a lack of cheek pieces in those helmets from the non-Roman, indigenous burial contexts, with the view that, in the case of ex-Roman 'booty', these may have been 'discarded' as 'inconvenient or useless'. This suggested that, even after the Roman introduction of cheek pieces, Celtic/non-Roman users continued with a deliberate preference to the contrary (Quesada Sanz, 1997, 155).

Although the presence or lack of cheek pieces may help to differentiate Roman and non-Roman use, Russell-Robinson also identified six variants (A to F) within the Montefortino typology, based on the helmet bowl and neck guard shapes, which he used to suggest a developmental progression. Even within this framework, however, the basic features remained constant, with little to differentiate at first glance until the much later examples.

Montefortino – Types A and B

Types A and B helmets represent the standard Montefortino types which remained in use from the fourth to the second centuries BC by both Roman and non-Roman users, with a bulbous, conical bowl, drawn up to an integral hollow knob, and with a short, sloping neck guard. The only difference between these two categories lies in the level of decoration, Type B having very simplified or no decoration, with a plain, conical knob with flattened top. The knob of type A, however, may be hemispherical, decorated with scale pattern and the knocked-back, half-round sectioned neck guard decorated with cable pattern and filed horizontal lines. As both of these types appear to coexist within the same time-scale, the only difference being the quality and level of decoration, this probably represents the purchasing power of the individual.

At this time each soldier was equipped at his own expense (Polybius, 6.26.1–2), his equipment being his own personal property, commissioned on request from local metalworkers when called up for service, on a small-scale, ad hoc basis (Paddock, 1985, 143). If he survived to return home at the end of the campaign, his helmet, being his personal property, may end its days close to his home and close to its point of original manufacture. It is therefore possible that similarities in styles of decoration occurring in similar locations may represent the work of particular armourers, or at least of regional cultural styles. To support this view, Paddock cited two groups of almost identical helmets from around Perugia, Etruria, from grave contexts, dating to the fourth and third centuries BC, which may represent individuals returning from Punic campaigns, and may identify a local manufacturing centre (Paddock, 1985, 143). He also referenced three helmets with stamped markings overlying decoration which he believed to be more than simple scratched or engraved ownership markings and which may represent manufacturers markings, used to identify the work of individual armourers (Paddock, 1985, 144).

Montefortino – Types C and D

While the individual Roman soldier remained responsible for the purchase of his own equipment, the quality of manufacture remained consistent, individual items being

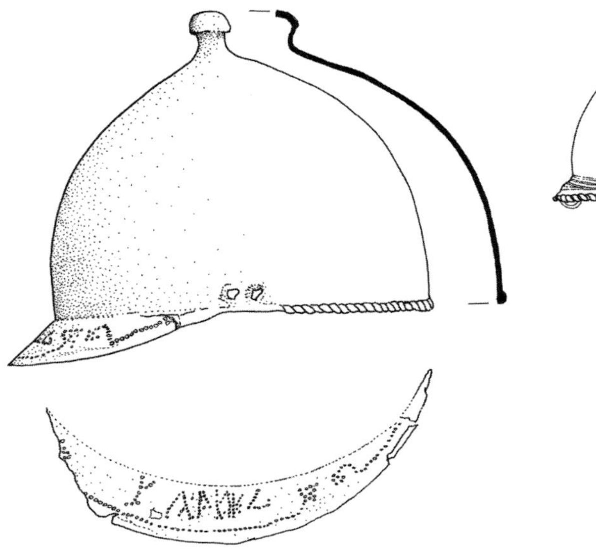

Fig. 33. Montefortino helmet (with engraved writing on neck guard). Bronze helmet, type B, as used by Roman legionaries during Punic Wars. Roman, *c.* 220–170 BC. Originally had cheek pieces (hinges visible), leather chinstraps, horsehair crest and padded lining (possibly of felt). British Museum (GR1975.6–3.1). (Artwork by J. R. Travis)

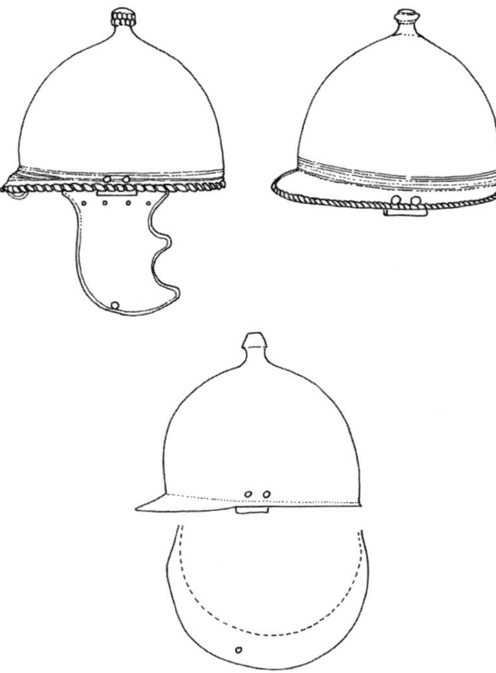

Fig. 34. Montefortino helmets types A to C (from Russell-Robinson, 1975). (Artwork by J. R. Travis)

commissioned as required from skilled craftsmen. However, with the reforms to the structure of the army by Marius, and later by Augustus, swelling its strength with an influx of poorer citizens to meet the demands of Civil Wars and the Social War, the responsibility for the purchase of equipment would have fallen on the state. With commissioning of large quantities to meet this increased demand, new large-scale factory production methods were introduced to speed up processing, and quality consequently suffered. Some helmet bowls were asymmetrical, thinner-walled and more crudely formed during the raising process, edges were left un-thickened and some bowls were insufficiently planished to remove larger hammer marks, as can be seen on one helmet from Montenerodomo (Paddock, 1985, 145).

Those helmets from the Russell-Robinson typologies C and D first appeared during the first-century BC period of mass production, as do the early 'Coolus' style of helmets. The type C helmet, also identified under the Continental system as 'Buggenum' (after the find site of one example from the Netherlands), is a simpler, slightly less bulbous but otherwise very similar shape to the earlier types A and B. Crest knobs are small, plain and mostly pierced to accommodate a plume. Neck guards are also slightly broader and flatter than their predecessors (Russell-Robinson, 1975, 18). One helmet of this type found at Sisak, Croatia, carries an inscription (SCIP IMP), interpreted by Waurick and Schaaf to suggest a mid-first-century BC date, consistent with the Caesarean campaigns (Feugère, 2002, 96). Other finds from around the Rhine and Meuse have been associated with the Germanic campaigns of 12 BC, Russell-Robinson suggesting that it may have remained in use until at least AD 70, into the Early Imperial period.

The type D helmet is stylistically and chronologically similar to the type C, other than in the treatment of the crest knob. Where previously this had been formed as an integral part of the bowl during the raising process, now it was cast separately and soldered on to the bowl (Russell-Robinson, 1975, 22). Paddock also reported this as another area where reduced-quality mass-production methods can be seen, with crest knobs being fixed to bowls 'off-centre' and insufficiently finished to remove flash marks from the casting process (Paddock, 1985, 145). Some crest knobs were drilled for plumes, as on type C helmets, although one example from Nijmegen was provided with a separate tube soldered behind the knob, presumably post-manufacture. There is also some evidence for helmets, from this period at least, being tinned (Russell-Robinson, 1975, 22). This cannot have been for protection purposes, however, and must have been a stylistic choice, perhaps to emulate the appearance of iron helmets, which were also beginning to appear around this time.

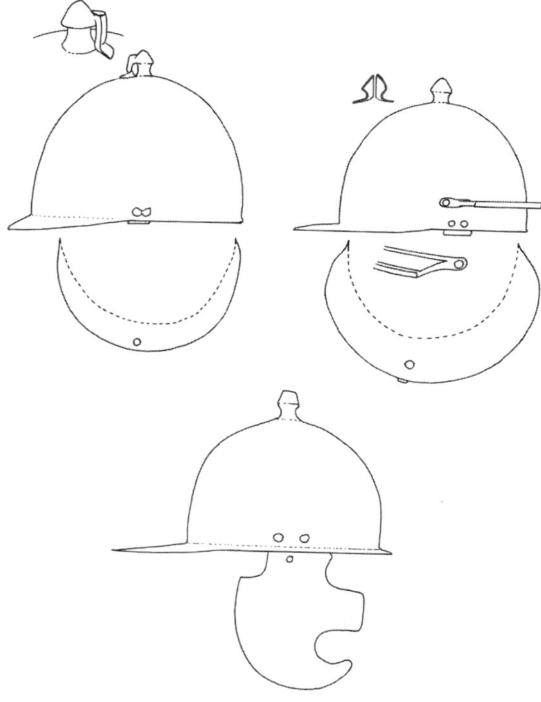

Fig. 35. Montefortino helmets types D to F (from Russell-Robinson, 1975). (Artwork by J. R. Travis)

Montefortino – Types E and F

Paddock identified a break in the continuity of helmet production, coinciding with the Augustan reforms of the early Principate, around 27 BC, when the number of legions was reduced (Paddock, 1985, 145). Pre-existing equipment remained in use, with spares stockpiled for reuse, so there was little call for the commissioning of new kit. With the types E and F, a progressive widening and flattening of the neck guard can be seen, along with the additional appearance of a reinforcing peak on the type E, similar to that on its Coolus contemporary (Hagenau types), the purpose of which, as suggested by Russell-Robinson, being to strengthen the weak point produced at the point of maximum thinning during the raising process (Russell-Robinson, 1975, 26). While most peaks are flat plates, the peak on one example of type E from Mainz was made from thinner metal, folded into a right-angled section to strengthen, in similar fashion to Italian helmets, which Russell-Robinson sees as Italian artistic style (Russell-Robinson, 1975, 63). In both E and F types the crest knob reverted to being produced integral to the bowl, forged in one piece, then lead-filled (Russell-Robinson, 1975, 25). In the type F, the influence of contemporary Coolus style can be seen in the extra-wide neck guard, to the extent that the two styles become almost identical; at more than just a passing glance, the only real difference is the bowl shape – hemispherical for Coolus and slightly conical for Montefortino.

Russell-Robinson interpreted these later changes, in widening neck guards and adding reinforcing peaks, as being a response to confrontations with new opponents making use of new slashing weapons. He cited evidence for large numbers of dead and seriously wounded troops with head injuries caused by downward cuts from long iron swords of the Celtic/La Tène people (Russell-Robinson, 1975, 26). Paddock, however, did not agree, as he felt that opponents had made use of these types of weapons throughout the period of use of the Montefortino, preferring to attribute the changes to contemporary reduction in *scutum* size (Paddock, 1985, 147). It is possible that both viewpoints are not so divergent or dissimilar. In any event, it is clear that these changes were introduced following a period of relative peace, allowing the opportunity to research and develop equipment improvements prior to the new active phase of Germanic campaigns. These German initiatives coincided not only with innovations in helmet design (including the introduction of different metal types, with the adoption of the use of iron by Gallic neighbours), but also with changes in *scutum* design, along with more widespread use of *lorica segmentata*, all perhaps reflecting new fighting methods and strategies.

COOLUS – TYPES A TO I

The bronze 'Coolus' helmet, as defined by Russell-Robinson's nine categories, was in use from the third century BC to the first century AD. However, under the Continental system, these are separated into two subtypes: the 'Mannheim' and the 'Hagenau', the former and earlier (represented by Russell-Robinson's categories A to C) not being provided with any crest knob at all. Like the Montefortino, the Coolus was a 'jockey cap'-style simple bronze helmet, although with a more rounded (rather than conical) bowl, was quicker (and presumably cheaper) to produce, and was again adopted from Celtic cultures, this time Gallic. In its earliest form, appearing around the third century BC, following its Celtic tradition, it had no cheek pieces, being pierced each side for simple ties, as with the early Montefortinos, and similarly some examples may not necessarily be entirely 'Roman'. However, where the Montefortino helmet can be seen developing from an Italic-Celtic tradition, the Coolus appears to spring from a Gallic source.

Although appearing in its earliest form from the third century BC, the Coolus appears to become issued in greater quantity from around the time of Caesar's Gallic Wars in the first century BC. Russell-Robinson suggested that Caesar made use of Gallic armourers in the Coolus district of Marne, close to the Rhine frontier, to equip his men during and after these campaigns, proposing a production centre in that region (Russell-Robinson, 1975, 26).

As with the Montefortinos, the Coolus helmet can be seen passing through a developmental progression, as described by Russell-Robinson (Russell-Robinson, 1975, 29), whereby neck guards expand and peaks are applied to reinforce weak points created in the manufacture of the bowl. Types A to C, as already described, were not provided with any form of crest knob, type A also being without cheek pieces and type C having a slightly swollen neck guard at the sides (Fig. 36).

As with the Montefortino, most of the innovative features appear to coincide with the onset of Germanic campaigns of the early first century AD. This again confirms Paddock's perceived break in manufacture (Paddock, 1985, 142), suggesting that, following a period of relative peace and low levels of manufacture, legions were re-equipped with new kit ready for expansion into Germanic regions. This was supplied with a range of innovative features, perhaps geared towards the weapons and fighting styles of potential enemy forces.

The types D to G, from the first century AD, known collectively by the Continental typology as 'Hagenau' (Feugère, 2002, 94), feature central crest knobs, as with the Montefortino helmets. Russell-Robinson suggested that this may indicate a switch in production, originating from an Italic source rather than the previous Gallic. These armourers then incorporated features of their own style: Montefortino-style crest knobs (from type E being slotted for the crest and drilled horizontally for a securing pin); side tubes for plumes; and some with Italic-style peaks of right-angled section (these being a feature of the 'Italic' style of 'Imperial' helmets; Russell-Robinson, 1975, 26; Fig. 37).

However, Feugère suggested that these early types, without knob (Mannheim) and with knob (Hagenau), may not represent different origins of manufacture, but may indicate a status differentiation between legionary and auxiliary troops, the Mannheim helmets being heavier (around 1 kg as opposed to 500–800 g) and of better quality, citing examples of both types having been found contemporaneously at one site (Vieill-Toulouse; Feugère, 2002, 71).

While types D and E still have relatively small, flat neck guards, this then becomes progressively wider and more sloping in later styles. With the type H helmets an additional reinforcing brow band was added and the neck guard was also supplied with a ring at the centre back. This may have provided a more secure method of fastening the helmet, with ties passing from one cheek piece backwards

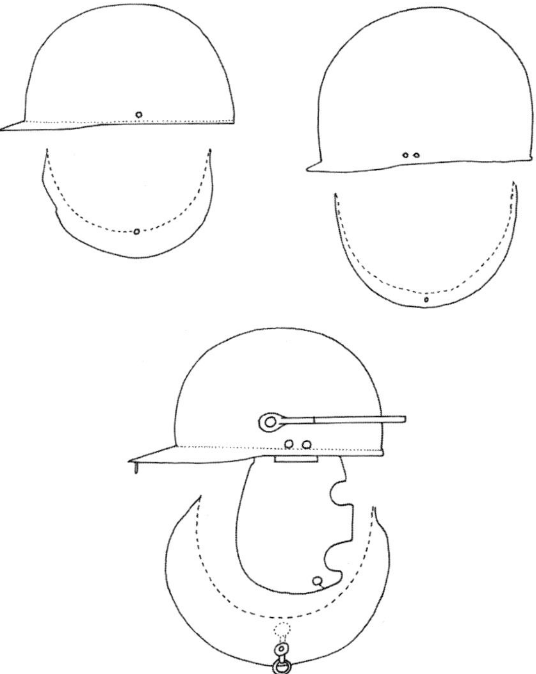

Fig. 36. Coolus helmets types A to C (from Russell-Robinson, 1975). (Artwork by J. R. Travis)

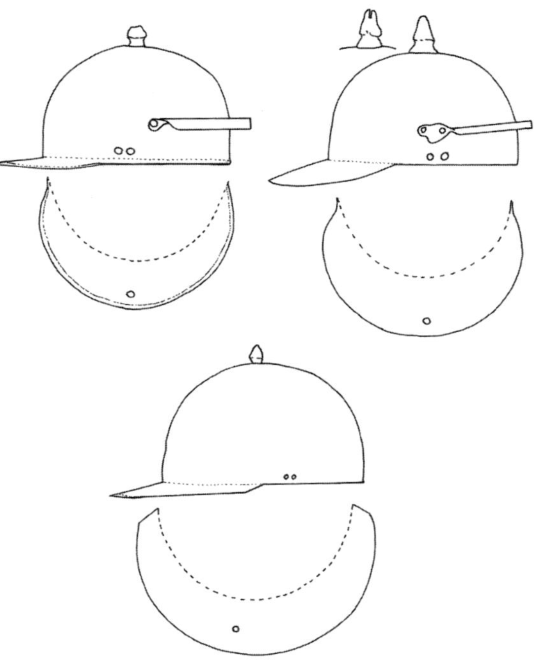

Fig. 37. Coolus helmets types D to F (from Russell-Robinson, 1975). (Artwork by J. R. Travis)

through this ring and forwards to the opposite cheek, or alternatively provided a means to carrying the helmet when not in use. In type I helmets, however, which appear to have coexisted with the type H, the neck guard featured an applied carrying handle on its centre-rear top surface. The type I helmets also differ from their predecessors in the shape of the bowl, in that it was extended, stepping down deeper at the back, in similar way to that seen on the iron 'Imperial' helmets. These later types H and I helmets were also further improved by the use of three rivets to secure cheek pieces to the bowl, rather than two rivets as previously (Fig. 38).

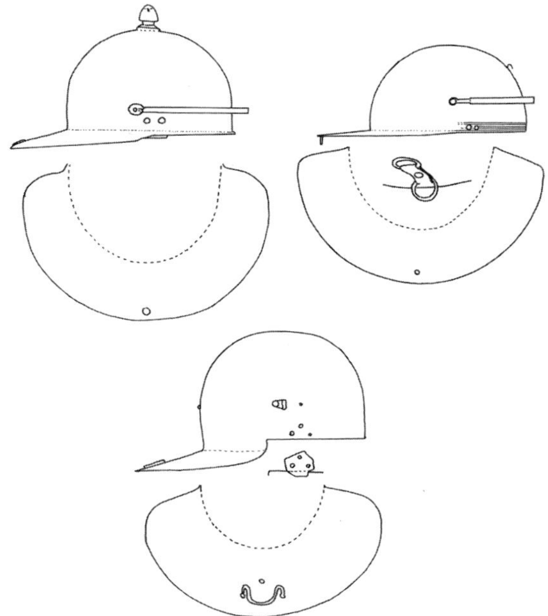

Fig. 38. Coolus helmets types G to I (from Russell-Robinson, 1975). (Artwork by J. R. Travis)

During the course of the developmental sequence of these 'Hagenau' Coolus helmets, therefore, innovative features can be seen being introduced, echoing those on the iron 'Imperial'/'Weisenau' helmets. The neck guard was widened and extended out to the sides, to protect against downward slashing blows or diagonal sweeping cuts with a sword or axe. The bowl was further strengthened against a direct overhead and frontal assault with the addition of first a reinforcing peak, then an applied brow band, and eventually with a deepening at the back, with a stepped occipital area. This brought the neck protection further down towards the shoulders and upper back, reducing the tendency for the helmet to dislodge with a direct strike in a downward direction. The movement away from crest knobs in the later helmets of this type may also reflect a change in enemy type and fighting styles. However, it appears to be more of a stylistic change along the lines of the new iron helmets, reverting once more to a Gallic influence, stemming perhaps from the earliest Roman/Gallic iron helmet, the Agen/Port type.

With the increased production necessary to meet the needs of the post-Marian and post-Augustan reforms, new methods of production were introduced, with evidence of a change from small-scale, ad-hoc production by local armourers to large-scale 'factory' production. The lighter Coolus helmets were generally of a lower quality than the earlier Montefortinos, being more crudely formed and finished, suggesting speed of manufacture being a priority over quality. Cast and applied crest knobs, rather than those worked in one with the bowl of the helmet, did not require the work of such a skilled craftsman. It was to achieve this increased production level that Paddock believed the process of 'spinning' was introduced at this time. He cited a number of helmets where he considered that spinning marks were evident – one Montefortino from Nijmegen and several Coolus/Hagenau helmets (Paddock, 1985, 146).

To 'spin' a helmet, a sheet of annealed metal would be pierced and set in a lathe between a 'former' and a 'follower'. With the lathe rotating, the metal sheet would be gradually directed towards the former, using stroking movements. The punch centring points would later be concealed by the applied crest knob, but evidence of the 'spinning' process may remain in the form of concentric tooling marks and in that the bowl would be rounded in form. Helmets made by drawing down, as a 'one off' by a craftsman for a specific individual, however, would be made more oval-shaped, to better fit the intended wearer (as the human head is not round). From his study of a number of Coolus Hagenau helmets, Paddock believed he was able to identify that the majority of these helmets had identical internal dimensions, suggesting the use of similar-sized formers, possibly indicative of factory mass production (Paddock, 1985, 146). He also suggested that the Pylos helmets of classical and Hellenistic Greece may similarly have been spun, due to consistencies in dimensions and roundness, although 'spin marks' were not evidenced (Paddock, 1985, 146). If this is the case, it is possible that this 'innovation' of manufacture was not new, but was a tradition adopted from the Italic armourers, through cultural influences from Etruscan/Greek origins, rather than from the Gallic. Indeed, Feugère suggested that the earlier Mannheim-style Coolus helmets were heavier and of better quality than the Hagenau style (Feugère, 2002, 71), which may support Russell-Robinson's view that the former were Gallic in origin and the latter Italic (Russell-Robinson, 1975, 26).

Certainly, the reintroduction of the crest knob would support this view of a movement back towards Italian manufacture, although with modifications for speed of production. The later loss of crest knob suggests that this focus of production may have moved back to Gallic regions, but may also represent a stylistic change in the type of crest and method of attachment. The overall visual appearance of the helmet would be quite different to the early Montefortino, and even Attic-style helmets, which are seen in artistic depictions with individual feathers inserted into tubes and central cascading horsehair plumes, either tied to, or inserted into drilled holes in the central crest knob. The crest knobs on these later helmets were slotted, suggesting a different type of crest altogether, perhaps by appearance more towards the flat crests of the iron 'Imperial' helmets (Fig. 122). The appearance of front and rear anchoring hooks on the later helmet bowls certainly suggests that by this time crests were of the 'flat' type. Side tubes for feathers are not universal, but do continue in use, suggesting that they may have been a badge of office, denoting rank, making officers more easily identifiable in combat situations.

Type	Form	Neckguard			Brow reinforced	Tubes	Knob				Cheek pieces
		Shape	Decoration	Peak			Pierced	Hollow	Cast & solder	Description	
A	Bulbous	Short sloping	Decorated	No	No	No	No	Yes	No	Round scale pattern or conical, plain flat top	Yes
B			Plain							Plain, conical	
C	Conical	Flatter, broader	Plain or rough pattern			No	Yes	Yes	No	Small, plain, conical	
D	Rounded conical		Strong tip			Behind knob on 1 eg	No	No	Yes		
E		Broad, flattened	No	Yes		Side on 1 eg	Yes, or slot	Yes	No		
F	Bulbous rounded	Large, flat	No	No		No		Yes, lead-filled			

Table 3. Montefortino helmets – description of H. Russell-Robinson typologies.

<table>
<tr><th rowspan="2">Type</th><th rowspan="2">Form</th><th colspan="2">Neckguard</th><th rowspan="2">Peak</th><th rowspan="2">Brow Reinforced</th><th rowspan="2">Tubes</th><th colspan="4">Knob</th><th rowspan="2">Cheek pieces</th></tr>
<tr><th>Shape</th><th>Decoration</th><th>Pierced</th><th>Hollow</th><th>Cast and solder</th><th>Description</th></tr>
<tr><td>A</td><td>Rounded, low</td><td>Short, sloping</td><td rowspan="9">No</td><td rowspan="2">No</td><td rowspan="7">No</td><td rowspan="3">No</td><td colspan="3" rowspan="3">No</td><td>None</td><td>No, just holes for ties</td></tr>
<tr><td>B</td><td>Bulbous, globular</td><td>Very small</td><td>None. Small hole centre top, possibly spun</td><td rowspan="6">Yes, two rivets</td></tr>
<tr><td>C</td><td>Bulbous, low</td><td>Small, flat, swelling at sides, curving inwards</td><td>Yes</td><td>None</td></tr>
<tr><td>D</td><td rowspan="2">Round, moderate height</td><td rowspan="2">Small, flat</td><td>Yes, right-angle section</td><td>Yes</td><td>Slotted</td><td rowspan="4">No</td><td>Yes</td><td rowspan="4">Small, solid, conical or slotted</td></tr>
<tr><td>E</td><td>Yes, flat and tongued to bowl</td><td>On side</td><td>Slotted, drilled horizontal</td><td>Yes</td></tr>
<tr><td>F</td><td rowspan="2">Rounded</td><td>Broader at sides, ends at short step (not rounded). Sloping</td><td>Possible</td><td>No</td><td>Slotted, drilled horizontal</td><td>Yes</td></tr>
<tr><td>G</td><td>Large, rounded corners, sloping</td><td>Yes</td><td>On side</td><td>Slotted, drilled horizontal</td><td>Yes</td></tr>
<tr><td>H</td><td>Rounded, low</td><td>Broad, flat (at right angles). Ring at back, underside.</td><td>Yes, right-angle section</td><td>Yes</td><td>No</td><td colspan="3" rowspan="2">No</td><td>None, front & rear hooks</td><td rowspan="2">Yes, three rivets</td></tr>
<tr><td>I</td><td>Deep, stepped back (like Imperial)</td><td>Broad, sloping. Carrying handle</td><td>Yes</td><td>No</td><td>On side</td><td>None</td></tr>
</table>

Table 4. Coolus helmets – description of H. Russell-Robinson typologies.

V

IRON HELMETS OF THE LATER REPUBLICAN AND IMPERIAL PERIOD

Although in his analysis Russell-Robinson (1975) classified the iron helmets of the Imperial period as 'Gallic' and 'Italic' (with their predecessors, the Agen and Port helmets), based on features which he perceived as indicators of area of manufacture, these are alternately identified as 'Weisenau' and later 'Niedermörmter' types under the Continental typology, their names based on find sites of the original exemplars.

AGEN/PORT HELMETS

The Gallic Celts were famed metalworkers. They pioneered the use of iron helmets (Warry, 1980, 143), although there is no evidence to suggest any use of 'spinning' in production, iron not lending itself to this method as readily as bronze (Paddock, 1985, 147). The two early types of Gallic, iron helmet, the 'Agen' and the 'Port', are not immediately similar, but each exhibits features that became standard on subsequent iron 'Imperial' descendants. Both helmets have deep, rounded bowls, with flattened top and straight sides. The Agen type (named after the find spot of the first example) flares out to a narrow brim (at first glance, similar to a bowler hat, or a First World War British helmet), although this brim doubles its breadth at the rear to provide a neck guard. This widened neck guard could have been a weak point, with a tendency to bend and crumple, so it was then embossed with two shallow, semi-circular steps, a feature retained on the Imperial helmets, designed to increase rigidity. Perhaps for similar reasons of rigidity, or perhaps to increase ventilation, the helmet was also provided with a prominent, triangular sectioned, horizontal rib all around the bowl, just above the brim/neck guard. Four helmets of this type are known (Russell-Robinson, 1975, 42), only the one original from Agen being provided with a crest fitting (a simple tube, riveted through its circular flanged base), although from so few examples greater use cannot be excluded.

The Port type Gallic helmet (named after an example from Port bei Nidau), has an immediate 'Roman' look to it, the early features of the 'Imperial' descendant being easily recognised (Russell-Robinson, 1975, 42). The deep, straight-sided bowl is extended downwards at the rear, occipital area and is provided with two prominent, embossed ridges, just above the narrow neck guard flange. Across the front of the bowl

Fig. 39. (a) Agen and (b) Port helmets (from Russell-Robinson, 1975). (Artwork by J. R. Travis)

are a pair of simple, recurved, embossed 'eyebrows', a feature later to be more elaborately developed in the helmets of Russell-Robinson's 'Imperial Gallic' typology (Fig. 40). As with the occipital ridges, this would have developed as a strengthening/ventilating feature as much as for any aesthetic/decorative reasons.

At either side, on each type, Agen or Port, two iron rivets served to attach cheek piece hinges, and here, in the cheek pieces, a degree of commonality can be seen. Cheek pieces of both types are markedly similar, rounded to the rear, with recessed border, to follow the line of the jaw, and flat at the front with two semi-circular cut-outs for the eyes and mouth. The tie-ring attachment is towards the rear edge, allowing for a close fastening. Russell-Robinson (1975, 42) attributes these helmets to the mid-first century BC, citing finds of this type of helmet and cheek piece from contexts dating to Caesar's siege of Alesia in 52 BC. A further feature, later developed in the 'Imperial' typology, making an appearance on one much-damaged example from Vie Cioutat, France, is a shallow cut-out above the wearer's ears (Russell-Robinson, 1975, 42), and must have looked transitionally not unlike the Imperial Gallic type A, but without the strengthening peak.

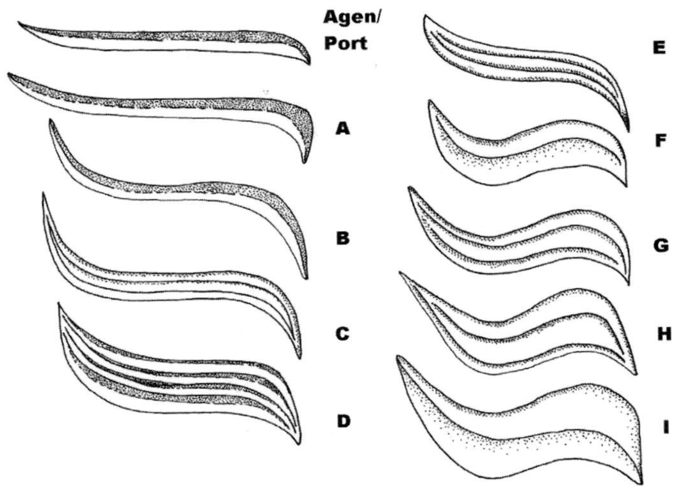

Fig. 40. Development of eyebrows on Imperial Gallic helmets from earlier Agen/Port form (from Russell-Robinson, 1975). (Artwork by J. R. Travis)

THE STARA GRADIŠKA HELMET

A well-preserved iron helmet was found, at a time of low water, in the River Sava, near Stara Gradiška in 2003, and has been identified as being late La Tène, of 'east-Celtic' or 'Novo Mesto' type (described as 'bronze' in the subsequent report, although being mostly iron with bronze additions; Mihaljević & Dizdar, 2007, 117).

'East-Celtic'-type helmets ('Novo Mesto' type) are usually made of three parts: a hemispherical bowl, a forehead guard and a neck guard, the latter two reinforced at the point where they join by a jutting rib and decorated with many rivets. Most have cut-outs for ears. Cheek pieces can be rounded or squared, hanging from five-part hinges, and are decorated with images of animals. The helmets are usually of iron, with forehead band, neck guard and cheek pieces of bronze (*ibid.*, 127).

Unlike the 'east-Celtic' helmets, the 'west-Celtic' ones were made in one piece, with prominent mouldings at the bottom, a flanged neck guard and rounded cheek guards (the 'west-Celtic' helmets being found in settlements and graves in France and Switzerland). Late La Tène helmets (of 'Port' type) are found in western and eastern Celtic regions. They have embossed eyebrow features on the front of the bowl and two ribs on the neck guards.

The Stara Gradiška helmet was formed from sixteen separate parts altogether, including bowl, neck guard, cheek pieces, reinforcing strips and decorative motifs and rivets (*ibid.*, 120). The helmet had a smooth, hemispherical iron bowl (or 'calotte'), with three narrow ribs with grooves at the edge, and had been forged from a double layer of sheet iron for extra strength.

A moulded bronze reinforcing strip was fitted over the apex of the bowl, from front to back, terminating in small human-face mask motifs and triskels (three-branched raised swirls, embossed onto rounded rivet shapes, surrounded by a raised outer ring). Small iron rivets on the inside attached a protective bronze forehead brim and a neck guard. The forehead and neck guards were also soldered together where they met on the helmet sides (*ibid.*, 120).

The bronze cheek pieces were almost rectangular, with rounded corners and at two points along the front edge (one at the mid-point and one at the bottom) suspended from the forehead guard by hinges (made in five parts, with an iron shaft). They were held fastened by a strap, a fixture which was soldered to the inside of each plate. Each cheek piece was decorated with a highly stylised embossed representation of a water bird, and three ornamental rivets (with cross-shaped incisions and traces of red enamel).

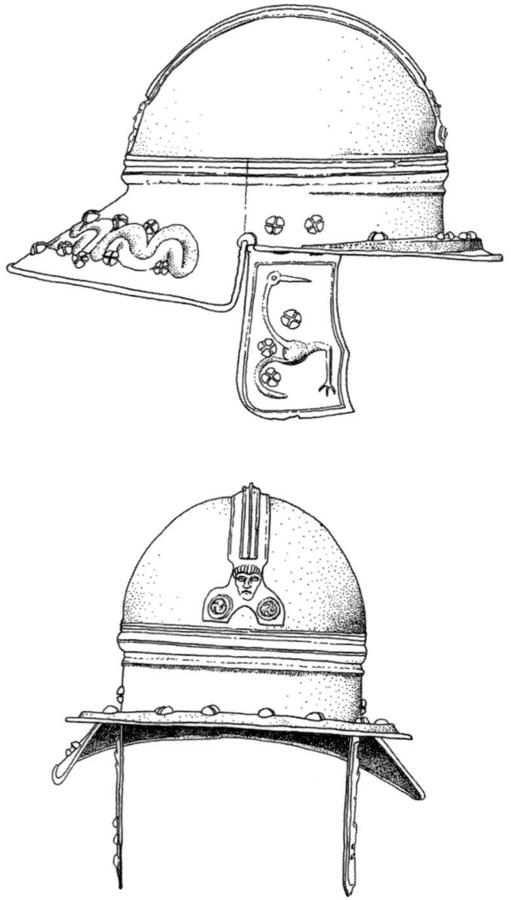

Fig. 41. Late La Tène Helmet from the River Sava, near Stara Gradiška. (Artwork by J. R. Travis)

A crescent-shaped reinforcement plate was soldered to the horizontal part of the forehead brim, held by seven more of the decorative rivets. The wide, sloping neck guard was also decorated with a chunky embossed decoration, resembling four letter Ms and similar decorative rivets (placed in two rows: seven on the inside and eleven on the outside; one in each of the 'bumps' and 'dents' of the Ms). There is an established custom of putting helmets in graves in the La Tène culture, and fragments of similar 'M' motifs have been found on these, dated to the end of the first half, or the second half, of the first century BC.

From the method of construction and the style of decoration, the helmet has thus been identified as an 'east-Celtic' form of a 'Port' helmet (Mihaljević & Dizdar, 2007, 127). Other similarly dated 'east-Celtic' 'Novo Mesto'-type helmets have been also found from Slovenia and Croatia, with some also further afield, including one from central Poland (from a cremation grave at Siemiechŏw), which contained a helmet and *gladius* of a Roman legionary, suggesting some cultural contacts and exchanges of ideas and goods (Jazdzewska, 1986, 57–62).

THE SIEMIECHŎW HELMET

The Siemiechŏw helmet was found in 1982, in a grave in a late La Tène, early Roman cemetery, dating from the first century BC to the second/third century AD, at Siemiechŏw, on the Warta River, central Poland (Jazdzewska, 1986, 57). It came from one of thirty-nine cremation graves which had produced Celtic-style weapons and pottery, indicating contacts between local Celtic inhabitants and the Roman province of Noricum. One burial, however, was found to contain an iron helmet, used as an urn, containing cremated remains, along with two knives (one on top and one inside the contents). Also found with the burial was a ritually bent sword (*gladius*), a spearhead and a shield boss.

The helmet has been identified as belonging to a Roman legionary, and as being of Celto-Italian design. It had a hemispherical bowl, with a horizontal, angular neck guard, a pronounced peak, and two cheek pieces (12 cm long), attached by hinges, with iron loops on the inner side for a closure strap. Jazdzewska (1986, 58), proposed that its closest comparative would be to Russell-Robinson's Coolus type C (dating from the late first century BC to early first century AD), citing a similar 'legionary' Coolus type G first-century AD helmet from Burlafingen, Munich. However, being that the Coolus helmet was of bronze and this helmet was of iron, it would probably be closer to the early iron 'Port' helmet (Jazdzewska also reporting that the cheek pieces, also of iron, are similar to those on the Gallic Agen/Port helmets).

Although describing the helmet as a 'Roman legionary helmet', Jazdzewska (1986, 58) suggested that the owner at the time of deposition had probably not been 'Roman', believing that the deceased had been an important person of local origin, and that it would have been 'unacceptable' for him to have become a 'Roman' soldier, as he would not have been a citizen; instead Jazdzewska proposes that the helmet would have reached the Warta region through trade (probably through sale of war booty, illegally sold to the northern peoples).

IMPERIAL GALLIC – TYPES A TO K

Iron helmets first appear to be used by the Roman army following Caesar's Gallic Wars, although they had been in use by Gallic Celtic people prior to this, suggesting either the adoption from their example, or commissioned manufacture by Gallic armourers. As previously mentioned, in his perceived developmental progression, Russell-Robinson believed that the Imperial helmet was a descendant of the Gallic 'Agen' and 'Port' helmet types, exhibiting features from both (Russell-Robinson, 1975, 45).

The bowl shape, flattened on top and straight-sided, is similar in the Imperial to the Agen-Port types, and displays the embossed, recurved 'eyebrows' derived from the 'Port' helmets (Fig. 40). In common with Port types, two raised 'occipital' ridges can be seen at the back, with a third step defining the commencement of the outward-flanged neck guard. Drawing from the 'Agen' predecessor, the neck guard is then provided with semi-circular embossed steps for increased rigidity, forming an indent for the suspension ring on the lower surface. Where this style does differ from the Agen-Port types, however, is the appearance of a heavy reinforcing peak at the front.

Although under the Continental system these helmets are generally grouped under the 'Weisenau' heading, as with the previous bronze helmet types, Russell-Robinson attempted to group these into eleven categories by apparent developmental progression seen in minor feature variations.

Imperial Gallic – Type A

In its earliest form this helmet appears as a full hybrid of the two earlier styles, the Agen and the Port, resembling in profile the Port, but with a deeper neck guard to the rear. As seen on some later Port examples (for example that from Vie Cioutat), this type as standard featured small, semi-circular sections of the lower bowl cut away for the ears to improve hearing. The enlarged neck guard protruding to the sides, combined with the heavy peak to the front, would have in some way deflected blows to this new area of vulnerability. The attachment of the peak was aligned to the upper 'occipital' ridge, to create the impression of a continuous line encircling the helmet, aesthetically reflecting the fully encircling ridges of the 'Agen' predecessor, while practically reflecting its defensive properties in facial protection and strengthening the bowl from overhead frontal attack. The cheek guards are again similar in shape to those on the Agen/Port types, the edges cut away for the eyes and mouth, but without any form of 'cut away' for the ears and fastened using conical studs, as on the Montefortino. Russell-Robinson saw similarities in the shape of these cheek pieces to those from Coolus type D helmets, proposing an Augustan date, pre-AD 14, for this variant (Russell-Robinson, 1975, 51; Fig. 115).

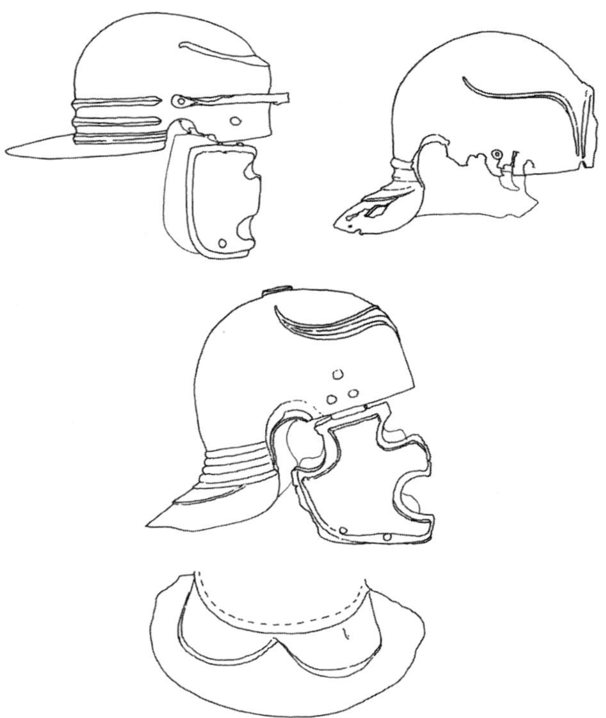

Fig. 42. Imperial Gallic helmets types A to C (from Russell-Robinson, 1975). (Artwork by J. R. Travis)

Imperial Gallic – Type B

Differences in this type to type A are that the bowl shape is more rounded on top, ear 'cut-aways' are slightly flanged outwards (for increased protection) and the moderately sized neck guard now slopes downward slightly. The cheek pieces, while similar in shape at the front to the Agen/Port and to type A, were provided with additional semi-circular cusps, cut away at the upper rear to accommodate the ear, and outwardly flanged at the lower rear to protect the throat (Fig. 115). Russell-Robinson also suggested that this variant may also have been supplied with a decorative and reinforcing brow band at the front. He cited evidence of riveting holes for its attachment on the front edge of the type B helmet from the Kupa, near Sissek (formerly in the Salzer Collection, but now lost), as seen on an illustration by Lipperheide (Russell-Robinson, 1975, 52).

Imperial Gallic – Type C

This type is again similar to type B in its rounded, hemispherical shape, but stepping down lower at the back, with three occipital ridges instead of two as previously, and lacking the flanged ear guards. There is no evidence for a reinforcing peak, but this does not exclude its original presence. The eyebrows are more elaborately embossed, with a medial step, and the neck guard slopes down, as with the type B, but is wider, flaring forwards at the sides, covering the flanged cheek guards and affording greater protection to the throat and neck from diagonally directed overhead blows. At top centre, the bowl is provided with a rectangular plate, riveted at each corner and raised to form two ridges (front to back), to serve as attachment for a two-pronged crest support (Fig. 122).

Cheek pieces are similar in form to their predecessors, although with cut-away cusp for the ear, outwardly turned throat flange and slight rounding to the straight leading edge between eye and mouth cusps. On the example from the River Kupa, in the Archaeological Museum Zagreb, the cheek piece has an embossed semi-circle below the hinge and is provided with tie rings, instead of the previous studs, riveted to the centre lower edge (Russell-Robinson, 1975, 53). Russell-Robinson also reported traces of a 16 mm-wide bronze brow band and bronze U-sectioned edging around the neck guard, ear recesses and cheek pieces (Russell-Robinson, 1975, 53).

Imperial Gallic – Type D

Robinson reported only one known example of this helmet type, found in the Rhine at Weisenau, originally intact but destroyed during the Second World War and surviving now only in photographs, drawings and fragments in the Museum of Mainz (Russell-Robinson, 1975, 53). Similar in profile to the type C, with rounded bowl, three occipital ridges and sloping, flaring neck guard, it is of fine quality and highly decorative, suggesting to Russell-Robinson use by an officer of rank, perhaps a centurion. It has rectangular crest support but no trace of front/rear rings, so could have supported a centurial *crista transversa* (Russell-Robinson, 1975, 53). The eyebrows are large, boldly recurved, with four equal ridges. The leading edge of the peak was inlaid with a bronze herringbone pattern and the helmet further reinforced by the addition of a bronze brow band with five ribs of reeded decoration, the outer ribs beaded; the central one with upwardly turned crescent shapes (Russell-Robinson, 1975, 53). In addition, all exposed rivets on the bowl and cheek pieces were surrounded by decorative silver bosses with red enamel centres. The cheek pieces have more rounded edges than previously, and these, along with the main body of the helmet, were provided with slender bronze edge binding (Fig. 115). The other major new feature of this type was the addition of applied iron ear guards, increasing ear protection, although not as prominently as in later examples.

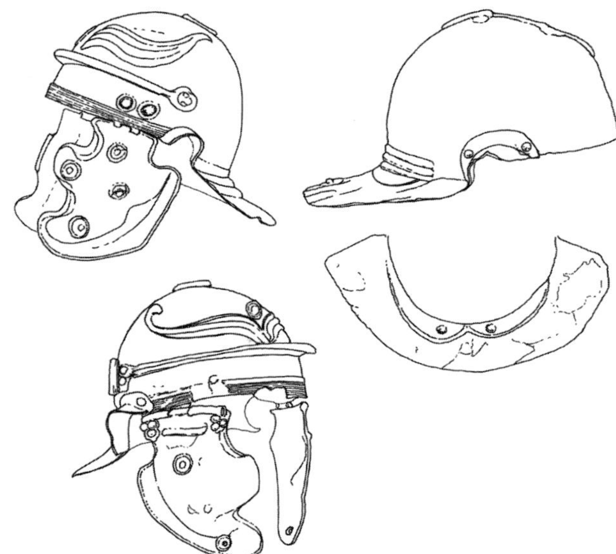

Fig. 43. Imperial Gallic helmets types D to F (from Russell-Robinson, 1975). (Artwork by J. R. Travis).

Imperial Gallic – Type E

This helmet is similar in shape and features to the type D (with three occipital steps and two on the neck guard), and also in the type of crest support, reeded brow band decoration, edge binding and cheek piece shape. The neck guard projects more at the sides, however, and has more angular, rounded corners. Of the two examples cited by Russell-Robinson, the applied ear guards on the Valkenberg helmet (dated to AD 39–42/43) are of bronze (rather than iron, as on type D), and are missing on that from the Celtic cemetery at Idria, but may have been originally present. The latter helmet is devoid of any form of ear shaping, although it is heavily distorted from extensive (and, as suggested by Russell-Robinson, overly enthusiastic) renovation, which appears to have removed this ear section altogether and closed the gap where it had once been (Russell-Robinson, 1975, 54).

Imperial Gallic – Type F

Dating to the second quarter of the first century AD, this helmet is essentially similar in form to types D and E. However, it is much simpler in decoration. The eyebrows are wide and simplified and embossed steps at the occiput and on the neck guard are shallower, while embossed decoration on the cheek pieces is confined to the jawline and a horizontal rib below the hinge. The neck guard is more rounded and does not project as widely at the sides. The crest attachment is again rectangular in form, but with only a single ridge, and with additional anchor loops on the front and rear of the bowl. On one example, however, from Sisak, a different type of crest holder can be seen – a round plate with a central slot (an attachment type usually associated with the Italic type helmets), which Russell-Robinson (1975, 56) suggested may have been a later addition or sloppy repair.

Imperial Gallic – Type G

This helmet bears all of the features of a typical mid-first-century AD Imperial Gallic helmet, a complete example of which, from the Rhine at Mainz, can be seen in the Museum at Worms. It has a rounded, hemispherical bowl, embossed with broad, stylised, leaf-like eyebrows. It has three shallow, occipital steps and two on the neck guard, one indented into two semi-circles for the central rivet and decorative boss. Further decorative bosses can be seen at either end of the neck guard, covering two hinge rivets above the cheek piece (on each side above the applied brow band), and three on each cheek piece (the two in the middle serving no purpose, and the lower one anchoring the tie ring). In addition to these three decorative bosses, the cheek pieces are rounded in form and provided with bronze edge binding, throat flanges and a raised semi-circular embossed reinforcement below the hinge, as had been seen on type C helmets (Fig. 115).

Fig. 44. Re-enactor wearing a reconstruction of an Imperial Gallic type F helmet. This helmet differs from others of Gallic type, as it has an 'Italic'-style round, 'turnkey' crest fitting and side tubes for single-feather plumes. (Photograph by H. Travis)

Imperial Gallic – Type H

This helmet is a further variation of the type G and contemporary in date, examples of both having been found in Colchester, in clearance pits from the Boudiccan revolt of AD 61. Its main difference to the type G helmet is that the neck guard is set at a deeper angle of around 50°. There is also the possibility of surface silvering having been used, traces of which were found beneath the brow band rivets on an example from Augsburg (Russell-Robinson, 1975, 57).

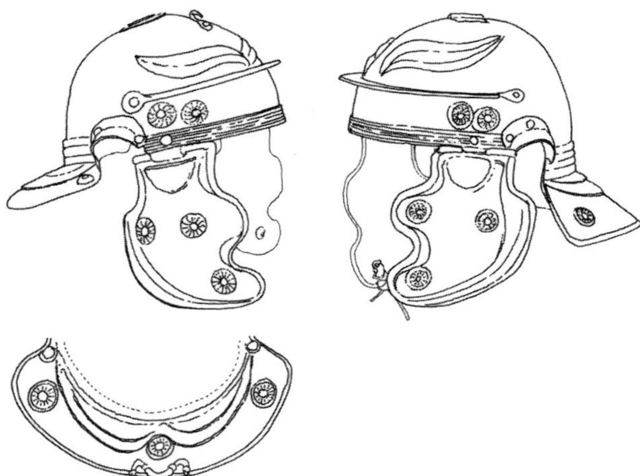

Fig. 45. Imperial Gallic helmets types G to H (from Russell-Robinson, 1975). (Artwork by J. R. Travis)

Imperial Gallic – Type I

Again, this Imperial style helmet follows the same basic design as the type H, but was produced in bronze rather than iron. It features broad, leaf-like embossed eyebrows, with medial ridge, three occipital ridges and two neck guard steps. It has applied ear guards, simple reeded brow band and flat reinforcing peak. The example cited by Russell-Robinson (1975, 59, pls 136–139), found in the River Rhine at Mainz, featured traces of a twist-on crest holder, and had also been provided with plume holding tubes applied to each side, next to the peak attachments. This helmet bears the inscribed name of its owner, 'L. Lucretius Celeris', a member of *legio I Adiutrix*, who were stationed at Mainz (*Moguntiacum*) between AD 71 and 86. Its loss in the river was attributed by Russell-Robinson (1975, 8) as being probably prior to AD 83, when the less reliable ferry was replaced with the safer bridge crossing.

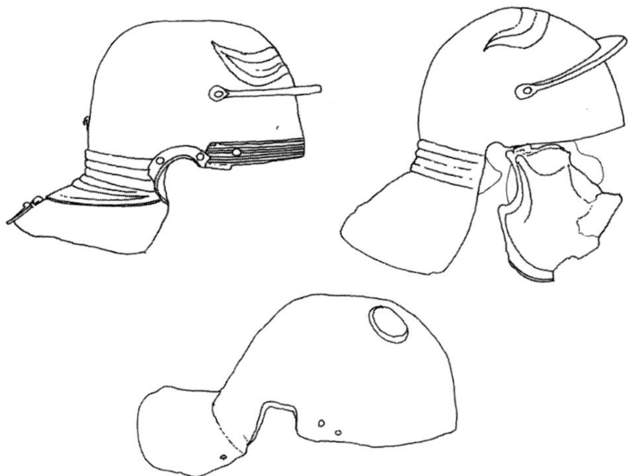

Fig. 46. Imperial Gallic helmets types I to K (from Russell-Robinson, 1975). (Artwork by J. R. Travis)

Imperial Gallic – Type J
Russell-Robinson (1975, 61) reported only one known example of this type of helmet, from Brigetio, Hungary, with a suggested date of AD 100–125. It is very similar in shape and decoration to types G, H and I, but the neck guard is much larger, sloping down at 45°, and the cheek pieces are simply decorated, each with only two decorative bosses, one in the centre and one at the lower edge (Fig. 115).

Imperial Gallic – Type K
Although categorised among the helmets of Imperial Gallic type, Russell-Robinson described this as a transitional type between Imperial Gallic type J and Imperial Italic type G. It broadly resembles in shape the Imperial Gallic type J, although with more rounded corners on the neck guard. It also featured four bronze crescent-shaped *luna* ornaments, applied as decoration on the crown, as seen on the Imperial Italic type G, although without the cross reinforcements (Russell-Robinson, 1975, 61).

Fig. 47. Imperial Gallic type J helmet from Brigetio, Hungary, now in Caerleon Museum. (Photo by J. R. Travis)

IMPERIAL ITALIC – TYPES A TO H

Although under the Continental system the iron helmets of the Imperial period are categorised under the term Weisenau, with the same basic features (shape, occipital ridges, stepped neck guard and cheek pieces), Russell-Robinson identified some features which he considered to have a Gallic origin and others which he felt also exhibited an Italic influence, although some of these were actually bronze rather than iron. These Italic features, he believed, may represent manufacture of the new Gallic-style helmets in Italian workshops, who then introduced features of their previous Greco-Etruscan and Italian tradition, identifying similarities to the Attic helmets of the fourth to third centuries BC (Russell-Robinson, 1975, 62). Those features that he felt to be specifically Italic were the reinforcing peaks (of right-angle section rather than solid, flat plate), the round plate twist-on crest fixture (rather than the Gallic-style slide-on method), and the lack of eyebrows and throat flanges (Russell-Robinson, 1975, 63). Again, within this range of helmets of deemed Italic style, Russell-Robinson also suggested a developmental progression, spanning the first two centuries AD, producing eight subcategories, A to H.

Imperial Italic – Type A

The only two examples of this category are easily dated, being found in Herculaneum, attributed by Russell-Robinson as belonging to the cohorts of *vigiles* (the city guards or firemen), their archaic style being perhaps in part due to their ceremonial nature. Russell-Robinson attributes these helmets to his Imperial Italic category, despite both known examples being made of bronze rather than iron, as he felt that they exhibit features more of common origin to this type than any other, drawing on the Greco-Etruscan 'Attic' tradition (Russell-Robinson, 1975, 65).

The skull shape on these helmets is straight at the back, curving around the ears, as with the earlier Attic, rather than following the contours of the head, although lacking in the medial ridge. Just below the ears, a 90° flange then turns outwards to form a small neck guard. The helmets do not bear the Gallic-style eyebrows, but are embossed with a scrolling, inverted V shape. The cheek pieces still fasten with the early-style simple studs, as seen on the Montefortino, Coolus and Early Imperial Gallic helmets (Fig. 117). The method of crest fastening, however, varies from these by using the cruder twist-on style of round plate with a central slot, which Russell-Robinson (1975, 65), identified as typically Italic, used with bronze hooks attached to the bowl front and back for additional crest anchorage.

Imperial Italic – Type B

This iron helmet more closely conforms to the true Imperial Italic style, with its plain, undecorated, deep, straight-backed skull and occipital ridges. The narrow neck guard, with rounded, angular corners, turned out at 90° to the skull, has a single embossed reinforcing step for half of its width, although, unlike the Imperial Gallic style, this has no central recess for a corresponding suspension loop on its lower surface, which is instead set further out towards the rim. Whereas on type A the back of the helmet simply curved around the ears, on this helmet the ear recesses are flanged outwards slightly. On the example from Klakanje, featured by Russell-Robinson (Russell-Robinson, 1975, 67, pls 152–154), there are no remaining traces of either crest plate or hooks, although these may have been lost. Traces can be seen, however, of a simple reeded brow band, bronze edge binding and enamelled bosses, one on the centre of the neck guard and one on the lower cheek piece, securing the tie rings. Based on the comparison of style of these bosses and brow band with their equivalents on Imperial Gallic type D and E helmets, Russell-Robinson (1975, 67) estimated a contemporary date around AD 25 to 50.

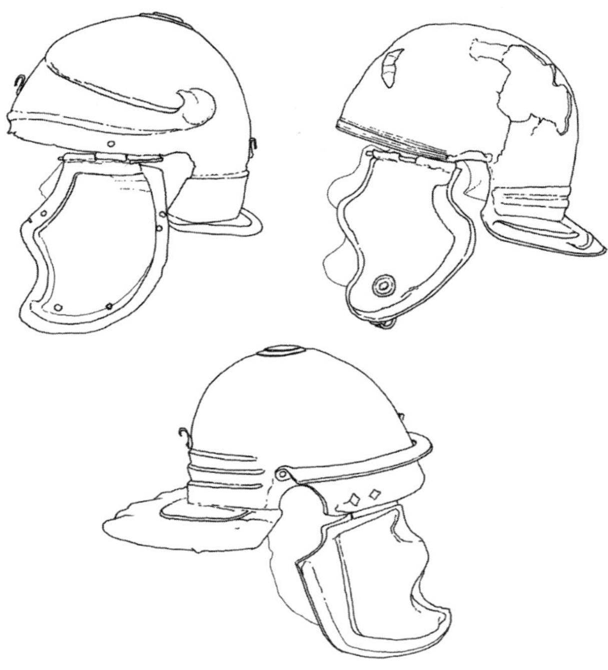

Fig. 48. Imperial Italic helmets types A, B and C (from Russell-Robinson, 1975). (Artwork by J. R. Travis)

Imperial Italic – Type C

In this category of helmets (all of which are of bronze), there are once more no Gallic-style eyebrows. The three occipital ridges are widely spaced and flattened out. The widened neck guard again is broad and flat, with angular corners and a reinforcing step, although now this has the central recess as seen on the Imperial Gallic types. The crest attachment is of the round, slotted plate twist-on type, with front and rear hooks, in typical Italic style and the ear recesses are once more flanged outwards. This helmet is the first in the Imperial Italic category to feature a reinforcing peak, although, unlike those of thick, flat Gallic style, these are of right-angle section, as seen on Montefortino and Coolus examples, which Russell-Robinson (1975, 67) suggested points to a common Italic origin.

Dating for this category is relatively secure (for the end date at least, with the provision that length of service is unknown), in that two of the helmets cited by Russell-Robinson were found in the River Po at Cremona (as also was a helmet of Montefortino type F, a presumed contemporary), and is therefore attributed to loss during the civil war of AD 69. Russell-Robinson (1975, 67) also reported that these examples, and also cheek pieces deemed to have come from similar helmets, are all roughly finished, with visible hammer marks, and are of inferior quality, suggesting rushed mass production and lower-status ownership.

Imperial Italic – Type D

This helmet closely resembles the previous type C in profile, although it is much more ornate, with heavily applied brass decoration. The ear guards are of applied brass, as is a wide brow band and wider band to the rear, from level with the top of the ear guard, covering not only the three occipital ridges but also the embossed, recessed neck-guard step. Four broad applied bands also separate the bowl into quadrants, topped by a circular crest holder (this time with a T-shaped slot). Further applied decorations within these quadrants depict, to the front, spread-winged eagles carrying victory wreaths in their beaks, and to the rear, temples with altars. The cheek piece similarly bears a more stylised depiction of a temple, below a wide applied band immediately under the hinge (Fig. 117).

The neck guard is wide and flat, with angular corners (as with type C), and a broad edge binding (as also has the cheek piece). On its upper surface it is fitted with a carrying handle, with pear-shaped terminals, secured by split pins through two bossed washers (Fig. 50). On the under surface tie rings are riveted to each side, the tie thong passing from one cheek piece to the other via these rear rings. Although this helmet is also provided with a reinforcing peak, unlike that on type C, which starts above the midpoint of each ear, this is more slender

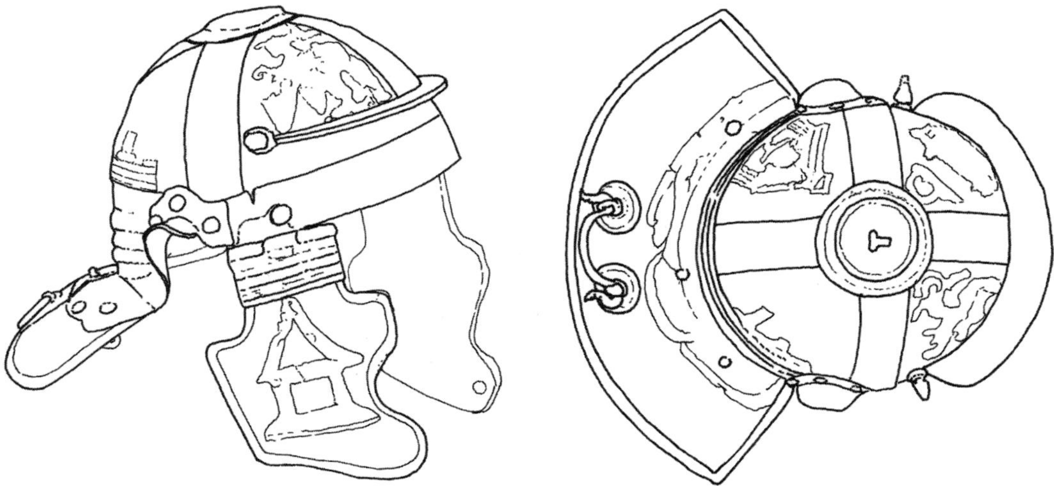

Fig. 49. Imperial Italic D (with 'temple' motif on cheek pieces) (from Russell-Robinson, 1975). (Artwork by J. R. Travis)

and is smaller, being riveted to the bowl further forward, in front of the transverse decorative bands. It also bears notches indicating combat damage and obviously was a working helmet that did not serve a purely ceremonial purpose.

Where the end-date for use of the type C helmets (*terminus ante quem*) was derived from a presumed loss date to civil war action at Cremona, similarly a roughly maximum date for this helmet was estimated by Russell-Robinson. As it was found from the River Rhine at Mainz, Russell-Robinson (1975, 69) suggested that its loss may probably be attributed to the overcrowded ferry crossing, rather than to the later, more reliable bridge crossing established in AD 83.

Imperial Italic – Type E

This iron helmet was found in the fort at Hofheim by H. Schoppa in the 1960s (Schoppa, 1961). Russell-Robinson described the helmet as being strongly comparable to type D (in bowl shape, profile and cheek pieces), other than its neck guard being sloping rather than flat. It is also noted that each cheek piece is provided with two fastening rings, and ties may have therefore crossed under the chin for a closer fit (Russell-Robinson, 1975, 70). It lacks any of the applied decoration of the type D, much of which Russell-Robinson suggested had been lost prior to deposition, the helmet being old and heavily worn when discarded (Russell-Robinson, 1975, 71). Based on personal communication with Schoppa, Russell-Robinson attributed the loss date for this helmet to AD 100 (Russell-Robinson, 1975, 70). However, in recent years the date of both this and the previous type D helmet have been disputed, with Junkelmann (2000, 84) suggesting a much later date in the middle or second half of the second century.

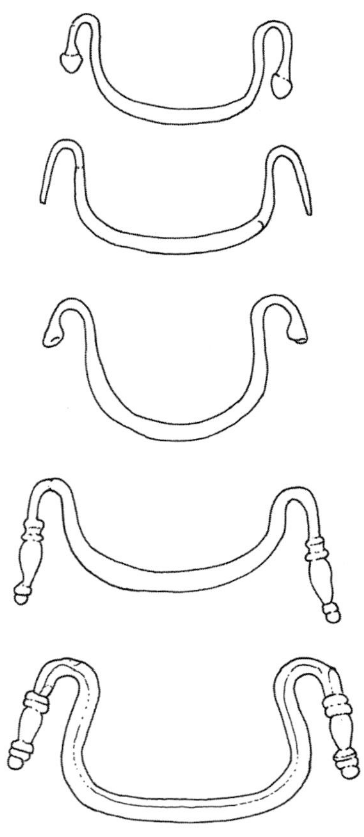

Fig. 50. Progression of helmet hook types (from Russell-Robinson, 1975). (Artwork by J. R. Travis).

The argument behind this later dating seems to centre around two areas of focus. Firstly, with the type E helmet, Russell-Robinson's assignment to AD 100 does not correspond with the date for abandonment of the fort at Hofheim, as published by Schoppa (1961, 5–6), who said that the fort (and possibly the vicus where the helmet was found) was abandoned in AD 120–121. This means that the end date for this helmet type at least may have to be extended slightly, although, as stated by Russell-Robinson, the helmet was heavily worn when discarded, so may not have been in use for some time earlier. The argument for the type D helmet belonging to a later date is based on the appearance of the decorative cross-bracings. Junkelmann (*ibid.*) suggested that these may have been an imitation of more functional cross-bracings, as seen on the type G Hebron helmet, the dating of which has been assigned to the Bar Kochba War of AD 132–135, which would then suggest a later date in the mid-second century AD or later for the type D.

However, this argument is based on interpretation of the method of 'quadranting' the helmet with decoration. These decorative strips are in no way functional, in contrast to those on the Hebron, so the comparison ends at that point. The basic shape of the helmet itself bears far more resemblance to other helmets from proven first-century AD contexts than it does to the deep Niedermörmter helmets of types H onwards.

Although there have been a relatively large number of helmets found, the very fact that Russell-Robinson felt it necessary to describe so many categories is indicative of the range of variety seen among them. Not all of these helmets are necessarily derived from each other, many coexisting within the same time framework, and clearly not all helmets belonged to owners from the same social class or military rank, or served the same purpose. This type D helmet is highly decorated and would not necessarily resemble lower-status helmets of the same dating, but at the time of its use would not have been as unique as it is today. In addition, the very nature of helmets, as being intended to withstand substantial attack, led to their remaining in use for considerable lengths of time. At any one moment, a great variety of helmets would therefore have been in use simultaneously. Although the dates put forward for many of these helmet types are subjective, and can only be used to indicate possible and rough developmental progression, Russell-Robinson did provide us in this particular case of the type D helmet with a well-reasoned date as a basis from which to work.

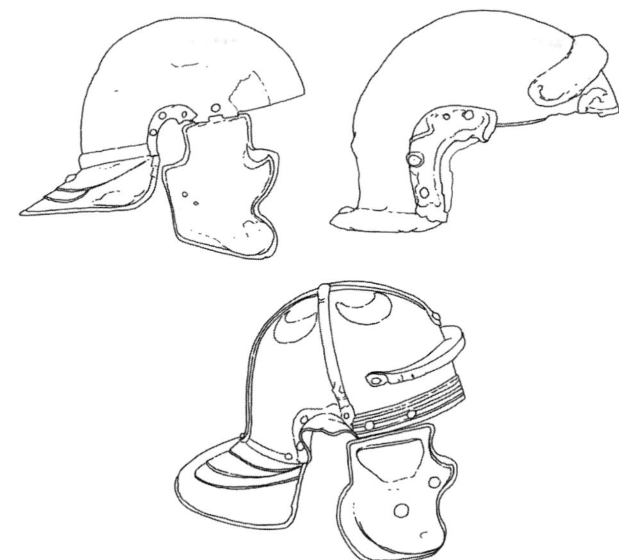

Fig. 51. Imperial Italic helmets types E, F and G (from Russell-Robinson, 1975). (Artwork by J. R. Travis)

Imperial Italic – Type F

Russell-Robinson (1975, 71) reported only one example of this type of helmet, found in the Rhine at Mainz (unfortunately destroyed during the Second World War); this was iron and heavily corroded, lacking the majority of its diagnostic features, including most of the neck guard, other than its applied ear guard and its unique peak reinforcement. Unlike the flat, heavy Gallic style, and the preceding Italic right-angle sectioned peaks, this example carries a demi-oval sectioned strip, tapering in at each end, which Russell-Robinson saw as an attempt to reduce weight without impeding strength.

Imperial Italic – Type G (Hebron)

This second-century AD iron helmet is best known by its Continental name, 'Hebron', derived from its find site in Israel. It is similar in profile to the earlier two types D and E, with a broad, sloping neck guard, but with its rounded hemispherical bowl being slightly deeper, sitting higher on the wearer's head. As with its predecessors, it retains the three embossed occipital ridges, but three semi-circular embossed steps now reinforce the neck guard. The central area of the neck guard was damaged, although Russell-Robinson (1975, 71) believed it may have originally had a carrying handle attached, as on type D. As with type E, the cheek pieces for this variant have two rings on each side, and may have been tied by crossing under the chin (Russell-Robinson, 1975, 73).

The most noticeable features of this helmet, however, are the two semi-circular sectioned iron strips, applied front to back and side to side, separating the crown into quadrants, each of which is then decorated by a crescent-shaped applied bronze motif. This separating of the bowl into quadrants was also seen on the earlier type D, in that category serving a largely decorative function, executed in wide brass strips, whereas in the type G (Hebron) these are more substantial and functional. The increased thickness where these bars cross, on top of the helmet, makes the application of any form of crest support difficult, and there is no trace of any form of crest fitting.

It is not that this helmet is devoid of all decoration, however. Unlike the type F, this helmet again is fitted with a reinforcing peak of right-angle section, the front face of which is covered with an applied bronze strip, decorated by alternating punched bosses and circles of dots. Below this, the helmet is further strengthened with a brow band of iron strip, covered by thin reeded bronze, with stamped laurel leaves and berry decorations. This further suggests that this cross bracing now serves a functional purpose (possibly in answer to some new threat, or new enemy weapon), at the expense of more decorative features, such as crests, wherever these conflict. However, this apparent trend away from crests is also evident in the later-period Imperial Gallic helmets.

Imperial Italic – Type H (Niedermörmter)

Taking its Continental name from the find site of the best and most complete known bronze example (Niedermörmter, near Xanten), this helmet is markedly different to its predecessors, culminating in an exaggeration of all of their basic features. In profile it has a deep, well-rounded bowl, extending further than any previous examples at the back of the head, with five prominent occipital ridges, leading to a broad, convex, sloping 'skirt' of a neck guard, 12 cm wide with a narrow, slightly indented step, providing greatly increased protection for the neck and shoulder areas. This neck guard is then provided with a large, ornate carrying handle, with a decorative 'toffee wrapper'-shaped panel (*tabula ansata*), and with further L-shaped decorative panels in the corners, the rim being bound by U-sectioned bronze/brass strip. The applied ear guards stand proud on each side, curving over the ear for increased protection, deflecting blows on to the broad neck guard. The brow band is wide, with four semi-circular scallops cut into its upper edge. The bowl is divided into four wide, applied panels with central ribs, topped by a large, domed button on a double-stepped base and a wide, round base plate. The peak is wide and of right-angled section, curved at the ends and fixed by two prominent studs. All of the decorative reinforcing panels are soldered to the bowl, and the joins decorated by applied pearled strip.

Although the type H helmet from Niedermörmter is the most complete and ornate example, a less decorative and less complete iron example is known from Hessen. Broadly similar in profile, with its deep occipital area, the neck guard is still not quite as wide as in the Niedermörmter example, and it is heavily corroded, lacking the applied decoration. It is missing its brow band and peak, and its ear guards are of iron, being directly flanged out from the helmet bowl (Russell-Robinson, 1975, 74). It is probable that this helmet had always lacked the ornate decoration of the Niedermörmter example despite being similar in shape, the bowl having a simple bronze reinforcing strip remaining on the left side, closer in dimension to those on the type G Hebron. Fragments of applied bronze decoration from a further example are known from Faurndau, in the form of a *tabula ansata*, a carrying handle, ear guard, neck-guard trim, pearled strip and a brow band with punched decoration of eagles and victories.

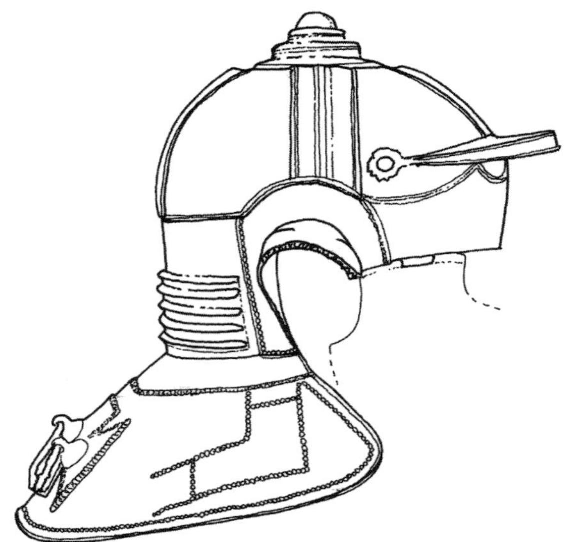

Fig. 52. Imperial Italic H (from Russell-Robinson, 1975). (Artwork by J. R. Travis)

From the bowl shape, Russell-Robinson attributed the helmet to legionary rather than cavalry use, despite the increased depth of neck guard (normally a feature of cavalry helmets), estimating its date to the late second or early third century AD, based on the style of decoration in the Faurndau and Niedermörmter panels (Russell-Robinson, 1975, 74). He also considered that the helmet would probably have used simply shaped cheek pieces, with only shallow recesses for eyes and mouth, as he felt that the larger, cavalry-style cheek pieces could not have been used with the protruding, rounded ear guards (Russell-Robinson, 1975, 73).

		Neckguard		Peak	Brow reinforced	Plume tubes	Crest support	Eyebrows	Stepped occiput	Ears			Decorative Bosses	Cheek recess
Type	Form	Shape	Decoration							Recess	Flanged	Ear Guard		
A	Vertical sides, flattened top (like Agen)	Wide	Indented step	Heavy, flat	No		No	Simple			No			No
B	Rounded	Moderate		n/k	Possible		n/k	Simple, slender			Yes	No	No	
C		Broad, sloping	Deep indented step		10 mm bronze	No	Rectangular, 2 prongs	Slender, recurved						Yes
D	Rounded, deep, flat at temples	Slightly sloping	Indented step	Broad, bronze reinforced	Reeded, bronze, 5 ribs			Recurved, 4 ridges				Iron	Yes, 3 silvered & red enamel	
E	Low, rounded		2 steps, 1 indented	Flat				Recurved, 3 ridges					Yes, 3 on cheek	
F	Rounded	Slightly sloping, sharp corners			Multi-reeded, silver	Sides	Rectangular, 1 prong (1 eg has round twist-on)					Bronze	Yes, 3 silvered & enamel	Yes, edges bound
G	Rounded, two bosses at temple	Moderate size, almost flat. Rounded corners, carry handle	2 steps, 1 indented, 3 bosses (centre & corners)			No	Single tube	Broad, leaflike	Yes	Yes			Yes, 3 on cheek	
H	Rounded	Angled lower set at 50 degrees, no carry handle	2 steps, 1 indented, 3 bosses	Flat, tongued to bowl			No	Broad, recurved, horizontal, low relief, 3 ribs			No	n/k	n/k	n/k
I	Rounded, bronze	Wide, carry handle			Reeded bronze	Sides	Round, twist-on, with slot	Broad, recurved, horizontal, stepped						
J	Rounded	Slopes down at 45 degrees, larger. Decorative bosses, carry handle	2 steps, 1 indented	Flat		No	No	Very broad, flat, stepped				Bronze	2 on cheek	Yes
K	Rounded, applied bronze lunae (like Hebron), but no cross bars	Rounded corners		n/k	n/k		n/k	n.k				n/k	n/k	n/k

Table 5. Imperial Gallic helmets – description of H. Russell-Robinson typologies.

Type	Form	Neckguard		Peak	Brow reinforced	Plume tubes	Crest support	Eyebrows	Stepped occiput	Ears			Decorative bosses
		Shape	Decoration							Recess	Flanged	Ear guard	
A	Rounded, deep back, straight down, Attic style	Small flange at right angles to bowl	No	No	No but embossed rib		Round, twist-on, hooks front & back	No, but embossed inverted V					No
B	Rounded, deep back	Narrow, rounded corners	Single embossed step. No indent for suspense rivet, bronze edging & dec. bosses	n/k, missing	Reeded, notched, central rib		No, but hooks front & back		No		Yes	No	Yes
C	Rounded	Wider, moderate width	Single, indented	Right-angle section	n/k		Round, twist-on, hooks front & back						n/k
D	Rounded, applied decoration. Wide cross strips with motifs in quadrants (eagle, temples, columns)	Wide, sharp corners, carry handle	Applied edging & on 'step'	Flattened peak, conical-headed rivets at sides	Wide	No	Round, t-shaped slot, no front/back hooks	No	Yes	Yes	No	Yes, bronze	No
E	Rounded, shallow	Wide, sloping down	Brass edging. Stepped, indented	n/k, missing	n/k				Shallow		Yes	No	
F	Rounded, shallow, deep at back	n/k, missing	n/k	Wide, demi-oval section					n/k				
G	Rounded, deep, hemispherical, cross supports. Lunae decoration	Wide, slightly sloping, carry handle	3 semi-circle steps	Right-angle section, with applied bronze strip	Reededm stamped laurel leaves		No		3 ridges		No	Yes, iron	n/k
H	Bronze, deep. Applied ornament. Wide cross strips	Wide (12 cm) sloping down, carry handle	Toffee-wrap & L-shapes at sides - embossed dec.	Right-angle section, with conical-headed rivets	Wide				5 ridges, deep			Yes, wide	No

Table 6. Imperial Italic helmets – description of H Russell-Robinson typologies.

VI

HELMETS OF THE LATER EMPIRE

THE EMERGENCE OF LATE EMPIRE HELMETS

Towards the end of the third century and the beginning of the fourth century AD, the helmet designs previously seen in the first and second centuries appeared to disappear, along with their embellishing removable crest boxes and tubes for feathered plumes, and were replaced by a new style of helmet construction and design, with an adoption of Sassanian- and steppe-influenced composite helmets. These were very different to the previous helmet types used before the mid-third century, which had been formed in one piece with integral neck guard and hinged cheek pieces (the later bowls reinforced with cross bars or plates). After a lengthy break in the archaeological record, the new helmets then appear fully developed, with no apparent ancestors.

Klumbach (1973, 51–83) proposed that these changes were part of an 'orientalisation' of styles under the Tetrarchy, although James (1986, 131) considered this to be only partly the case, attributing the main cause to a decline in the economy and the collapse of coinage from the mid-third century AD. Armourers, who had previously been legally required to supply the army, could no longer do so as the currency was not available for their payment. Under Diocletian, the supply of equipment was therefore nationalised, with state arms factories (*fabricae*) set up at strategic locations, with a requirement for simplified new designs in order to achieve monthly quotas. An illustration from the *Notitia Dignitatum: insignia viri illustris magistri officiorum* (from a sixteenth-century copy of the fifth-century AD manuscript) depicts some of the items of armour, including helmets, produced from the state-run *fabricae* listed within the document (see Fig. 53). The new styles were described by Stephenson (1999, 25) as offering an increased level of protection, but with a reduced level of 'flamboyance', with protection as a priority over display, and would have met that requirement for quicker, more economical production.

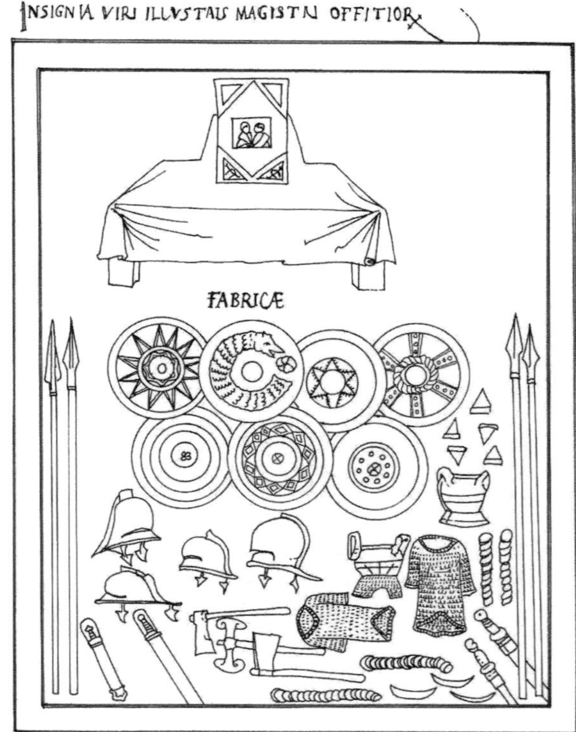

Fig. 53. Illustration from *Notitia Dignitatum: insignia viri illustris magistri officiorum*, from sixteenth-century copy of fifth-century AD manuscript. (Artwork by J. R. Travis)

Klumbach (1973, 51–83) had suggested that the 'Simple' Intercisa-type helmets had been intended for infantry use, with the 'Heavy' Berkasovo type being for cavalry. Stephenson (Stephenson & Dixon, 2003, 24), however, disagreed with this simplification, citing the fifth-century AD mosaic *Crossing the Red Sea* from Santa Maria Maggiore, Rome, which shows cavalry wearing Intercisa-type helmets. He also noted that an inscription on the 'Berkasovo'-type helmet from Deurne, Netherlands, identified its owner as belonging to the '*equites Stablesiani*'. He therefore proposed that both types of 'Ridge' helmets would have been used by Late Roman Cavalry (Stephenson & Dixon, 2003).

The new helmets fell into two main classifications: 'Spangenhelm' and 'Ridge' helmets, the latter further falling into two subcategories (the 'Simple' or 'Intercisa' helmet; and the more complex 'Heavy' or 'Berkasovo' type; Southern & Dixon, 1996). All known examples of 'Ridge' helmets date to the fourth and early fifth centuries AD, with a number found in Europe. It was originally believed that the new helmets were probably imported from Persia, all known pieces up to the early 1970s having been published by Klumbach (1973, 51–83). Common features were composite, 'bipartite' bowl construction, with two half-skulls joined by a front-to-back strip, or 'ridge' piece. Each half may be single piece or in up to three plates. The 'Spangenhelm' in contrast were of 'radial' construction, with no front-to-back ridge, but with vertical iron strips converging at the apex.

THE 'SIMPLE' OR 'INTERCISA' HELMETS

The 'Intercisa' or 'Simple'-type 'Ridge' helmets were named after the find site in Hungary of fifteen to twenty such helmets, the helmets falling into four different types (Klumbach, 1973, 103–109, figs 45–57; Figs 54–57). Further examples are also known from Trier, Augst and Worms (Southern & Dixon, 1996, 93). Despite a variation in designs, they had a range of common features. The helmet bowls were of composite, 'bipartite' construction, with two single-piece sections riveted to a ridged strip running from front to back (Stephenson & Dixon, 2003, figs 9 & 10). James (1986, 111) reported that hinges were not used, with cheek pieces and neck guards attached to the linen or leather lining of the helmets using straps or laces, and not to the bowl itself.

Both the lower edge of the bowl and the upper edge of the cheek pieces had matching semi-circular or oval shapes cut for ears. The bowl edge, neck guard and cheek pieces were pierced for the attachment of a lining, and to fix the pieces of helmet to each other.

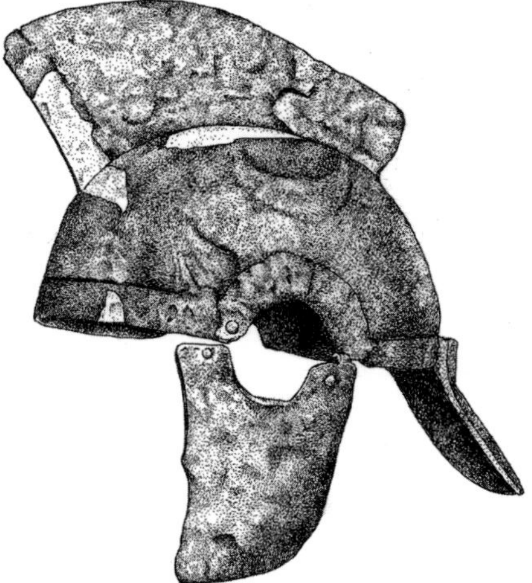

Fig. 54. Intercisa 1 (with crest). (Artwork by J. R. Travis)

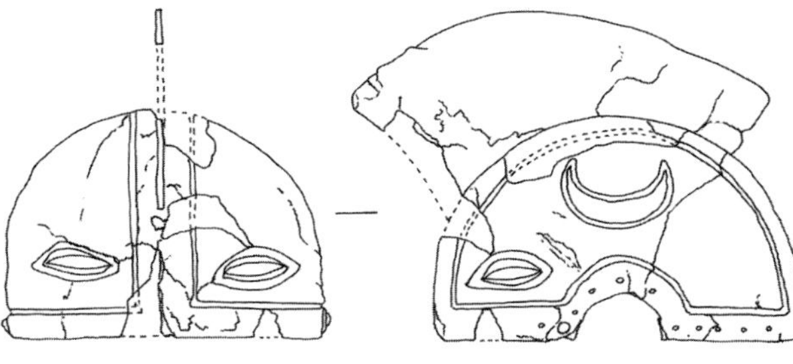

Fig. 55. Intercisa 2 (with crest), no neck guard. (Artwork by J. R. Travis)

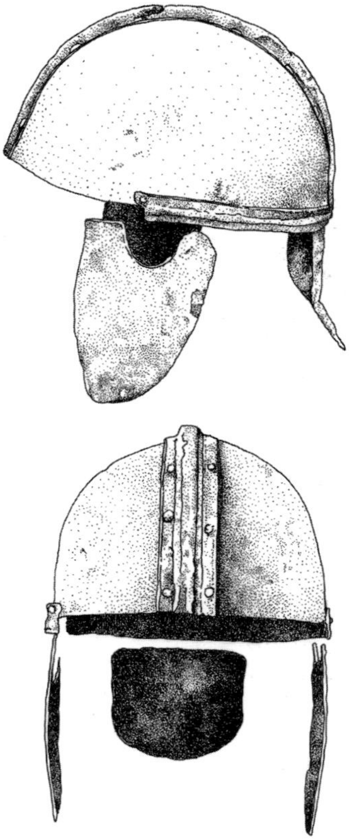

Fig. 56. Intercisa, no crest. (Artwork by J. R. Travis)

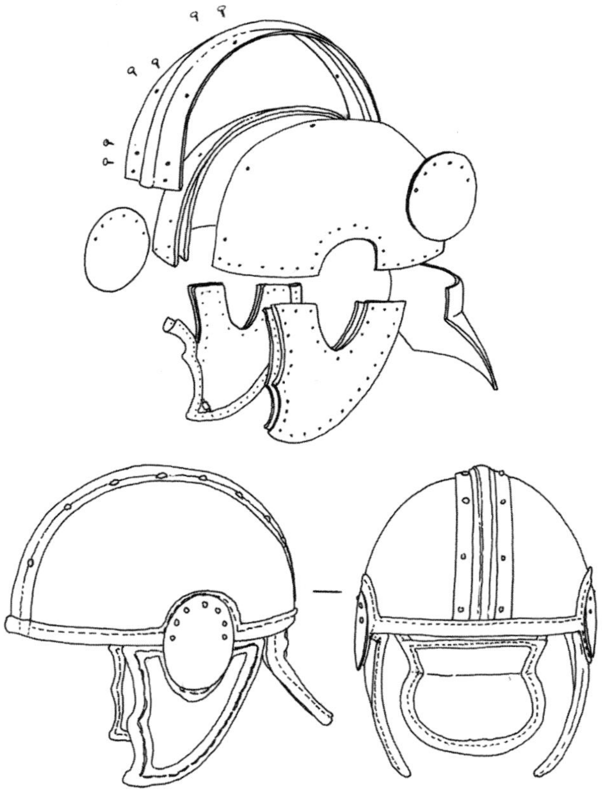

Fig. 57. Expanded Intercisa. (Artwork by J. R. Travis)

One example from Intercisa was also provided with a crest (Southern & Dixon, 1996, 92, fig. 10). Most examples are very plain (as recovered), but traces of silver around rivets on examples from Intercisa and Worms, along with silver sheathing from two more examples from Augsburg-Pfersee (Fig. 58), suggests that helmets were not plain iron, but were highly decorated (some also with incised, chiselled or embossed 'eye' shapes to the front of the bowl). Also some of the Intercisa helmets depicted on the *Crossing the Red Sea* mosaic in Santa Maria Maggiore appear to have been gold or gilded. A further image of an infantryman in an Intercisa-style helmet, along with a rider wearing a *pileus*-type hat, can also be seen on a grave *stela* from Gamzigrad, dating to the time of the Tetrarchy (Southern & Dixon, 1996, 93, fig. 11).

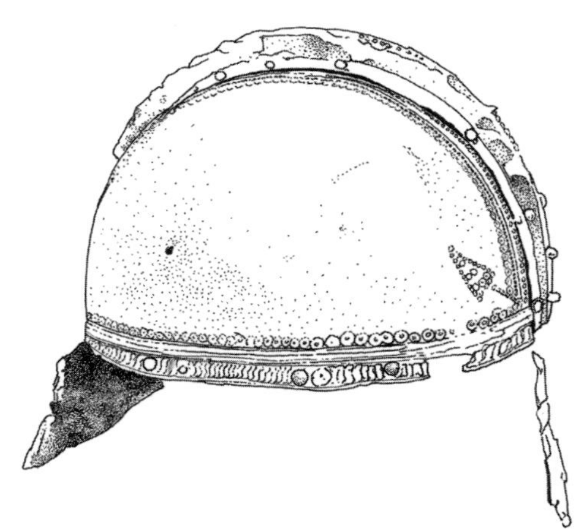

Fig. 58. Augsberg Pfersee helmet. Fitted with a nasal guard, as is more commonly seen on the Berkasovo type. (Artwork by J. R. Travis)

The Augsburg-Pfersee examples were unusual in that they were fitted with a nasal guard, as is more commonly seen on the Berkasovo type. Stephenson (Stephenson & Dixon, 2003, 27) noted that nasal guards were not a feature of previous Roman or Celtic helmets, their last appearance being on fourth-century BC Greek 'Chalcidian' helmets, although he did not consider these to be their origin in this case. Instead he viewed the influence being from third-century steppe and Sassanian helmets, with diffusion across the Danubian and eastern frontiers.

THE 'HEAVY' OR 'BERKASOVO' TYPE HELMETS

At Berkasovo two examples of complex 'Heavy'-type 'Ridge' helmets were found, although these each had different types of bowl formation. Their bowls had been of iron, now corroded away, with only their silver surface sheathing remaining (Southern & Dixon, 1996, pls 4–9).

In the first example, the bowl was divided into four quarters (Stephenson & Dixon, 2003, plate 15; Fig. 59), as on the helmets from Burgh Castle, Deurne and Conçesti (Johnson, 1980 303–312; Stephenson & Dixon, 2003, pls 12 & 11; Figs 64 & 61), whereas the second Berkasovo example (Fig. 60), had a two-part bowl (bipartite), like the Budapest helmet. On both helmets, an additional band, curving over each eye, was riveted to the inside of the rim. A Sassanian-style T-shape nasal guard was also riveted to the front of the helmets (Stephenson & Dixon, 2003).

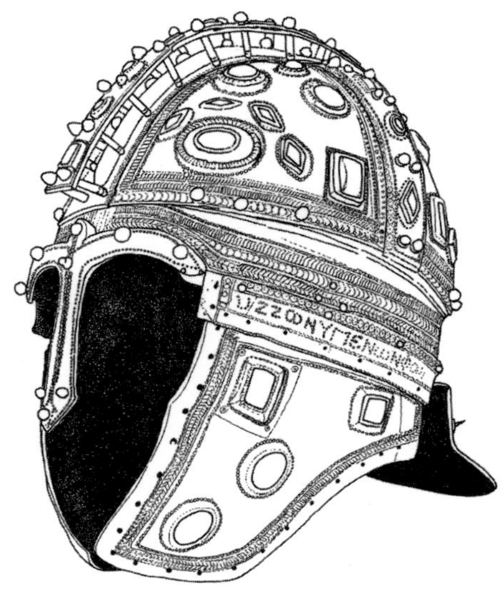

Fig. 59. Berkasovo: Helmet 1. The iron bowl, now corroded away, with highly decorated silver surface sheathing, was divided into four quarters. A brow band, curved over each eye, was riveted to the inside of the rim; and a Sassanian-style, T-shaped nasal guard also riveted to the front. (Artwork by J. R. Travis)

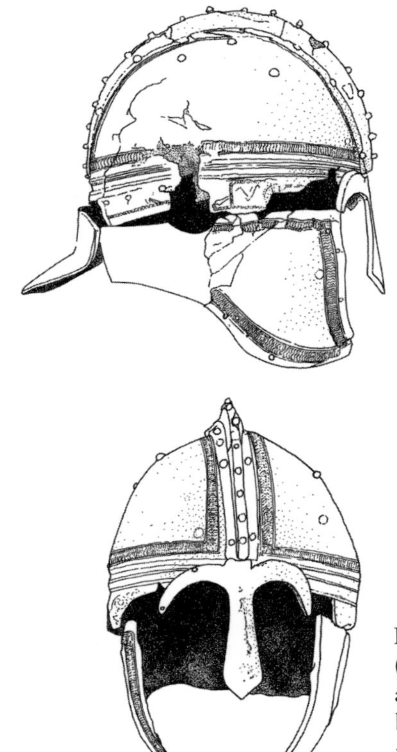

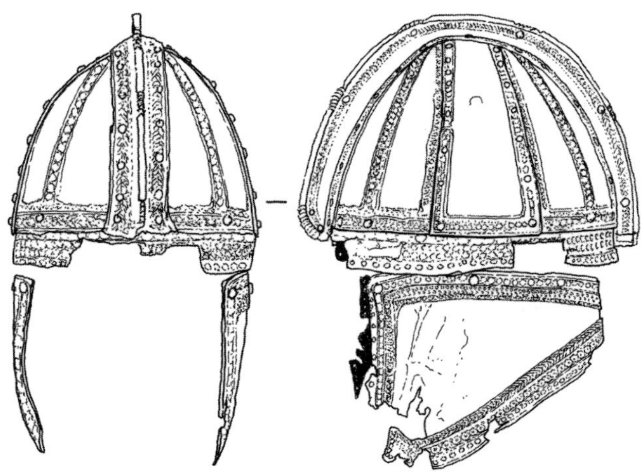

Fig. 61. Conçesti Intercisa/ridge helmet. (Artwork by J. R. Travis)

Fig. 60. Berkasovo: Helmet 2. As with Helmet 1, the iron bowl (this time being two-part, bipartite construction), is corroded away, with highly decorated silver surface sheathing. Again, a brow band, curved over each eye, was riveted to the inside of the rim; and a Sassanian-style T-shaped nasal guard also riveted to the front. (Artwork by J. R. Travis)

The Berkasovo helmets, in common with that from Deurne, were also provided with additional metal bands masking the joint between the rim and the cheek pieces. Cheek pieces were attached by the same method as on the Intercisa helmets, but were much larger, covering almost the entire side of the wearer's head and neck; with no 'ear' openings to improve hearing, but providing better throat protection. A neck guard was attached to the brow band (similar to that on the Simple type), not by hinges but by way of leather straps hung from the inside of the bowl, attaching to buckles on the neck guard. A crest was then held above the ridge by long shafted rivets.

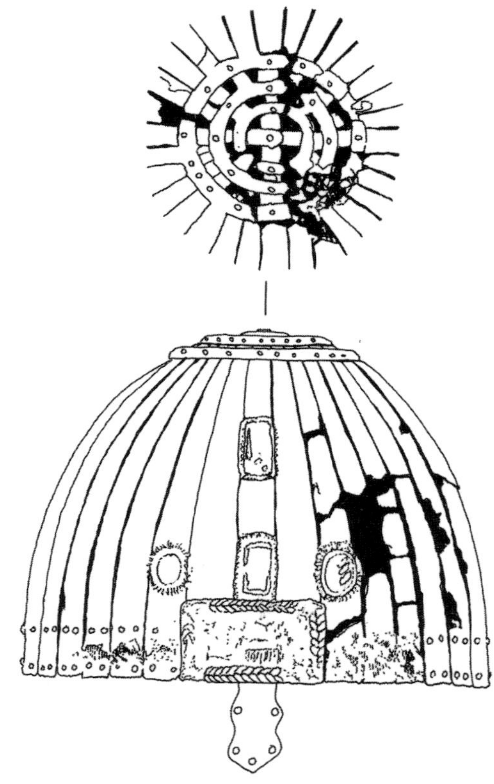

Fig. 62. Steppe helmet. (Artwork by J. R. Travis)

The sheathing was decorated either with a combination of decorated rivet heads and embossed motifs (as on the Conçesti, Deurne and Berkasovo Number 2 helmets); or with embossing combined with glass-paste settings (as on examples from Budapest and Berkasovo Number 1). Stephenson (Stephenson & Dixon, 2003, 29) noted that the embossing derives from a Mesopotamian-Iranian tradition, as seen on a number of Parthian and Sassanian helmets, whereas the glass paste gems were a steppe innovation (citing by example a third-century AD helmet, also with glass paste settings, from a horse grave at Kerch in the Crimea; *ibid.*, 27, fig. 13; Fig. 62).

Another example from Heddernheim, Germany, shows an improvement in design in the greater coverage of its cheek pieces, so that only a small area of face was exposed. The cheek pieces were large, overlapped at the chin, leaving only a small, T-shaped face opening. They were hinged on the upper edge, fastened by a hook on the front-left cheek piece, passing through a hole on the front of the right cheek piece (Stephenson, 1999, 26). The iron (or copper alloy) bowl extended down to the base of neck, where an angled neck guard was attached. The front of the bowl had a pointed peak, either horizontal or angled upward, and reinforcing bars crossed over the crown, extending to the base of the neck (both peak and cross bars being attached by cone-shaped or dome-headed rivets). The out-turning, sloping neck guard deflected weapons, as also did the curved cheek pieces. Reinforcing cross bars and peak also acted to absorb any blow from above before it could contact the bowl, minimising the shock of any impact reaching the wearer. Further impact absorption would have also been provided by internal padding from a helmet liner or hat (possibly a *pileus*, or 'pill-box' hat). Another variation of this helmet type, from Buch, Germany, had a peak but no crossed reinforcing bars, although it did have embossed cross ribs (Stephenson, 1999).

The helmets are also seen on third-century AD grave *stelae*, including one of a legionary from Brigetio, Hungary; and another of Aurelius Surus, from Istanbul (Stephenson, 1999, 25). They can also be seen on the Dura Europos Synagogue frescos. However, other contemporary figures depicted on the Battle of Ebenezer fresco (Fig. 63), also from Dura Europos, are shown to be un-helmeted, wearing instead coifs constructed from scale. Further evidence for use of coifs can also be found in the illuminations of a fourth-century manuscript, *Vergilius Vaticanus* (*Cod. Vat. Lat.* 3225; Coulston, 1990, 145). Stephenson (1999, 27)

Fig. 63. Part schematic of the 'Battle of Ebenezer' fresco from the Synagogue, Dura Europos, depicting infantry soldiers in loose-fitting, long-sleeved, knee-length mail or scale coats, some bareheaded and some wearing coifs (from James, 2004, xxvi, plate 4). (Artwork by J. R. Travis)

suggested that the coif may have been used as an alternative to a helmet, further suggesting that these may have also been constructed of mail.

THE DEURNE HELMET

The Deurne helmet was found in 1910 by peat diggers at De Peel, near Deurne (North Brabant, Netherlands), now at the Rijksmuseum Oudheden, Leiden (Iriarte, 1996, 51; Fig. 64). The main iron core had corroded away completely, with only the gilt, silver-plated outer sheathing remaining, described by the finders as 'golden'. The sheathing (and similarly the now missing core) was constructed in fourteen parts: four bowl quarters; two bowl side bands; a central joining band; neck guard; nasal guard; a crest; two cheek pieces; and two narrow horizontal bands, to cover the small gap at the cheek attachment point (estimated at approximately 5 mm by Iriarte; 1996, 53). Holes pierced the outer edges of the bowl, neck guard and cheek pieces, with two silver rivets remaining on one cheek piece.

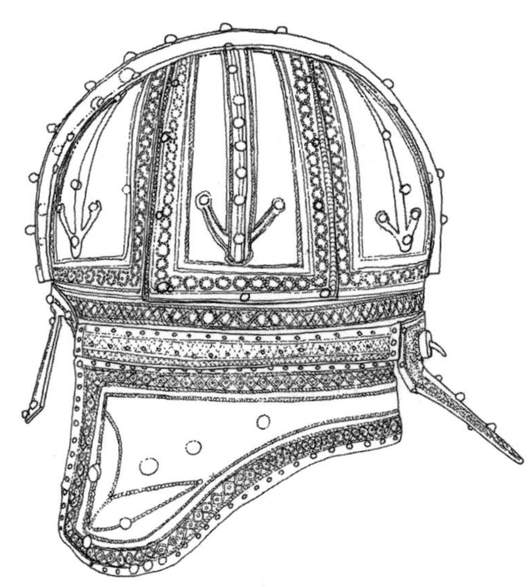

Fig. 64. Deurne helmet (Berkasovo style) (from Stephenson & Dixon, 2003). (Artwork by J. R. Travis)

In the original publication of the find, Braat (1973, 51–83) had previously proposed that these holes served for attachment of a lining, using rivets. Iriarte (1996, 53), however, on reassessing the finds prior to producing his reconstruction, proposed that the lining should have been laced in place, using thread or straps, alternately interpreting the rivets as being anchorage for cheek-piece hinges (despite the indications on similar helmets for hinges not being used). The neck guard would have been attached to the bowl by suspension straps, riveted to the inside of the bowl, and buckles on the outer face of the plate.

In the course of his reconstruction, Iriarte (1996, 53) concluded that the sheathing and linings would have been attached prior to assembly of the component parts. He further reported that in order to engage the strap holes in the buckles, they would have been fastened with a looser fit than had been anticipated, allowing greater movement, but permitting the neck guard to fold to the inside for storage. He also estimated that the thicknesses of the core plates would have been approximately 2 mm for the bowl, and 1 mm for the crest, this being thinner for easier working, based on rivet measurements and on comparisons with the Augsburg-Pfersee and Conçesti helmets (Fig. 58 & 61).

THE RICHBOROUGH HELMETS

A Late Roman shore fort, which had been a supply base during the Claudian to Flavian periods (dating between the late third and early fifth centuries AD), was excavated between 1922 and 1938 in Richborough, Kent. The site produced a large amount of material (metal, glass, bone, etc.), but not all finds were published and not all had been correctly identified. Lyne (1994, 97–105) later reassessed these finds, comparing with reports in the excavation notebooks, suggesting that a number of supposed 'fragments of armour' were in fact the remains of four Late Roman helmets, along with small fragments and fittings of others.

Richborough Helmet 1

One collection of pieces Lyne identified as belonging to a neck guard from a post-270 AD Intercisa-type helmet. Another nine pieces (including some recorded in the notebook as having 'bronze strapping'), he fitted together to form part of a left-side cheek piece, reporting that the neck guard and cheek piece had both been provided with a riveted copper alloy edging strip.

Some fragments with a 'brown-surfaced layer of whitish material' (which was identified after analysis as being gypsum, faced with resin or brown paint) were found to be the remains of a crest. However, Lyne (1994, 97) proposed that this would differ from that on the Intercisa type 4 helmet, in that it was 'three-dimensional', and would have had plumes of horsehair fixed permanently in the gypsum. This 'crest' was interpreted in his subsequent reconstruction as being fixed directly to the bowl, but he also acknowledged the possibility that it may have been in a separate, removable holder, as on helmets of earlier periods.

Further fragments (including one which had been recorded as part of a shield boss, or '*umbo*'), following x-ray examination, were then found to form most of the left side of the helmet. The bowl had been 'cut away' for the ear, and small holes pierced the lower edge, presumably for the purpose of securing the lining and affixing the cheek pieces. Lyne (*ibid.*) also reported that decorative 'emblems' or 'patches' were visible in the x-rays, but they may have been either iron or organic, as they were not found by x-ray fluorescence. From the remains of the cheek piece, Lyne (*ibid.*, 99), suggested that it appeared to belong to a variant of the Intercisa type (Fig. 65). The cheek piece also had rivet holes, which Lyne (*ibid.*) interpreted as being for the attachment of lining material.

Lyne (*ibid.*, 99) noted that this particular helmet exhibits some peculiarities from other Intercisa-types, in that the lower edge of the bowl rises at a slight angle from the ear forward. He suggested that this may have originally been an auxiliary cavalry type H helmet, dating to the second to early third century, which had been modified by the removal of its original integral neck guard, and replacement with one in the post 280 AD Intercisa style. To correct the upward slope on the original rim of the bowl, so that the new Intercisa-style cheek pieces could be attached, he believed that a separate brow band would have been added (now missing) to level off the rim to the new horizontal. To further support his view for remodelling of an older helmet, he also noted what appeared to be the remains of a projecting iron boss above and in front of the cut away for the ear, which he interpreted as having originally served as one of the fixing points for the peak (now removed). The helmet also appears to show signs of combat damage, which Lyne proposed to have been the reason for it being eventually discarded, sometime between AD 280 and 400 (although probably closer to the earlier of the two dates).

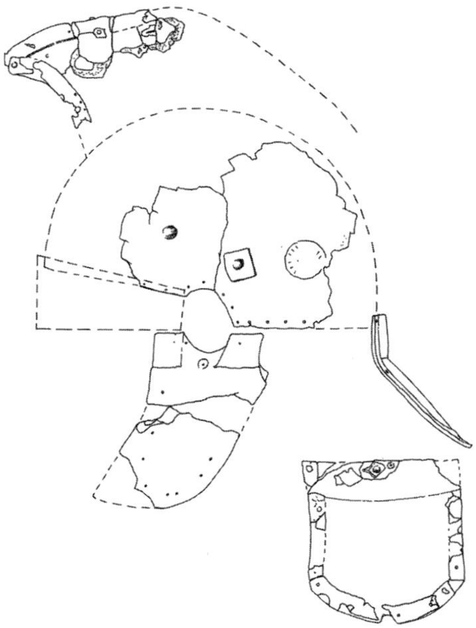

Fig. 65. Richborough: Helmet 1. (Artwork by J. R. Travis)

Richborough Helmet 2

Helmet 2 was less complete than the previous example, in that it consisted of just several fragments of bronze plating: one 'heart-shaped' piece, approximately 3 by 2.5 inches; one 'strip' 1.1 by 11.5 inches; and four further fragments, now missing. Lyne (1994, 101) suggested, based on the lack of iron corrosion on the fragments, that the helmet to which these fittings belonged may have been made of leather, noting that similar fragments had been found separately within the same ditch context, which may indicate two further such leather helmets. He also cited Vegetius (1.20), reporting an abandonment of body armour and helmets during the reign of Gratian, to back his proposal for leather helmets.

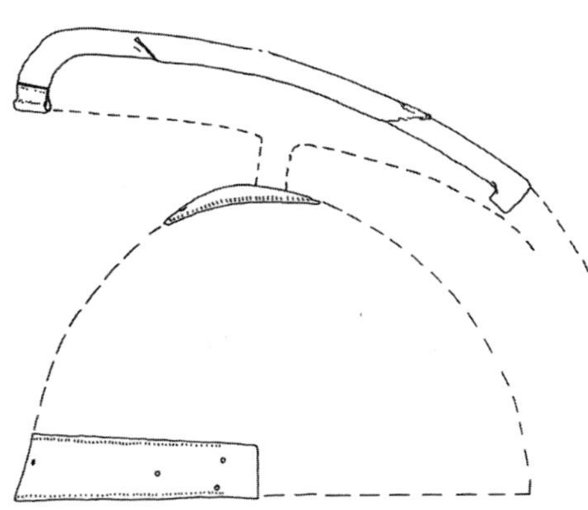

Fig. 66. Richborough: Helmet 2. (Artwork by J. R. Travis)

The slightly convex heart-shaped plate with its central hole, its edges decorated with repoussée dots, was interpreted by Lyne (1994, 99) as possibly being a fitting from the helmet's apex for the anchorage of a removable crest holder. The long strip, similarly decorated with repoussée dots, he interpreted as a brow band which would originally have extended around the helmet from each ear, expanding in width at the centre forehead. From the curvature of this brow band, he further estimated the bowl shape as being similar to that of an Attic helmet (Fig. 66).

In addition, a separate find of a copper alloy strip, 21 cm long, from a nearby location was suggested by Lyne to be the possible remains of a stiffening piece for the missing removable organic crest, which would have been raised from the bowl by a stem fitting (not present). Lyne (1994, 101) further interpreted marks on the 'crest' as possible traces of leather or fabric which would have been glued to each side of the strip.

Richborough Helmet 3

The excavation notebooks report a number of fragments (all from Pit 314) from a helmet bowl, with ribs running down from the apex. One of these fragments Lyne (1994, 101) identified as belonging to the front or back of a late fourth-century helmet with central narrow ridge, but without a crest, either of Intercisa type 3, or of Deurne/Conçesti variety. The same pit also contained an artefact described as an 'iron spoke shave', or 'lathe', which Lyne (*ibid.*) believed to have been the remains of the combined brow and nasal guard from this helmet. Also in this same pit context, a helmet crest holder had been found which had been interpreted as Imperial Gallic type, dating to the first century, although, uniquely, this had apparently been soldered into place. Lyne (*ibid.*) assigns this also to Helmet 3, although describing its similarity to the Imperial Gallic style as being 'an archaicism'.

Richborough Helmet 4

Helmet 4 consists only of a badly distorted length of gilt copper-alloy sheathing, which from its shape appears to come from the top of the ridge (Lyne, 1994, 104). Although not really sufficient to call a 'helmet' in itself, due to its fragmentary nature, it is different enough to the other finds to identify it as a fourth helmet, of Deurne/Conçesti type, possibly being for cavalry use. From the same context were also found three further fragments of copper alloy foil appliqué, possibly being parts of the same helmet. Other finds identified by Lyne (*ibid.*) as belonging to 'helmets', included what may be two parts of an iron cheek piece, some possible helmet 'finials', and several glass 'jewels', black with pale-blue centres, which may have belonged to a highly decorated Berkasovo type helmet.

THE DURA EUROPOS HELMET

All of the above Ridge helmets have been dated to the fourth or early fifth centuries AD, but one other possible example has also been found from Dura Europos dated to the third century AD (Southern & Dixon, 1996, 95, fig. 13; James 1986; Fig. 67). While not exactly the same as the above, and possibly being non-Roman, this helmet does exhibit some features placing it under the same identification category, and possibly being instrumental in determining the developmental history and area of origin for this helmet type.

Dura Europos was attacked and destroyed by Persian forces around AD 255 to 257 and has produced a wealth of archaeological material, mostly Roman, from a precisely datable context. Much of the material (bodies and equipment) came from the Tower 19 countermine, where Roman defenders were defeated in an underground battle attempting to prevent the Persian/Sassanian attackers undermining the tower. One body was found separate from those more easily identified as Roman. From his position, he had fallen backwards, facing towards the city, so potentially may have been one of the Sassanian attackers. This identification is further strengthened by the equipment found with him. His iron mail shirt bore a pattern of bronze rings forming a 'trident' motif, which has been identified as similar to a known Sassanian device. In addition, his sword was not of Roman type, with an imported, possibly Chinese, jade pommel. A helmet was found close to, and has been associated with, this body. It was unlike all others found at Dura (which were

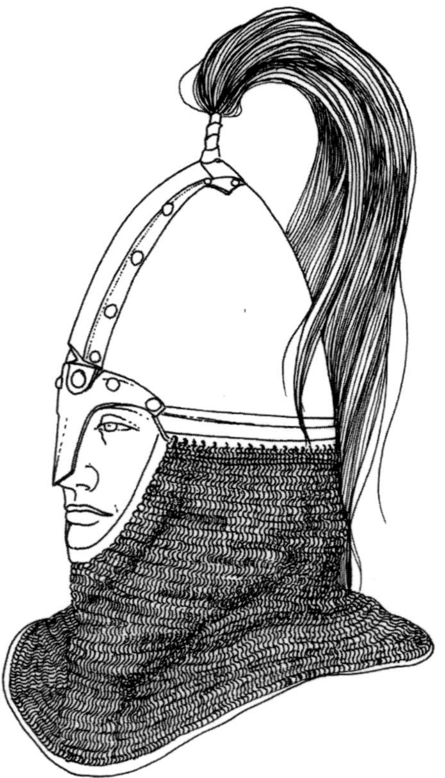

Fig. 67. Dura Europos helmet (from James). (Artwork by J. R. Travis)

of the standard mid-third-century Roman types), and has therefore also been identified as Sassanian, James (1986, 123) proposing an origin from lower Mesopotamia or Afghanistan.

Although crushed when found, approximately 80–90 per cent of the helmet remains, and it is still possible to estimate its original shape. The bowl was iron, 4 mm thick, of bipartite construction, the two halves riveted (in pairs 65 mm apart) to an external front-to-back joining strip, 3–4 mm thick and 30 mm wide. The strip had been shaped to the contours of the bowl: flatter at the rim and V-shaped at the apex. The overall shape of the bowl when constructed was parabolic from the side, but narrower and more pointed from the front. At the apex, a cylindrical 'spike', 51 mm long, dividing into two flat tabs at the base, was attached to the bowl by two rivets on each side. Also running from the 'spike' towards the brow was a curved vertical plate. At the top end it was riveted through a flat, teardrop-shaped tab, and the now missing lower end would have ended just above the brow (there is no sign of a similar back plate). On the front edge, the bowl had two shallow cut-out shapes in line with the eyes, and a single shaped plate above these to form 'eyebrows', held by four rivets. James (1986, 124) also reported the possibility of this plate having possessed a now snapped-off nasal guard.

Around the edges of the bowl were the remains of a curtain of mail ('camail'), formed from 9 mm rings, protecting the neck and cheeks. At the back of the bowl, four more rivets matching those for the eyebrow plate were suggested by James (1986, 127) as being for attaching a lining (of fabric or leather), which he believed would have been necessary to prevent the very tall helmet slipping down over the wearer's eyes.

THE SPANGENHELM TYPE

Sarmatian Spangenhelm

Existing parallel with the Ridge helmets described above was a further type of helmet, the Spangenhelm ('Ribbed helmet'), which also bears little resemblance to the earlier Imperial Gallic and Italic standard helmets of the first three centuries AD, although its appearance and origins can probably be traced through non-Roman finds (Scythian/Sarmatian). Actual examples of Sarmatian *cataphracti* armour do not exist, although some remains of possibly similar Scythian armour have been found in barrow deposits (Negin, 1998, 68). The remains of one such helmet were found in Burial Mound 4 at Nekrasovskaya Stanitsa. Only the side plates and the top knobbed round plate remain (the ribs and horizontal bands were gone), but the shape could be seen to be conical (Fig. 68). However, it is of note here that, despite other aspects of the Scythian/Sarmatian assemblage having remained relatively constant over considerable periods, this helmet exhibits no features of commonality with the much earlier sixth-century BC Scythian helmet (Fagan, 2004, 46; Fig. 18), which was of entirely scale construction, with no cheek guards. This may then pose the question as

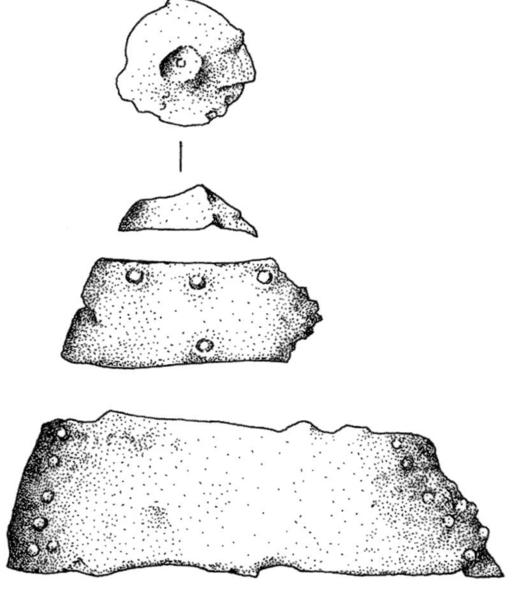

Fig. 68. Remains of Scythian helmet of composite, 'Spangenhelm'-type construction, with transverse ribs, found in Burial Mound 4 at Nekrasovskaya Stanitsa. Only the side plates and the top knobbed round plate remain (the ribs and horizontal bands missing), but the shape can be seen to be conical (from Negin, 1998, 68). (Artwork by J. R. Travis)

to whether these Scythian/Sarmatian composite helmets may have other ancestral roots (possibly these also deriving from the East).

Similar helmets to these northern (Sarmatian) composites can also be seen in imagery on earlier-period monumental sculptures, such as Trajan's Column (as worn by Syrian auxiliary archers, and as depicted in captured Dacian equipment). They appear as either egg-shaped or conical, made of several ribs converging upwards, secured by two transverse bands (Fig. 69). The lower band may sometimes widen into a neck guard. The main bowl plates were then attached to the ribs with nails. Occasionally the helmet would be provided with cheek pieces, and a metallic knob or ball at the apex, where the ribs met.

Fig. 69. Sarmatian helmets from Trajan's Column. (Artwork by J. R. Travis)

Fig. 70. Funerary stele from the Bosphoran centre of Tanais, of third-century Sarmatian lancer wearing scale armour and conical helmet. (Artwork by J. R. Travis)

Several forms of segmented helmets can be seen on Trajan's Column, and on Sarmatian 'cataphracts' on Trajan's Column, where the front-to-back and side-to-side outer ribs and two transverse bands are clearly visible, in addition to base bands secured to the main plates by large, round rivets; no visible apex knob, but small cheek pieces; and no neck or nasal guards. Similar helmets also appear on first- and second-century AD Bosphoran crypt frescos and on grave *stelae*, such as the Triphon relief (Negin, 1998, 68, plate 68; Fig. 70). Negin (1998, 65) suggests that this type was widespread with first-century AD Sarmatians, although he believes that they had adopted it from the East (with there being no indication of local origin from barrows).

By the third and fourth centuries AD, this helmet type can be seen worn by Roman cavalry (*equites cataphractarii*) on the Arch of Galerius (it is known that Galerius made use of Sarmatian-style *cataphractii* as his personal bodyguard during his Persian campaigns; Negin, 1998, 74), although these have a large, round apex knob; no transverse bands except for a wide brow band, with integral nasal guard; and small cheek pieces with a possible out-turned flange to the jawline.

Tacitus had told of the invasion of Moesia in AD 69 by 9,000 Sarmatian horsemen (*cataphracti*) of the Rhoxolani tribe, defeating two cohorts of Roman troops, describing the armour of their 'chiefs and nobles' as being 'made of tough leather and iron strips', covering their bodies, arms and legs, all being 'impervious to blows' (Fig. 90BA; Tacitus, *Hist.* 1.79; Feugère, 2002, 142; Negin, 1998, 65). The Sarmatians had redeveloped their riders into heavily armoured '*cataphracti*' following defeat by Mithridates VI Eupator of the lightly armoured Rhoxolani horsemen at the end of the first century BC. This style of armour assemblage was then taken up by the end of the first century AD, first by other Sarmatian tribes, closely followed by a number of other Eastern peoples, such as Bosphorans, Bactrians, Parthians and Scythians (as evidenced in various artistic and archaeological sources).

The Romans were so impressed with the success of their opponent's armour type and fighting style that they developed units of their own *equites cataphractarii* by the time of Hadrian. The Roman cataphract equipment, however, was more uniform, avoiding the disadvantages of leather scales in favour of metallic plate, as had been described by Tacitus, Arrian and Ammianus (Feugère, 2002, 142). By the third and fourth centuries these cataphract units had increased in number, with Emperor Galerius using them for his personal protection during his Persian campaigns, and as depicted for his guard on the Arch of Galerius, where they would have continued to make use of their own style of armour, including their Spangenhelm-type helmets (Negin, 1998, 74; Fig. 71).

Fig. 71. Graffito image from Dura Europos of a heavily armoured horse and rider (*Clibinarius*). (Redrawn by JR Travis)

The Egyptian Spangenhelm

Two undated helmets of Spangenhelm-type design were found in Egypt, and it had been suggested that these may bridge the gap between second-century Spangenhelm depictions and fifth- to sixth-century Baldenheim helmets (also between Ridge and Baldenheim types). However, Stephenson's view (Stephenson & Dixon, 2003, 29) was that these were of parallel construction to the Baldenheim helmets and did not agree with Ridge comparisons either (describing them as 'too little evidence stretched too far').

The first of these helmets, from Der-el-Medineh (Dittmann, 1940, 54–58; Southern & Dixon, 1996, Plate 11; Fig. 72), has a bowl formed from six plates riveted to six bands, topped by a circular disc/plate riveted to the apex. A ring was also secured to this disc, possibly to assist with carriage, or for the attachment of decorative

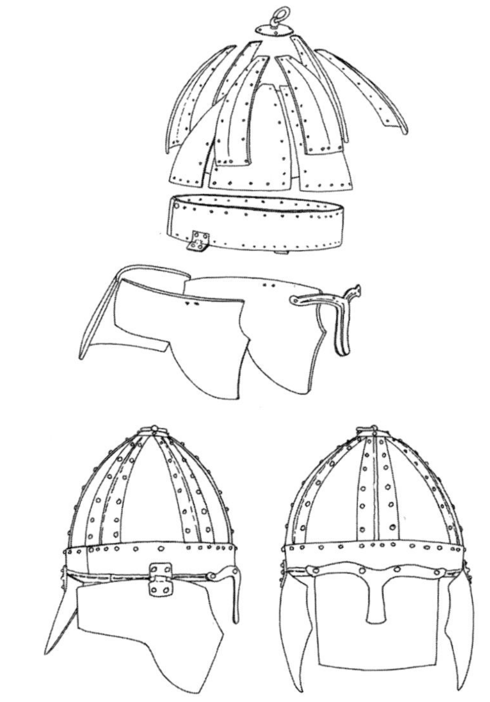

Fig. 72. Expanded Spangenhelm-type helmet, from Der-el-Medineh, Egypt (Bittmann, 1940, 54–8; Southern & Dixon, 1996, Plate 11). The bowl is formed from six plates riveted to six bands; topped by a circular disc/plate riveted to the apex; a ring secured to the disc, either for carriage, or for decorative ribbons or streamers; brow band riveted around the rim, arching over the eyes; with T-shaped nasal guard. (Artwork by J. R. Travis)

ribbons or streamers. A brow band was then riveted around the rim, arching over the eyes, and a T-shaped nasal guard was attached. Finally, the helmet had large Berkasovo-style cheek pieces and neck guard, attached to the bowl by hinges (Southern & Dixon, 1996). Stephenson (Stephenson & Dixon, 2003, 29) considered that this was 'Roman' and 'Tetrarchic' in date, viewing it as a regional variation rather than a missing link.

Fig. 73. The second Egyptian Spangenhelm-type helmet (the Gepid helmet), now in the Rijksmuseum van Oudheden, Leiden. The bowl is made of four plates riveted to four broad bands, topped by a disc; the cheek pieces are narrow, hinged to the bowl, and it had no neck guard or nasal guard. (Artwork by J. R. Travis)

The second of these helmets, the Gepid helmet, now in the Rijksmuseum van Oudheden, Leiden, was reportedly 'purchased' in Thebes 1828, where it had been 'found' on the head of a mummy (Fig. 73). Stephenson (Stephenson & Dixon, 2003, 29) believed that it could be Roman, but may also date to the ninth century AD, and be of Uighur Turkish origin, as it is similar to wall painting from Kumtura in Turkish central Asia. It had a bowl formed by four plates riveted to four broad bands, topped again by a disc. Unlike the previous example, this helmet had narrow cheek pieces (again hinged to the bowl), punched with holes for attachment of a lining (as also is found on the brow band). Furthermore, this helmet had no neck guard, nor was it provided with a nasal guard (Ebert, 1909, 163–170; Southern & Dixon, 1996; Negin, 1998, 71).

Both helmets had been initially attributed with rather dubious dating to fifth/sixth centuries AD, but were later reassessed by James (1986, 134) to potentially much earlier, possibly contemporaneous with a mid-third-century helmet from Dura Europos (all material at Dura dating to the Persian siege of the city in the mid-250s, and belonging mostly to the defending Roman troops). Reassessment of these helmets, along with that from Dura (Fig. 67), prompted James (*ibid.*) to propose a new model for development of these late Roman helmets (the Dura helmet providing 'evidence' that Ridge helmets may have been of Partho-Sassanian inspiration, with reassessment of the two Spangenhelm from Egypt as having been Danubian in origin).

The Baldenheim Spangenhelm

Another type, similar to the Egyptian helmets above, is the Baldenheim type. As described above, Spangenhelm first appear in Roman use in the fourth century AD, as seen on the Arch of Galerius (Stephenson & Dixon, 2003, 28, fig. 14). The later fifth- to sixth-century finds, however, are of a different type of Spangenhelm: the Baldenheim type (*ibid.*).

They were constructed from four or six iron plates, not touching but shaped to form a bowl. These iron plates were silvered on several examples (Southern & Dixon, 1996). The plates then overlapped and were attached to a gilded brow band, which was shaped to curve over the eyes, although without a nasal guard. Gaps between the iron plates were bridged by four or six inverted, T-shaped, gilded copper plates/ribs, or 'spangens', then riveted to the iron plates. At the apex, an inverted T-shaped, gilded copper alloy disc with protruding fungiform button in the centre was interpreted as being possibly for a plume (Southern & Dixon, 1996, 95).

The bottom edge of the brow band and the entire perimeter of the gilded cheek pieces were pierced with holes for attaching a lining, and to secure the gilded copper alloy cheek pieces to the bowl. The gilded copper parts were decorated with classical and Germanic patterns in punched decoration. James (1986, 134) noted that all other Baldenheim-style helmets are similar in design, which he suggested indicated centralised production, probably by Roman craftsmen for Ostrogothic masters.

Stephenson (Stephenson & Dixon, 2003, 31) suggested that simple Intercisa-type helmets remained in use in the early Byzantine period (indicating some continuity with the Dominate), citing one find from Korak, Jordan. He also cited Theophylact Simocatta's statement (ii.4.3) of 'distinctive and conspicuous' helmets still worn by some Roman troops, from which he proposed that Berkasovo and Baldenheim types were still being worn. He also suggested that images of Byzantine cavalrymen on the Isola Rizza dish may have been wearing these later, Baldenheim-type Spangenhelm, suggesting that increasing Avar influence in the sixth century led to the introduction of lamellar helmets, such as those at Niederstotzingen and Kertsch; and that helmet styles from the Dominate period continued in use to early Byzantine and were supplemented in the sixth century by Avar lamellar helmets (Stephenson & Dixon, 2003, 31, pls 11 & 14). He further cited Maurice (*Strategikon*, 1.2) that cavalrymen wore 'helmets with small plumes on top', but believed that this could apply to both lamellar helmets and Spangenhelm.

SUMMARY OF DEVELOPMENT AND POSSIBLE ANCESTRY

James (1986, 127) compared the construction of the Dura Europos helmet to that of the Roman Ridge helmets, all having an iron body, formed from two half-shells, joined by riveting to a central front-to-back 'ridge' strip. The Dura helmet also had the additional applied nasal and eyebrow plates present on some, but not all Ridge helmets (its structure being the same as that of the 'simpler' Berkasovo II variant). He considered that the 'more complex' Berkasovo I and Deurne helmets therefore should be seen as one end of a variant line, with the 'simpler' Augst and Intercisa at the other end, with the Dura helmet (and possibly many other variations) as prototypes from which they derived, with the assumption therefore for an oriental, possibly Partho-Sassanian origin.

James (1986, 117) also reviewed features common to existing Partho-Sassanian helmets (with a view to finding possible prototypes for the Roman Ridge helmets, other than that of the Dura helmet, also identified as probably being Sassanian), identifying two regional groups: one group being from North Iran (four examples); and the other from Mesopotamia (one example). All were from later periods (fifth to seventh centuries AD), so none could have been viewed as 'prototypes' in themselves, but did show probable common ancestry. He found that all were of similar construction (composite bowls, joined by front-to-back strip), some also exhibiting the shaped rim and applied eyebrow/nasal guard, although their shapes were taller and more parabolic (as with the Dura helmet). Most had holes pierced around their rims, which had been identified as being for the suspension of a 'camail' (again, as on the Dura example), although James (*ibid.*) considered that these were more probably just for attachment of the lining.

James (1986, 119) also noted one further example, from the British Museum, which differed from the others, being of radial construction, similar to the Spangenhelm type (four plates attached to four vertical strips), and this helmet did still possess the remains of an iron 'camail', similar to that on the Dura helmet. However, he discounted this example as being post-Sassanian, due to its similarities to much later Russian and Tibetan helmets.

Klumbach (1973) had proposed that the Spangenhelm had derived from earlier Roman Ridge helmets. However, this was disputed by James (1986, 128). He challenged the previous dating of fifth century AD assigned to the two Egyptian helmets with 'radial' construction, proposing instead a date in the third century, or earlier.

James (1986, 128) cited the appearance of Spangenhelm, almost identical to the Egyptian examples, in use by Roman troops at the beginning of the second century, as being worn on Trajan's Column by auxiliary archers (usually described as Syrian, but whom James suggested may have been locally recruited auxiliaries). The helmets can also be seen on the column's base among captured enemy equipment and being worn by Dacian/Sarmatian cavalry opponents, the latter helmets being bullet-shaped, of radial construction, with cheek pieces but without neck guards. These are also constructed with additional transverse bands, similar to the Scythian/Sarmatian helmet found at in Burial Mound 4 at Nekrasovskaya Stanitsa (Negin, 1998, 65; Fig. 68). As indicative of Spangenhelm being in use by Roman troops around AD 300 (this being the date attributed by James to the Egyptian helmets), James (1986, 131) cited reliefs on the Arch of Galerius, where helmets can be seen with pointed-shaped bowls of radial construction, neck and nasal guards, and cheek pieces (the use of hinges on the Egyptian cheek pieces probably being an early feature, residual from the previous Imperial helmets). He then concludes that they would have begun to replace the traditional Imperial helmet types in the latter half of the third century AD, but would not have been widely used outside the band of AD 260 to 320, although appearing prior to the bipartite Ridge helmets (which then began to replace them after that time).

In his proposed developmental model, James (1986, 134) proposed that there was not just one direction of influence in play, but that features can be identified which were sourced from the earlier Roman Imperial (such as the reinforcing plate on the Dura Ridge helmet and the cheek hinges on the Egyptian Spangenhelm helmets); from above the Danube and steppe region (for the helmets of radial construction); and Ridge helmets from across the Euphrates; with influences from all three origins passing in both directions via the nomads of central Asia. However, with regard to the radial helmets, he did not see the Dura or Egyptian examples as being ancestral to some of the later Spangenhelm (such as the early medieval Baldenheim type, which he saw as a continuance of traditions from eastern Europe, central Asia and Russia, made for Ostrogothic masters by Roman craftsmen), but he did identify commonality with other northern European helmets of the sixth to eighth century AD (such as those from Sutton Hoo, Valsgärde and Coppergate), which he described as being 'very different' (James, 1986, 134; Bruce-Mitford, 1978; Tweddle, 1984; Addyman *et al.*, 1982).

VII

AUXILIARY HELMETS

AUXILIARY HELMETS – TYPES A TO D

It would appear that armour quality suffered at times when mass-production methods were being used to meet increased demand (from the Civil and Social Wars, and following the Marian and Augustan reforms), although the armour was still destined for legionary use, the auxiliaries continuing to use their own kit in their own native style. However, Russell-Robinson identified some helmets, dating to the Augustan and Imperial periods, which were also of marked inferior quality. These, he considered, may have been for auxiliary infantry use rather than legionary issue, in part due to the poor quality and also in that none are inscribed with the names of owners, suggesting equipment being passed down from retiring veterans to new recruits (Russell-Robinson, 1975, 82). A number of helmets were found from the Augustan period onwards inscribed with the names of not only the owner but also their legion and commanding officer, indicating legionary use, although it must be acknowledged that not all helmets are so inscribed. However, where this lack of inscription coincided with poor-quality manufacture, Russell-Robinson felt that these may not have been intended for legionary use, and within this framework he felt able to define four typologies of auxiliary infantry helmets.

Auxiliary Helmets – Type A

Dating to the mid-first century AD, this helmet resembles the Coolus type I, although it is much cruder (or simpler) in form and finish. Russell-Robinson considered this helmet was probably produced by spinning, from the concentric rings of tool marks and punched centre to the straight-sided bowl, probably used for location on the lathe. The helmet is generally more poorly finished, with visible spinning marks, lack of thickening of the rim and uneven shaping, with the neck-guard rim stepping down at the ears at an angle of 45° on one side and 90° on the opposite (Russell-Robinson, 1975, 83).

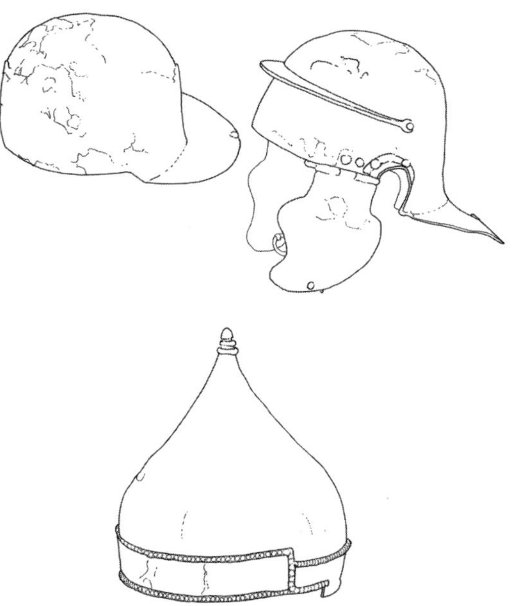

Fig. 74. Auxiliary infantry helmets types A, B and D (from Russell-Robinson, 1975). (Artwork by J. R. Travis)

Auxiliary Helmets – Type B

This again has a very simple, rounded bowl, with straight sides and sloping neck guard, similar in profile to an Imperial Gallic helmet but much plainer, without any decoration or any occipital ridges. It has applied ear guards and a reinforcing peak, set high up on the bowl. This helmet was also found in the Rhine at Mainz, suggesting loss before AD 83 when the bridge replaced the unpredictable ferry crossing (Russell-Robinson, 1975, 85).

Auxiliary Helmets – Type C
This second-century AD bronze helmet bears close resemblance to the auxiliary cavalry types D and E helmets with crossed reinforcements on top of the bowl. However, on this helmet the four ends all finish on the same level, whereas on the cavalry examples the one at the back reached down further than the other three. The helmet also has a short, flat reinforcing peak, but this is fixed by a central 'tongue', passed through a slot in the bowl and bent over on the inside (Russell-Robinson, 1975, 85). The example cited by Russell-Robinson, from the Museo Archaeologico Florence, has been radically modified in antiquity, being truncated all the way around at the ear level, part of the ear recesses remaining, and pierced with holes, possibly for mail attachment. In his reconstruction, however, based on representations on Trajan's Column, Russell-Robinson (1975, 85) suggested a short, sloping neck guard and simple cheek pieces without any throat flanges.

Auxiliary Helmets – Type D
This is a bronze, bulbous, conical helmet, which looks more Eastern than Roman, resembling Syrian, Sarmatian or Dacian models depicted on Trajan's Column, but with some distinctly Roman features. The bowl has an applied brow band (decorated with images of Roman deities, Victory, Jupiter and Mars), stepping down at the back to a separate riveted neck guard. The presence of cheek pieces (hinges for which would have been riveted to the inside) is similarly a Roman feature, although the form of these is not known. From this combination of Roman and Eastern features, and in view of known use of Eastern auxiliary archers (depictions of which are seen on Trajan's Column), Russell-Robinson (1975, 85) proposed that this may have belonged to a Levantine auxiliary archer.

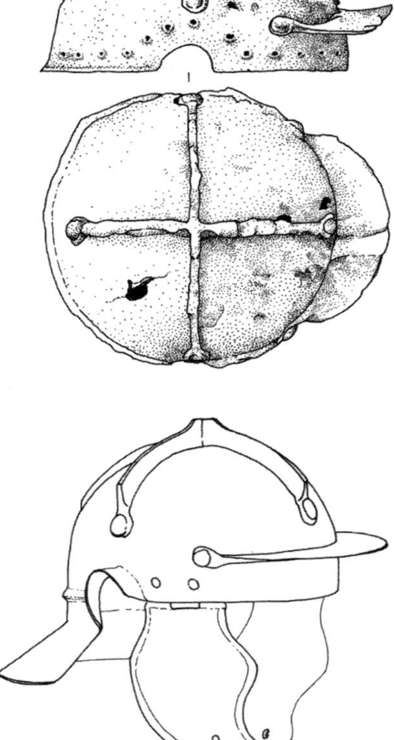

Fig. 75. Auxiliary infantry helmet type C (from Russell-Robinson, 1975). (Artwork by J. R. Travis)

COMPOSITE HELMETS

A further type of Eastern-style helmet (although more egg-shaped than conical in profile) was in widespread use by first-century AD Sarmatian 'cataphracts'. This composite helmet is described by Negin as the prototype for Roman *equites cataphractarii*, and may have formed the basis of later composite Spangenhelm and Intercisa helmets discussed in greater detail in the previous chapter. The body of this helmet was formed by a ribbed frame, converging on a metal-knobbed terminal, and separated by two rows of transverse bars. Metal plates were then secured to these bars with nails or rivets. Occasionally these helmets were also fitted with cheek pieces (Negin 1998, 72). Examples are seen in sculptural representation, such as first- or second-century AD Bosphoran crypt frescos, and also found archaeologically, as in fragments from a burial mound context from Nekrasovskaya Stanitsa (*ibid.*).

VIII

CAVALRY AND FACE HELMETS

During the Republican period, up to the first century BC, cavalry were, as with the legionary infantry, drawn from Roman citizens who met the wealth criteria (cavalry being made up of men defined as being of equestrian rank), and would have been responsible for the supply of their own equipment. However, from the first century BC, after first the Marian and later the Augustan reforms, the structure of the legions changed, and the majority of active cavalry forces were drawn from auxiliary sources (Russell-Robinson, 1975, 89). Although Russell-Robinson (1975, 82) argued for auxiliary infantry helmets generally being less ornate and of inferior quality, the same is not the case for cavalry equipment. However, this is perhaps not too surprising, as these individuals would have been drawn from the wealthier 'equestrian' ranks of their own native societies, and would have had the resources to afford better-quality equipment. Much of this equipment followed Roman traditions, with features adapted to better suit cavalry purposes. With fully enclosed cheek pieces, covering the ears and flanged to protect the throat, and with bowls extending down to the base of the neck, the rider was protected from backwards-sweeping cuts from mounted adversaries (this often combined with greatly widened, sloping neck guards). For example, on an Imperial copy of a Republican relief of Mettius Curtius, at the Lacus Curtius in the Forum, the cavalryman can be seen wearing a close-fitting Attic-style helmet, the bowl reaching down to the base of his neck, where it meets and covers any gap with the back plate of his cuirass. He is also provided with an unusually shaped crest, which may be intended to represent a flowing horsehair plume (Fig. 76).

However, within this framework, individual traditions can be seen in styles of decoration, particularly in the Sports-type helmets, including Eastern-looking faces. In his study of cavalry helmets, Russell-Robinson identified nineteen types of cavalry helmet which he separated into two distinct groups, and which he categorised as auxiliary cavalry (types A to I) and cavalry sports helmets (types A to J), the latter being highly decorative, often provided with full-face masks. It has been suggested that these parade or sports helmets, because of restricted vision, were only used for equestrian exercises in the *Hippika Gymnasia*, as described by Arrian (*Ars Tactica*), although other sources suggest their use also on the battlefield (Ammianus 16.10.8; Heliodorus, *Aethiopica*, 9.15).

Fig. 76. Described as an Imperial copy of a Republican relief, sculpture depicting cavalryman Mettius Curtius, at the Lacus Curtius in the Forum, Rome. The rider can be seen wearing a close-fitting Attic-style helmet with an unusually shaped crest, which may be intended to represent a flowing horsehair plume. (Artwork by J. R. Travis)

Stephenson and Dixon (2003, 22), however, argue that the

Hippika Gymnasia, being a testing ground for battlefield techniques, would have required an equal level of vision and control. They suggest that the positive effect of a flamboyant, fully masked and equipped cavalry unit on the morale of the army, and the corresponding negative effect on the enemy, would justify the reduction in vision. This reasoning is also suggested by Russell-Robinson for why, at a time when equipment was state funded, such additional expense would be lavished on auxiliary equipment (Russell-Robinson, 1975, 107). Stephenson and Dixon also propose that cavalry may have been issued with two helmets, one of each type, the sports for ceremonial and battlefield display and the plainer, more functional for everyday patrol purposes. To support this argument, they cite a burial from Nawa where both types of helmet were found together in one grave (Stephenson & Dixon, 2003, 24).

Again, a separate Continental system of typologies exists in parallel to that of Russell-Robinson, based on names of location of some typical examples. The Weiler type of iron helmet, dating to the first century AD, equates most typically to Russell-Robinson's auxiliary cavalry type A. The Niederbieber, dating from the second century AD, equates to auxiliary cavalry types C onwards, and the Guisborough relates to the cavalry sports helmets (with the archaic Attic-style bowls), the example from Guisborough, Yorkshire, being specifically of sports type I (Russell-Robinson, 1975, 132, pls 391–393; Fig. 92).

AUXILIARY CAVALRY HELMETS – TYPES A TO I

Auxiliary Cavalry Helmets – Type A

This first-century AD helmet type, as previously mentioned, equates to the Continental Weiler type, although examples are also known from Newstead, Scotland, and Northwich, Cheshire (Plate 7.11; Curle, 1911, Plate XXVI; Russell-Robinson, 1975, 94, pls 246–249). It is hemispherical, with ear recesses, extended deeply at the occiput to a small, flanging neck guard at the nape. Russell-Robinson suggested that this would have been produced as a plain iron bowl, sheathed with bronze or silver moulded to resemble hair or other raised decoration (Russell-Robinson, 1975, 89, 95). At the time of his report, the Northwich example was still undergoing conservation work and features were not discernible. However, since that time, this has been found to have been decorated with rudimentary and stylised hair embossed onto the iron base. The undecorated area across the brow of the helmet suggests that this may have been fitted with a wide, decorative brow band reinforcement, and its cheek pieces

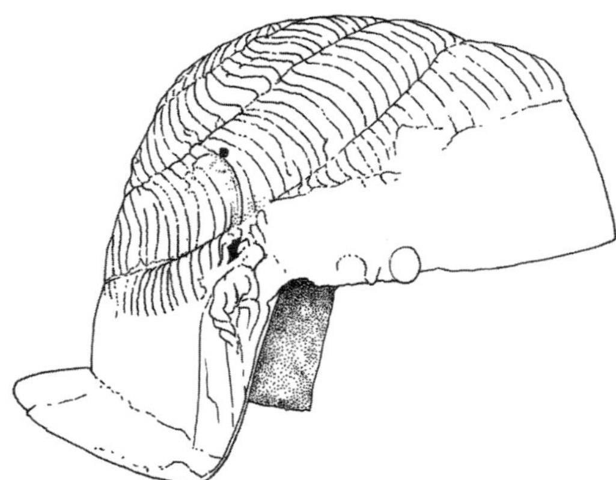

Fig. 77. Auxiliary cavalry helmet: type A ('Weiler' type), with stylised representation of curled hair and decorative cheek pieces (from Russell-Robinson, 1975). (Artwork by J. R. Travis)

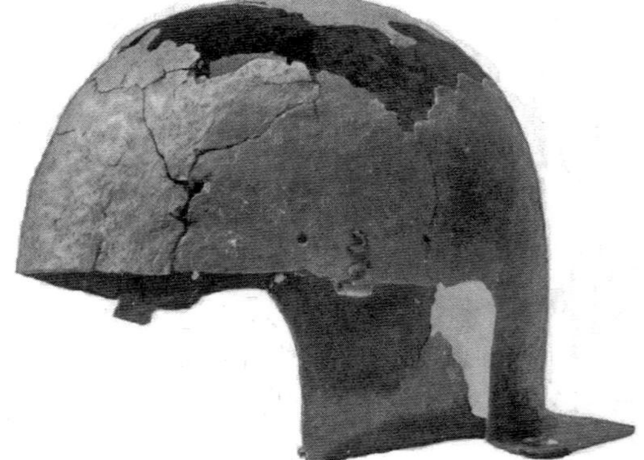

Fig. 78. Auxiliary cavalry helmet: type A ('Weiler' type) from Newstead, decorative outer layer gone, only the inner core remaining. (From Curle, 1911, Plate XXVI)

may have been enclosed, resembling those on the type B helmet from Witcham Gravel, Ely (Russell-Robinson, 1975, 94, pls 250–253).

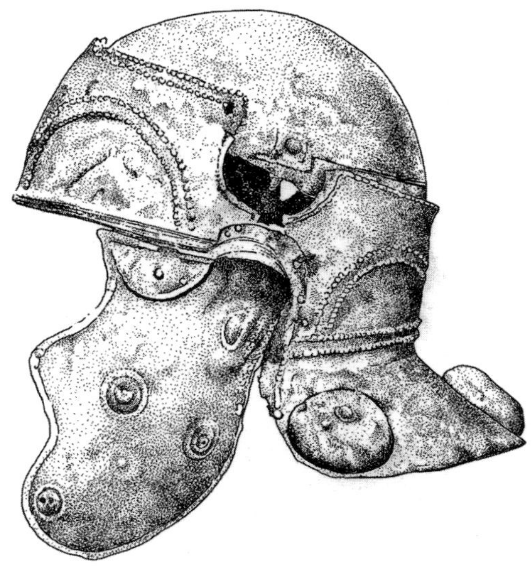

Fig. 79. Auxiliary cavalry helmet: type B from Witcham gravel, Ely (from Russell-Robinson, 1975). (Artwork by J. R. Travis)

Auxiliary Cavalry Helmets – Type B

This helmet is similar to the previous type, A, but has a deeper, sloping neck guard. Russell-Robinson reports only one known example of this type, from Witcham Gravel, Ely (Russell-Robinson, 1975, 94). The bowl is of iron, with an applied outer casing in four parts. The crown and neck guard were cased in white metal or silver and the wide, two-part band, with pearled, semi-circular decoration of punched, raised dots, covering the brow and occipital area, was in yellow bronze/brass, applied ear guards covering the join between, creating a two-tone effect (Russell-Robinson, 1975, 95). Four large, round bosses (resembling old-fashioned bicycle bells) covered the rivets attaching the brow band and occipital band, front and back and above each ear, with a further three such bosses on the neck guard. The cheek pieces were of bronze and were fully enclosed, with stylised, embossed simulated ear decoration, slightly cusped for eye and mouth, but with no throat flange. The helmet is now lacking any crest attachment, although a double line of rivet points across the crown, front to back, suggesting that it may have been fitted with a non-removable crest, lost prior to deposition (Russell-Robinson, 1975, 95).

Auxiliary Cavalry Helmets – Type C

With the second century AD, a new shape of cavalry helmet appears, described under the Continental system as Niederbieber, this helmet being an early form of that type. It is formed from a single plate of bronze with a small, triangular, raised point at the apex. The back of the bowl is straight and deep, reaching to below the nape, almost to the shoulders, terminating in a small, slightly sloping neck flange. It is decorated by two embossed parallel ribs, from the neck flange, up and around the ear, across the brow, and down behind the opposite ear (Russell-Robinson, 1975, 96).

Auxiliary Cavalry Helmets – Type D

Of similar shape to the type C, this helmet is also provided with applied ear guards (flanged outwards, bending around the ear, and continuing downwards to the neck guard), and a brow band, pointed on its lower edge. Instead of a raised point at the apex, as on type C, this helmet is fitted with a low crest, reaching from the apex to just above the neck guard, fixed at each end by a large, cone-headed rivet. The sloping neck guard is deeper than the previous type, bound at the edge in bronze, and the extremely large, enclosed cheek pieces have a deep throat flange which extends to meet the neck guard to form a wide, cohesive neck, shoulder and throat protection.

Auxiliary Cavalry Helmets – Type E

This helmet is almost identical in profile to the previous type, D, although it is also fitted with a transverse, flat reinforcement, in addition to that running from front to back, the plates being slotted at the apex, similar to those seen on the auxiliary infantry type C. As had possibly also been the case with the previous type D, above the applied brow band, a small peak was fitted, pointed at the centre, on some examples pointing upwards, on others pointing downwards. Some examples also feature a carrying handle on the centre back of the neck guard. Parts of this type of helmet have been found at Newstead, dated to AD 140–158 (Russell-Robinson, 1975, 97), and at Dura Europos, dated to AD 255–256 (James 2004, 107).

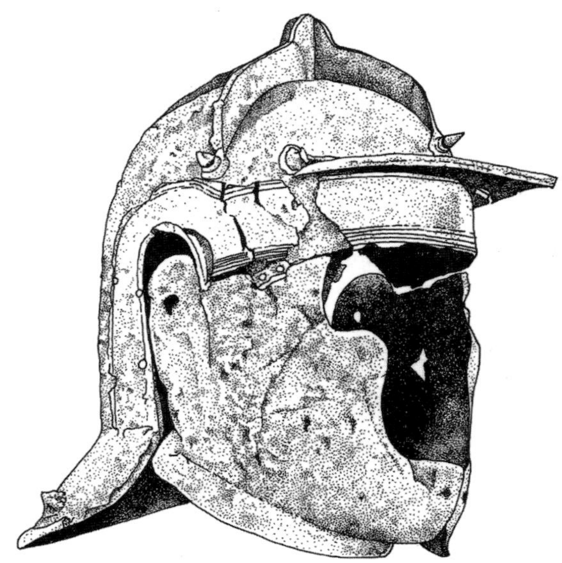

Fig. 80. Auxiliary cavalry helmet: type E (Heddernheim) (from Russell-Robinson, 1975). (Artwork by J. R. Travis)

Auxiliary Cavalry Helmets – Type F
This type is again very similar to its predecessor, of Niederbieber type, but being more simply made, lacking applied decoration, its ear guards and brow border being raised from the helmet body, and using ball-headed rivets to fix the peak and cross bracings. As with its predecessor, the neck guard was bound with a bronze rim and fitted with a carrying handle (Russell-Robinson, 1975, 99).

Auxiliary Cavalry Helmets – Type G
This iron helmet is unlike the previous Niederbieber types, and Russell-Robinson suggested a different point of origin (Russell-Robinson, 1975, 99). It is less deep at the back, closer to the types A and B, but dating to the later part of the second century AD (although the most complete example, from the Waal at Nijmegen, is now missing most of its neck guard, so possibly closer in profile to type B). It also features applied decoration, in the form of bronze ear guards and an elaborate brow band, with transverse ribs and a raised crown of embossed laurel and oak leaves (Russell-Robinson, 1975, 99).

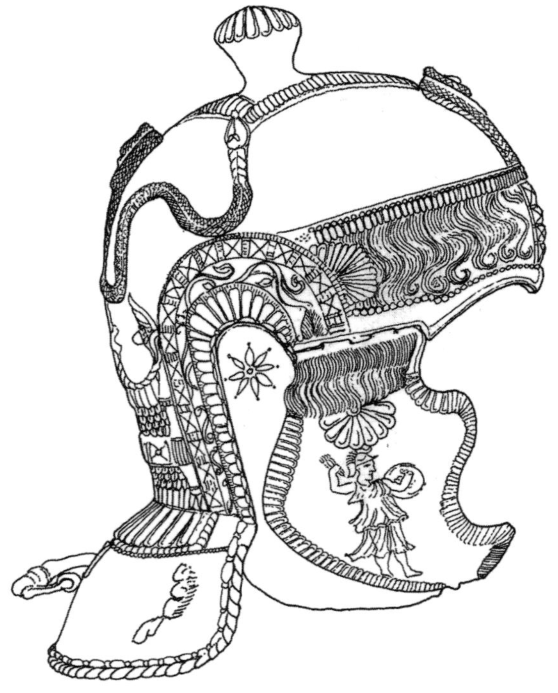

Fig. 81. Auxiliary cavalry helmet: type H (from Russell-Robinson, 1975). (Artwork by J. R. Travis)

Auxiliary Cavalry Helmets – Type H
This helmet, dating from the late second to the early third century AD, is again of the basic Niederbieber shape, of iron with applied bronze decoration, but with a wide, dished neck guard, and featuring a large, hollow bronze knob (or anther) on a convex square base, at the apex, made to resemble the head of a poppy seed and pierced for a crest or plume (Russell-Robinson, 1975, 100). Several examples are known, some with modest decoration, although one, from Heddernheim, is very elaborately decorated, with panels engraved across the brow, around the ear and across the occipital area, with featherlike scales and writhing serpents, which Russell-Robinson considered to show an Egyptian influence (Russell-Robinson, 1975, 100).

Auxiliary Cavalry Helmets – Type I
This is a plain, deep helmet of the basic Niederbieber type, with a large, dished neck guard, as on type H. Russell-Robinson (1975, 104) reported that only one example is known, from Osterburker, dating to the mid-third century AD. The ear recesses are very large and worked out from the bowl to form shallow ear guards. There is no brow band and the upturned, pointed peak is attached close to the rim. As there is no visible means to attach the cheek pieces, Russell-Robinson suggested that it may have used connected cheek pieces, as seen on sports type H, tucked under the brow and fastened with straps across the neck flange (Russell-Robinson, 1975, 100).

CAVALRY SPORTS HELMETS – TYPES A TO J

These highly ornate and lavishly embossed helmets, if not commissioned by the owner, would have represented a substantial financial investment of state funds (Russell-Robinson, 1975, 107). However, as not necessarily being purely ceremonial in function, they would have had a considerable value in battlefield conditions for the shock effect of their expressionless features on the enemy. Russell-Robinson (1975, 107) considered that these helmets more probably derived from Hellenistic Greek or Etruscan origins (citing as example the fourth-to-third-century BC Negau-style Etruscan helmet in the Vatican Museum), rather than those helmets of the third-to-second-century BC Persian *clibanarii*, which he felt more probably copied the Roman examples.

Cavalry Sports Helmets – Type A
Russell-Robinson (1975, 112) included this first-century BC helmet from Semendria in his typology of cavalry sports helmets as a potential prototype for later masked helmets, although being much cruder. Formed in two parts, the shallow skull reaches to just level with the top of the ears at the back, and overlaps the mask at the brow. The hair and face are naturalistically sculpted, in contrast to the later stylised representations, and there are no projecting ear guards. The back of the skull and the jawline are pierced, which Russell-Robinson suggested was for the attachment of a lining material.

Cavalry Sports Helmets – Type B
These helmets, dating to the late first and early second century AD, have a stylised, youthful male face, fashioned to appear as though wearing an ornamental Attic-type helmet, heavily embossed with scenes of soldiers, animals and mythological creatures. Russell-Robinson (1975, 112) considered that the embossed bowl decoration showed less artistic talent than the facial features of the mask, and that this part may have been executed by less skilled craftsmen. The bowls are fitted with high-projecting peaks (rounded on the Ribchester example, but pointed on others), and the masks, attached to the bowl by a hook and slot, extend around to include raised

Fig. 82. Cavalry sports type B helmet from Newstead. (From Curle, 1911, Plate XXVI)

ear protection (Fig. 83; Russell-Robinson, 1975, 112–113, pls 310–313).

Fig. 83. Cavalry sports type B helmet from Ribchester. (Photo by J R Travis)

Cavalry Sports Helmets – Type C

These late first- to third-century AD helmets also follow the archaic tradition for Attic shaped bowls, boldly embossed with all-over wavy hair, with the face again being of a stylised youthful male, the curls from the hair extending on to the forehead and sideburns (Russell-Robinson, 1975, 112).

Cavalry Sports Helmets – Type D

In this variant, both bronze and iron examples are known, and the mask is now affixed to the bowl by a hinge in the centre of the forehead. The bowl is fashioned to represent an elaborately decorated helmet, and on one example from Vize, Thrace, the facemask is also provided with simulated cheek pieces, fashioned to give the impression of cusps for ears, eyes and mouth (Russell-Robinson, 1975, 116–117). The face is again generally of a stylised, youthful, clean-shaven male, some plainly fashioned without ears, as on the example from Vechten, and also that more recently found at Kalkriese (Fig. 86), which it closely resembles. However, some fashion trends and regional cultural variances can be seen, with one example from Tel Oum Hauran, dating to the second half of the second century AD, sporting a moustache and heavy curled sideburns, whereas another from Emesa, Syria, exhibits distinctly Eastern features (*ibid.*).

Fig. 84. Cavalry sports type C (a) iron helmet and face mask from Newstead. (From Curle, 1911, Plate XXIX)

Fig. 85. Cavalry sports type C, tinned bronze parade mask, *c.* AD 100, from Aintab, Syria. The mask would have originally had a matching skull piece, similar to that from Newstead, to protect the rest of the head and back of neck. Now in the British Museum (GR1919.19–20.1). (Artwork by J. R. Travis)

Cavalry Sports Helmets – Type E

Whereas all of the previous helmet types had depicted male faces, Russell-Robinson grouped here a number of helmets with apparent female features, which he suggested may represent Amazons (Russell-Robinson, 1975, 124). However, some of those which he described as female are rather indeterminate and less easily differentiated from the males, as with one from Newstead, his identification being based on comparisons of known female hairstyles, some heavily plaited, others decorated with jewellery, diadems, or with their hair raised into high peaks.

Most of the evidence for this category of helmets is mask driven, with very few helmet bowls in the archaeological record. However, from the face masks available, most appear to belong to a rounded, head-shaped bowl (possibly influenced by the Attic), the mask just providing the simulated 'persona'. The bowls would then have been decorated, either with all-over simulated hair, as seen on several of the type D helmets, or with all-over embossed figures, as on the Ribchester helmet (type B).

However, some of the face masks appear to belong to an entirely different type of bowl (these being those examples listed by Russell-Robinson as dating to the second to

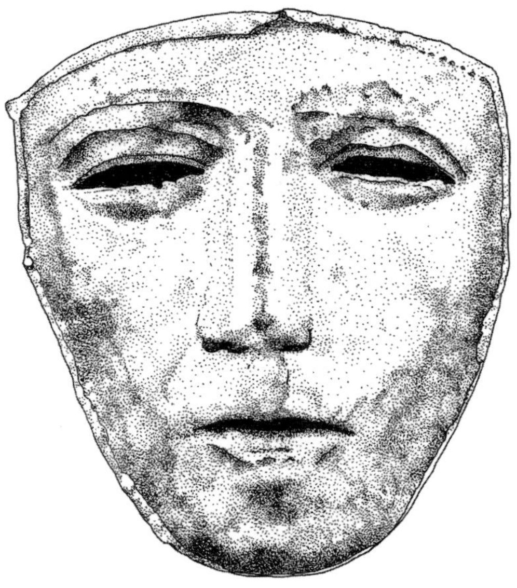

Fig. 86. Mask from cavalry sports type D helmet from Kalkriese (from Bunz & Spickermann, 2006). (Artwork by J. R. Travis)

Fig. 87. Brass mask from cavalry sports type E helmet from Newstead. (From Curle, 1911, Plate XXX)

Fig. 88. Bronze parade mask, cavalry sports type E, dating to second century AD. The mask was found on the face of a skeleton in a tomb at Nola, southern Italy. This would have belonged to a parade helmet, intended for cavalry displays, type E helmets being provided with a woman's face; the female masks possibly representing Amazons. Now in the British Museum (GR1824.4–7.10). (Artwork by J. R. Travis)

third century; 1975, 125, pls 364–366), the masks rising at the apex to at peaked shape, where presumably they would have met a similarly shaped bowl, for example on the helmet from Grafenhausen and the two from the Straubing Hoard. The latter two examples particularly differ from the others as the faces have an Eastern appearance, with simulated tight curls rising all of the way up to the pointed apex. These two examples, as on the example from Nola (estimated to be from a century earlier), have more realistic representations of eyes, with a circular ring inset to simulate the pupils. It is interesting here to note that, despite Russell-Robinson's tendency to create new 'types' within his categories for sometimes even the slightest differences, here, with helmets so clearly different, he still chose to group them with the other type Es.

If, therefore, we accept his designation of these helmets as still belonging to the type E group, based on the use of female features, we should probably look to this type for classification of the recently discovered Crosby Garrett helmet, with similarly female features, 'hair' reproduced in similar fashion to those from the Straubing Hoard, and its raised, peaked bowl (as discussed in greater detail below). However, we must also consider the integral crests on two of the following types (low on the type F, but higher on the type Hs – particularly high on the example from Heddernheim), and whether these helmets should be viewed as either a new type, or as transitional to the later types.

Fig. 89. Mask from cavalry sports type E helmet, bronze, second to third century AD, from the Straubing Hoard, Straubing Museum. It has a face of Eastern appearance and more realistic representation of the eyes, as seen on the more recently found Crosby Garrett helmet. It was originally classified as type E by Russell-Robinson, but possibly should be viewed as a separate type. (Artwork by J. R.Travis, after Russell-Robinson, p. 125, plate 366)

Cavalry Sports Helmets – Type F

These helmets are made in three pieces. The Attic shaped bowl divides from the front face section, on the line with the ears and across the top of the forehead. The central T-shaped part of the face, with the eyes, nose and mouth, is then removable, secured at the centre brow with a turning pin, and possibly with another near the lips.

Faces are again distinctly male, and bowls, where present, are close-fitting and Attic-style, with small neck guard,

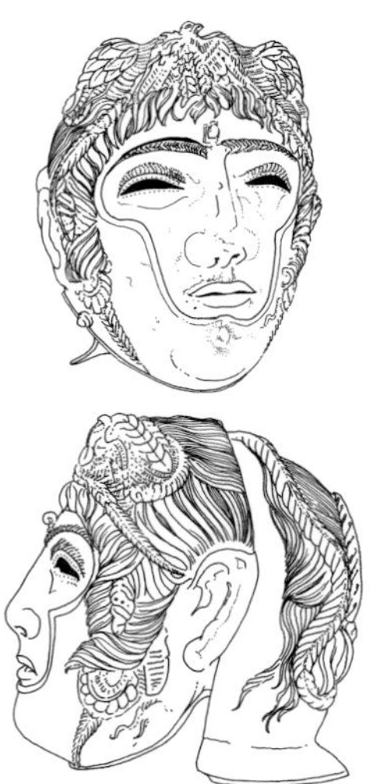

Fig. 90 Cavalry sports helmet type F, bronze, late second century AD, from Prondorf, in the Landesmuseum, Stuttgart. It is made in three pieces: an Attic-shaped bowl, divided from the front face section at the ears and along the forehead, with a central opening for a separate, removable T-shaped face section. (Artwork by J. R. Travis, after Russell-Robinson, p. 126, plate 368)

and either provided with simulated hair swirls or all-over embossed figures. One example, from Ostrov, Romania, differs in that, although also of close-fitting Attic style, it is provided with a low raised crest, running from the centre back down towards the neck.

Cavalry Sports Helmets – Type G

These helmets are again fashioned in three parts, with a T-shaped removable central face panel, as in type F helmets, and a close-fitting Attic-style bowl, but feature a high, arched crest and an integral pointed peak with a small embossed face, to give the impression of an archaic Corinthian helmet. The front part of the crest is usually decorated with a moulded head of an eagle, this being particularly finely reproduced on the example from Eisernes Thor on the Donau, in the Hungarian National Museum, where the full body of the bird can be seen, crouching forward, as though ready to take off for the attack (Russell-Robinson, 1975, 128, pls 381–383). On this same example, the crest itself has been extensively moulded, to represent a double row of standing feathers, and with writhing snakes up each side of the bowl.

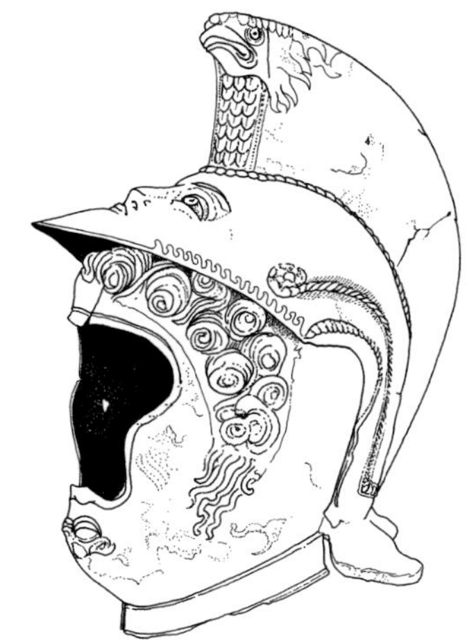

Fig. 91 Cavalry sports helmet type G, bronze, late second to early third century AD, from Heddernheim, in Frankfurt Museum. As with the type F, it is made in three pieces, with a separate T-shaped face section. The Attic bowl however, has a high, arched crest and integral pointed peak, with an embossed face similar to those seen on Corinthian helmets. (Artwork by J. R. Travis, after Russell-Robinson, p. 129, plate 376)

Cavalry Sports Helmets – Type H

These helmets, dating to the third century AD, have a bowl which is a debased form of the Attic style, with highly decorated cheek pieces connected at top centre and the chin to form an open face. As with the previous type G, it has an integral embossed crest, although not raised as high, and the brow is flat, without any Corinthian-style peak.

Cavalry Sports Helmets – Type I

This helmet, also dating to the third century AD, is of the type named under the Continental system after one of the few known examples, that from Guisborough, Yorkshire. It closely resembles the type H helmet, with an Attic form, but the embossed brow band is flat across the brow and raised into three rounded peaks.

A similarly shaped helmet exists, also dating to the third century AD, from the River Saône at Chalon (in the Musée des Antiquités Nationales, St

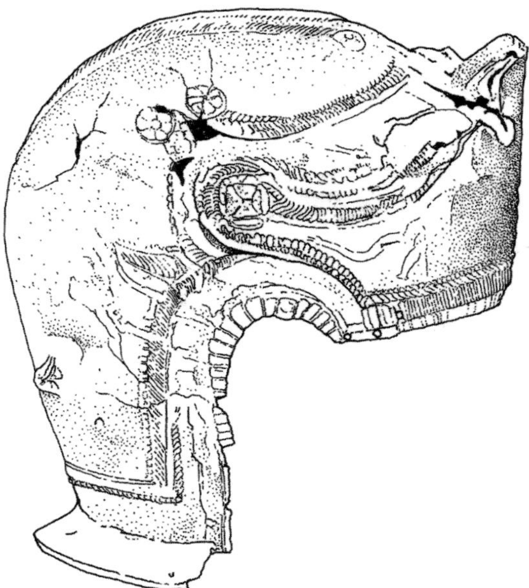

Fig. 92. Cavalry sports helmet type I, third century AD, from Guisborough, Cleveland. It was made from thin bronze, with embossed and lightly engraved decoration (figures representing deities on the brow plate include Mars and Minerva). The helmet would originally have had a cheek piece on each side. Now in the British Museum (PRB1878.9–10.1). (Artwork by J. R. Travis)

Germaine-en-Lage; Russell-Robinson, 1975, 134, pls 394–396). However, more recently, in 2012, the remains of a further example have been found at Hallaton in Leicestershire (Hill, 2012; Fig. 97). Both of these examples will be discussed further in the later chapter dealing with possible officer helmets, along with a further helmet from Theilenhofen, which presents features common to both types H and I (Fig. 98).

Cavalry Sports Helmets – Type J
Robinson reported only one known example of this type of helmet, dating to the second century AD, from Ostrov, Romania. It is radically different from all other known Roman helmet types, Russell-Robinson (1975, 135) describing it as being of Sarmatian form. It resembles a tall Phrygian cap, with forward-curving apex, in the form of an eagle's head, the skull encircled by snakes, and the brow and cheek pieces are embossed with mythological figures and horses.

THE CROSBY GARRETT HELMET

The Crosby Garrett helmet (Fig. 93), was found in 2011 in Cumbria, in a much-damaged condition, in over seventy fragments, some of the larger pieces folded and squashed. The visor, or face mask, however, was almost complete, found face down. A restorer was commissioned by Christie's to restore the helmet for sale, although before any intensive scientific examination could be carried out. The remains were, however, analysed using a portable x-ray fluorescence spectrometer which suggested that the bowl was formed from bronze consisting of 82 per cent copper, 10 per cent zinc, and 8 per cent tin. A moulded figure of a griffin, from the top of the crest, was found to be made from a different mix (of 68 per cent copper, 4 per cent zinc, 18 per cent tin and 10 per cent lead), which Worrell (2011, 20) suggested was likely due to it having been cast from scrap metal. However, this mixture was more likely to have been a deliberate choice, in order to improve the flow of the bronze for casting. When new, the face mask of the helmet would have had a silver appearance (from a thin layer of tin alloy found to have been applied to the face) and the bowl would have been a contrasting coppery-yellow colour.

Fig. 93. The Crosby Garrett Helmet, bronze, found in 2011 in Cumbria. It is described by Worrell (2011, 22), as being a cavalry sports type C, with a dating estimated to between the end of the first century AD and the mid-third century AD, although its features suggest a more plausible identification as a cavalry sports type E. (Artwork by J. R. Travis)

The helmet had a close-fitting Attic-style bowl, with a small, turned-out flange at the neck. Five engraved rosettes decorate the back and sides of the helmet's cap. The appearance of hair on the mask is provided by a mass of large raised swirls above the face and framing it down the sides (hiding the 'ears'). A further single row of swirls pass across the back of the neck, to appear as though the hair was just showing under the back of the helmet. The shape of the bowl is noted by Worrell (2011, 22) as 'unusual', being made to resemble a 'Phrygian cap', the bowl rising and bending forward in a crescent shape to a rounded point, where the griffin figure had been attached (the griffin, as seen also on the Thracian gladiator helmets, whose peaked crests curve forward in similar fashion, being traditionally a companion of Nemesis, the goddess of vengeance and fate).

The face mask was attached by a simple hinge at the centre brow, and fastened at the neck using a leather strap attaching to an iron stud beneath each ear. Whereas some face masks just have holes where the eyes would be, this mask has inset circular rings, to represent the pupils for added realism (a technique also seen on a small number of other helmets with high-quality realistic faces).

The helmet is described by Worrell (2011, 22) as being a cavalry sports type C under Russell-Robinson's typology (and as type V under a typology by Maria Kohlert), with a dating estimated to between the end of the first and the mid-third century AD. However, she also drew comparisons with the highly decorated Ribchester helmet (cavalry sports type B), suggesting that this may have once had a similar moulding. She reported a description from 1815 by Charles Townley, the local antiquary, that the helmet had been originally found with a 'sphinx of bronze' (which she suggested could have been a griffin), which appeared to have been soldered to a convex surface, and which she suggested may have been the apex of the Ribchester helmet. However, although the helmet shows some damage (with holes possibly resulting from corrosion), the all-over embossed decoration leaves little unused space where such moulding could have been attached.

Within the Russell-Robinson typology, the type C helmets (dated to the late first to third century AD), were described as being boldly embossed with all-over wavy hair, with the face, as on the type B, again being of a stylised youthful male, the curls from the hair extending on to the forehead and sideburns. Like the type B, dating to the late first and early second century AD (which are, however, fitted with high-projecting peaks, as seen on that from Ribchester), the masks were attached to the bowl by a hook-and-slot mechanism. In the type D variant however, as on the Crosby Garret helmet, the mask was affixed to the bowl by a hinge in the centre of the forehead. The face on the type D was generally of a stylised, youthful, clean-shaven male. However, in the structurally similar type E, whereas all of the previous helmet types had depicted male faces, Russell-Robinson included a number of helmets with apparent female features, which he suggested may represent Amazons, although noting that some are rather indeterminate and less easily differentiated from the males (Russell-Robinson, 1975, 124).

The face on the Crosby Garrett helmet is more like an early version of a type E, similar to that on the Nola example (Russell-Robinson, 1975, 124, plate 361). These type E helmets are described by Russell-Robinson as 'female', or as 'indeterminate', both the Crosby Garrett and the Nola examples appearing to be more 'female' than 'male'. Furthermore, two of the other type E helmets, from the Straubing Hoard (*ibid*, 125, pls 365 & 366), have similarly shaped, raised, pointed Thracian-style bowls, although their hair was achieved using smaller spiral 'swirls' covering the full apex. In addition, it is of note that the eyes on both the Straubing and Nola examples had been similarly formed, with 'ring' inserts to represent the pupils.

I should therefore prefer to offer an alternative interpretation of the Crosby Garrett helmet's original designation of type C, instead placing it within the designation of a type E.

IX

OFFICER HELMETS

The preceding chapters of this book have discussed a wide range of helmets, their origins and their developmental progression including the classification of Roman helmets under the systems devised by Russell-Robinson and the Continental system categorising under find location of a small number of exemplars. While within these systems there has been some distinction between cavalry and infantry, and indeed of citizen legionary and allied auxiliary equipment, there is generally an overlying and unreal assumption of equality, with little discussion of the differences between officer and ordinary soldier. However, it is obvious that the lower ranks, barely able to afford the most basic of equipment (in some cases having to be provided by the state), would not have afforded the same quality of protection as the higher-ranking officer. This chapter will therefore attempt to redress that balance, to try to identify possible ownership status.

Russell-Robinson (1975, 136) stated that there had been thousands of officers who served in the Roman army (and who must therefore have owned helmets), but that he was only able to identify one helmet as having been 'officer' equipment. He did, however, admit that some of the helmets that he had categorised as being for general use by cavalry may have belonged to officers, but did not consider them as being of such better quality that they could not have belonged to the lower ranks (a viewpoint with which I could not agree, as some of these are obviously of notably high status, for example the highly ornate helmets from Guisborough, Hallaton and Berkasovo).

Russell-Robinson (1975, 136) suggested that one helmet, of Imperial Gallic type D (*ibid.*, 52, pls 111 & 112; Fig. 43d), may possibly have belonged to someone of centurion rank, although conceded that there were no features on it to indicate positive ownership. Similarly, he proposed that the Imperial Italic type H helmet dating to the second to early third century AD, from Xanten (of 'Niedermörmter' type), in the Rheinisches Landesmuseum, Bonn (*ibid.*, 72, pls 179–181; Fig. 52), may also have belonged to an officer (a designation with which I would also concur), although this identification was only based on its superior quality and that it had been inscribed with the owner's name ('SOLLIONIUS SUPERIUS'). In his opinion, had the helmet belonged to a lower-ranking soldier, it would have also carried the name of his commanding officer.

In his discussion of potential officer helmets, Russell-Robinson (1975, 136–139) suggested that these may have probably followed retro-styled archaic forms (such as Etruro-Corinthian, Attic, etc.; Fig. 30), as these forms appear on sculptures, where 'officers' are generally depicted also wearing the equally retro-styled muscle cuirasses, citing as an example the carved column in Perigueux Museum (Russell-Robinson, 1975, 137, pls 411–412). The column features a collection of 'officer' armour at the base, including a muscle cuirass, embossed greaves and an Etruro-Corinthian helmet (the type made to mimic a Greek Corinthian helmet, as though when worn pushed up on to the wearer's head, with a simulation of the 'face' part of the archaic version on the visor area of the Roman helmet), with arched crest and cheek pieces; all high-status equipment. The helmet featured on this sculpture is then similar in style to one depicted as worn by a figure of an officer on the Altar of Ahenobarbus sculpture (Fig. 94), and also on a helmet found at Autun, in south-east France, now in the Musée Rolin (Russell-Robinson, 1975, 137, pls 413–415; Fig. 95).

The Autun helmet, dating to the first century, has a tall, narrowing bowl (a skull shape as seen in Etruscan representations), with an exaggeratedly large 'peak' embossed with a face (brow, eyes and nose), its lower rim reinforced with an applied band of acanthus leaves. A large laurel wreath is attached at the back, projecting forward on each side of the bowl, the leaves standing proud from the helmet like bird wings. From each side, around the ears and towards the back of the helmet, there is a broad neck guard made from three separate plates, their edges cut and embossed to resemble more acanthus leaves, each plate overlapping upwards. The helmet is also provided with long, narrow, curved cheek pieces, similarly with acanthus leaves as decoration. Russell-Robinson (*ibid.*, 139) reported that the helmet had originally been gilded, and, in view of its elaborate decoration, proposed that it was probably made for a *Legatus*, or provincial governor (at the least a very high-ranking, senior officer), considering it to be 'unquestionably a parade helmet'.

Fig. 94. Figure of an officer depicted on the Altar of Ahenobarbus, wearing officer equipment of retro-styled forms: muscle cuirass and Etruro-Corinthian style helmet with horsehair plume (mimicking a classic Greek Corinthian helmet, as though pushed up on to the wearer's head, with a simulation of the archaic helmet's 'face' on the visor area). (Artwork by J. R. Travis)

The only other object which he considered as being possibly for officer use is a brow plate from an Attic-type helmet, dating to the early second century AD, from the Rijksmuseum van Oudheden, Leiden. This had been embossed with five panels of decoration. Two rectangular panels, one on each side, were split horizontally into three layers (the top layer with a row of round 'pellets', the middle layer blank and the lower layer with a row of paired laurel leaves and single berries). The two rectangular panels were then flanked by a square panel at each end (each with a diamond shape, containing the head and shoulders of a clean-shaven man) and another square panel in the centre front position (this containing a bust of another clean shaven man, interpreted by Russell-Robinson as possibly the Emperor Trajan, this time within a circular border). At each end, the plate was terminated by a flattened tab, pierced for a rivet for attaching to the bowl in front of the ear-guard plates. Brow plates resembling this one can be seen on the helmets worn by the officers of the Praetorian Guards depicted on the Praetorian relief, in the Musée du Louvre (*ibid.*, 142, plate 154; Fig. 96), with Russell-Robinson (*ibid.*, 139), further suggesting that the 'pellet' border decoration on the Leiden brow plate also resembled those seen on the helmets on the Praetorian relief.

Despite Russell-Robinson's reported lack of officer helmets, I would rather suggest that several of his reported 'general-use' helmets appear to be too high-status to have belonged to low-ranking legionaries. I am sure that any legionary appearing with such a high-quality, heavily decorated helmet where his officer was wearing a less ornate version would rapidly have found himself on long-term latrine duty.

I would suggest as a possible candidate for an officer's helmet the Imperial Italic type D, dating to the second half of the first century AD, found from the Rhine at Mainz (now in Worms Museum) (Russell-Robinson, 1975, 68, pls 166–169; Fig. 49). The helmet had a two-tone appearance, its iron bowl embellished by contrasting bronze/brass additions: crest plate; brow band; crossed, wide bowl reinforcing strips; and deep, wide band covering the three ridges of the occiput. It was also provided with bronze/brass edging around the neck guard and cheek pieces, and brass plates covering the top of the cheek-piece edge (covering the hinge points). The four segments of the bowl, created by the crossed reinforcing bands, each contained a bronze/brass applied motif (eagles at the front and temples at the rear), with another motif on each of the cheek pieces (again of stylised 'temples'). The high level of decoration on this helmet is clearly far in excess of what one would anticipate on one intended for an ordinary soldier, and must have belonged to an officer (the amount of work involved in its manufacture would have placed it well outside the affordability of a legionary's pay).

The same argument would no doubt apply to the equally ornate Imperial Italic type H helmet, dating to the second or early third century AD, from the Rheinisches Landesmuseum, Bonn, this being the one that Russell-Robinson had conceded as an officer 'possible' (1975, 72–73, pls 179–186; Fig. 52). This helmet, too, has many silvered applied decorative 'patches' in contrasting coloured metals, including a *tabula ansata* panel soldered at the fixing pint of the carrying handle, in the centre back of the deep, wide neck guard, along with the similarly soldered L-shaped panels at each end of the neck guard, and the crescent-shaped panel above the visor. These were all elaborately decorated with figures and other symbols (including eagles, standards, the god Mars, ichthyocentaurs and dolphins), the designs slightly recessed (possibly stamped) and pounced, and the plates then edged with an applied pearled strip.

Fig. 95. Officer helmet of retro styled Etrusco-Corinthian type, with Acanthus leaves decoration from Autun (from Russell-Robinson, 1975). (Artwork by J. R. Travis)

Fig. 96. Officers of the Praetorian Guards depicted on the Praetorian relief (in the Musée du Louvre), wearing Attic-type helmets, with embossed brow plates similar to that seen on the Autun helmet. (Artwork by J. R. Travis).

Once again, this helmet would have been beyond the pocket of an ordinary soldier, and should be considered as being for officer use; the ordinary soldier at this time probably wore a less ornate and less elaborate version, still showing the developmental improvements in neck-guard shape, bowl reinforcement and ear protection but without this level of costly embellishment.

It may also be necessary to reconsider the classification by Russell-Robinson of two of his auxiliary cavalry and cavalry sports helmets, specifically the auxiliary cavalry type G from the Waal at Nijmegen, dating to the second half of the second century AD, with its ornate brow band of moulded projecting laurel and oak leaves (Russell-Robinson, 1975, 98, pls 269–271), and the auxiliary cavalry type H (Niedermörmter), dating to the late second to early third century AD, also from Nijmegen (*ibid.*, 100–101, pls 273–276; Fig. 81). The latter, as with the previous Imperial Italic type H described above, makes heavy use of contrasting coloured panels, again with decorated, engraved applied panels (on the brow band, across the occipital area and the top of the neck guard, on *tabula ansata* and on a diamond-shaped panel at the apex). It also has a large knob at the apex, moulded in the form of a giant poppy seed case, and has two moulded 3D applied snakes writhing up from the centre back, towards the knob, from the sides.

Clearly, this helmet once again is too extravagant to be within the reach of an ordinary soldier; the latter more likely possessed a less decorative version of the same style of helmet, as seen for example in the type H helmet from Bodengraven (Rijksmuseum van Oudheden, Leiden; Russell-Robinson, 1975, 102, 283–285).

Another example that has been the subject of reconsideration as being for possible officer use in more recent years, since Russell-Robinson first developed his helmet categorisations, is the Guisborough helmet (Russell-Robinson, 1975, 132, pls 391–393; Fig. 92). Listed by Russell-Robinson in his categories as a cavalry sports type I, this helmet, dating to the third century AD (currently in the British Museum) is fashioned in thin bronze (too thin to really withstand any considerable amount of combat conditions). It is of Attic form, with an embossed forehead plate rising along its upper edge into three rounded peaks and bordered with snakes whose heads meet at the centre. A similarly shaped helmet, also dating to the third century AD, from the River Saône at Chalon (in the Musée des Antiquités Nationales, St Germaine-en-Lage; Russell-Robinson, 1975, 134, pls 394–396), also has two snakes coiled around the centre of the head, with a second pair riding from above the ears curling forward, their heads projecting up above the brow. The brow band on this example is similar in shape to that on the Guisborough helmet, although the upper-edge peaks are less extreme, only appearing as slightly undulating, gentle curves.

In 2012, the remains of another helmet, of similar shape to the above Type I helmets, was found at Hallaton in Leicestershire (Hill, 2012; Fig. 97). It was found as part of a hoard, buried around the time of the Emperor Claudius' invasion in AD 43, along with 5,296 Iron Age and Roman coins (one of the largest coin finds in Britain), and was jokingly described by its finders as resembling 'a rusty bucket'. Its date of deposition was estimated as being probably sometime in the AD 40s, from the dates of the coins found with it. There was, however, no coin evidence to suggest that its deposition could be as late as the Boudiccan revolts from the AD 60s.

Suggested reasons for its deposition include that it may have belonged to a local man who had served in the Roman cavalry before the time of the conquest, and had been buried at a local shrine on his return. Other suggestions include that it may have been a diplomatic gift to the leader of a supportive population. However, arguments that it may have been captured during a battle or raid, as spoils of war, are considered unlikely. The British Museum view was that it had been made for an officer, but had been too flimsy for actual combat, proposing that it had more probably been made for 'parade purposes' (Hill, 2012). It would therefore have been unlikely to have been taken into battle and, from the dating evidence of the coins found associated with it, would have been deposited too early for capture during any raids connected with the Boudiccan revolt.

The helmet thus raises questions regarding Roman relationships with the local population, both before and just after the invasion, of the likelihood of a local recruit entering into the Roman auxiliary cavalry (the auxiliary cavalry at that time were mostly recruited from native troops and not Italians, but these may have been more likely to have originated from Gallic and Thracian allies in mainland Europe than from Britain), or whether this helmet may form part of the argument for diplomatic contacts between native and Roman leaders, and the exchange of gifts and trade prior to the conquest.

From results of examination during the process of reconstruction of the fragments, the helmet appears to have been made between AD 25 and AD 50, from sheet iron covered with silver sheet, and decorated in places with gold leaf. It was decorated with a large wreath embossed around the back of the skull, from the occipital, rising over the ears to above the brow band. The brow band was fitted with a large moulded bust of a woman filling the central position and rising to above the central peak. This was flanked by animal motifs below the two outer peaks. The cheek pieces feature two embossed figures on horseback, seated one behind the other, interpreted as the Emperor with the goddess Victory behind him, and with another small, cowering figure of a defeated enemy beneath its hooves. Hill (2012) suggested that the quality of the object, and its elaborate decoration, would have made it costly to produce, and so she was certain that it would have belonged to 'someone very important, perhaps a high-ranking Roman officer'.

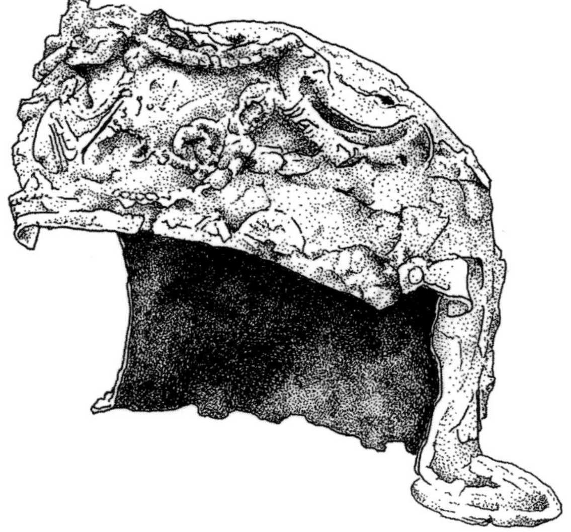

Fig. 97. The 'Hallaton Helmet', of cavalry sports type I (similar to the Guisborough helmet), dating to the AD 40s, made from sheet iron, covered with silver sheet and decorated in places with gold leaf. The high level of embossed decoration suggests that it may have belonged to a very high-ranking officer (perhaps a legate or a provincial governor). (Artwork by J. R. Travis)

Visual imagery of officers from sculptures normally depict them wearing the muscle cuirass, although those depictions of very high-ranking officers, generals and emperors are normally depicted bare-headed, so that their features may be immediately recognisable. However, one image of officers of the Praetorian Guard from the early second century (in the Musée du Louvre) demonstrates the quality of decoration on their uniforms, with ornately decorated shields, muscle cuirasses with raised moulded motifs and decorative ribbons and multi-layered pteruges, along with elaborately decorated helmets of similar type to the Guisborough and Hallaton helmets. On this particular sculpture, the helmets are also provided with lavish, tall, feathered crests, providing convincing imagery of just how high-status these helmets would have appeared in use (Russell-Robinson, 142 & 147, fig. 154 & plate 423; Fig. 96).

The level of decoration on the Hallaton helmet clearly far exceeds that displayed on the Praetorian relief, so it must have belonged to a person of even higher status, perhaps a legate or a provincial governor (all the less likely to have been captured in any native raid, so making the suggestion of 'diplomatic gift' more believable).

Another example which must be included in this section as a candidate for being a probable officer helmet is the cavalry sports helmet from Theilenhofen, in Bavaria, (*Iciniacum*), dating from the second half of the second century AD (the time of Marcus Aurelius), now in Weissenburg-Gunzenhausen Prähistorische Staatsammlung, in Munich (Fig. 98). It has a close-fitting, Attic-style bowl, with highly decorative embossed, triple-peaked brow band and cheek pieces that would place it clearly within the Russell-Robinson type I category. However, the bowl is also provided with a tall, elaborately moulded 'Thracian'-style crest (echoing the previous types G and H), decorated to simulate multiple layers of standing feathers, similar to, but much larger than, those on the type G example from Eisernes Thor on the Donau (Russell-Robinson, 1975, 128, pls 381–383). However, unlike the Donau example, the crest on the Theilenhofen example is even more elaborately moulded, fronted by an even more substantial seated eagle. In addition, each side of the bowl is further decorated by large, raised zoomorphic creatures (with head of a lion and a fishlike body), their heads sitting above the ears, above the ends of the brow band, their bodies and tails curving down the back of the bowl, behind the ears. Despite the elaborate crest, the helmet is clearly closer to the type I category, but exhibits a far higher level of decoration and status. Its classification must therefore be primarily designated as for high-ranking officer use, possibly, but not necessarily, belonging to a cavalry unit.

As discussed in the section dealing with helmets of the later Empire, there had been a substantial number of helmets in use up to and during the third century, all of which exhibit noticeable ancestral similarities and developmental progression in answer to whatever enemy weaponry and fighting style is prevalent (these being those helmets featured within the Russell-Robinson typologies). However, there then appears to be a lull in the appearance of new helmets (with the suggestion of a trend in some cases away from helmets, towards mail and scale coifs, as seen on the Battle of Ebenezer fresco; Fig. 63), until the sudden re-emergence of helmets of 'ridge' and 'radial' construction in the fourth century, these now exhibiting new and alien influences, possibly bidirectional, from Eastern provinces and the northern regions (of the steppes and the central plains inhabited by the nomadic people known under a range of names: the *Getae*, *Sarumatae*, and Scythians).

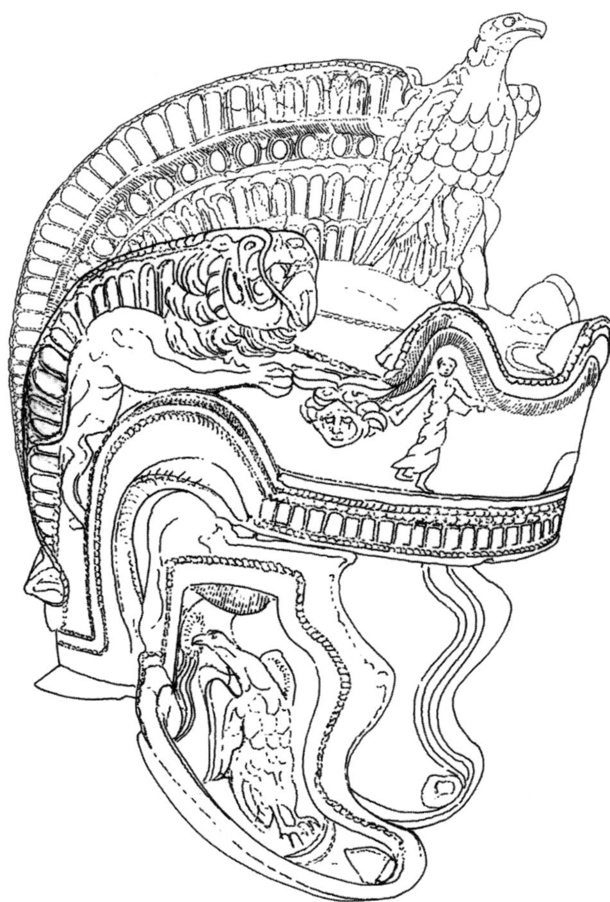

Fig. 98. Theilenhofen Helmet, possible officer helmet from either cavalry sports types H or I, dating to the second half of the second century AD. (Artwork by J. R. Travis)

Although the number of these later helmets still in existence is not great, several have been found preserved only through the resilience of their outer decorative layers (the harder iron core having corroded away). These are without doubt, then, the unusually decorative versions of what may have appeared in greater numbers but is no longer extant. Several of these helmets have been suggested to be for cavalry use, with features which would have developed more for the benefit of a rider than for a foot soldier, and it is well established that cavalry equipment was frequently more heavily embellished than the infantry equivalent. However, the level of decoration on some of these helmets does lend itself to the suggestion that these were more probably 'officer' equipment, and that similarly constructed yet less decorative versions may have originally been in circulation for lower ranks.

X

GLADIATOR HELMETS

GLADIATOR EQUIPMENT

Although this book (as with the two preceding volumes, dealing with body armour and shields respectively) is intended to deal primarily with origins and development of Roman military equipment, to review Roman helmets without consideration of gladiator equipment would mean leaving a glaring hole in the discussion. Gladiator games were an important part of the Roman way of life, appealing to all social rankings, from Caesar right down to the lowest members of society. As with the military, the equipment used by the gladiators owes much of its development to classical origins and the influence of neighbouring cultures (whether they were allies or enemies), also exhibiting a development progression over time. Initially, in the early years of gladiator contests, the equipment of both the military and gladiator were very similar, although, the games being all about display and exhibition, gladiator equipment became much more substantial and elaborate. In addition, although many of the gladiators nominally represented named ethnic groups (such as Samnites, Gauls and Thracians), their equipment owed more to an element of anachronistic fantasy than to offering an authentic historical view of that ethnic culture's warrior.

THE ORIGINS OF GLADIATORIAL COMBAT

There are two theories proposed regarding the origins of gladiator games: one being Etruscan, the other Oscan-Lucanian. It had originally been believed that gladiatorial combat had evolved from Etruscan death rituals, many aspects of Etruscan culture having no doubt merged with those of the Romans during the period of Etruscan rule. This proposal for Etruscan origins was based on literary sources (Athenaeus, *Deipnosophistai*, 4.153; Tertullian, *Ad nationes*, 1.10.47; *Apologeticum*, 15.5; and Isidore of Seville, *Origines*, 10.159). However, literary sources can be problematic, either through deliberate bias or through innocent and unintentional misreporting (particularly when authors were writing about events in their distant past), or by inaccurate modern translation; and in this case, the proposal could not be supported by any archaeological evidence.

Jacobelli (2003, 5), however, supported the alternate suggestion for an Oscan/Lucanian origin, as this was based on contemporary pictorial representations. The oldest known depictions of gladiatorial combat, with scenes of paired fighters, boxing and chariot races, come from frescos dating to between 370 and 340 BC from Oscan and Lucanian tombs in Capua and Paestum (a city in Campania, south of modern-day Naples). These depict paired men fighting with spears and lances, some wearing tunics, other in loincloths, and others naked. All wear Graeco-Italian-style helmets, as are found in similarly dated tombs (these always made of sheet bronze), and carry Greek-style large, round, convex hoplite shields. Also from Paestum, a necropolis in Laghetto produced a tomb plaque bearing a scene with paired combatants, with similar scenes on vases produced locally (*ibid.*, 6). Köhne & Egwigleben (2000, 15) also supported the view, based on these pictorial images, that Campania was the place of origin for gladiator contests, noting that it was also the location where the first stone amphitheatres were later built.

Initially, gladiator games appear to have been linked to funeral rites, as a tribute to the deceased (*munus*, meaning 'duty' or 'gift', being the name given to the service to honour the dead). In Rome the first known gladiatorial event was held in 264 BC in the Forum Boarium, as part of the *munus* for the funeral of Giunius Brutus Pera, arranged by his two sons, with just three pairs of gladiators (Valerius Maximus 2.4–7; Livy, *Periochae*, 16; Jacobelli, 2003, 5; Wisdom, 2001, 10). Following this modest event, *munera* then became widespread, leading to similar events but on an ever greater scale, with by 216 BC the funeral of Marcus Aemilius Lepidus, arranged by his three sons, involving twenty-two pairs of fighters; this rose to an event in 183 BC with sixty pairs, for the funeral of Publius Licinius, demonstrating how the 'custom' had become established in just over a century (Köhne & Egwigleben, 2000, 11).

The *munera* were usually held in December, coinciding with the festival of Saturnalia (the Roman equivalent of Christmas). These provided the audience with the opportunity to honour and grieve for the deceased person, heirs being instructed in wills of the deceased to offer games to perpetuate their memories (Seneca, *De brevitate vitae*, 20.6; Dio Cassius, 37.51). Performances were held in the Forum Romanum, where temporary wooden seating was erected, as there was no permanent amphitheatre. Over time, however, these events then began to change in nature into spectacles in their own right, not linked to any particular occasion (funerary or otherwise), the first of these being given in 105 BC by consuls P. Rutilius Rufus and Cn Manlius Maximus (Jacobelli, 2003, 6).

The public games, the '*udi plebeii* and *ludi romani* (held 6–13 July and 15–19 September respectively), were part-funded by the state, but with the balance to be found by the organisers, the *aediles* (the price of electioneering for future political careers, and of standing for election as *praetor*). They usually included criminal games, etc., and were dedicated to deities, whereas the gladiatorial events (*munera gladiatoria*) were separately timed, independent of state funding and held as a funerary honour. They invariably also began to develop into a platform for career progression and political propaganda, being popular with spectators (potential voters), as the deceased, in whose memory the games were being staged, were usually very wealthy noblemen or statesmen. They therefore became more elaborate to the end of the Republic, to such an extent that a law had to be passed after 63 BC (*lex Tullia de ambitu*), prohibiting their provision by public figures in the two years before becoming candidate for public office (Cicero, *pro Sestio*, 15.37).

Even Caesar had been guilty of manipulating the funeral games for his father, by delaying them for twenty years until he reached the position of *aedile* (in 65 BC). However, further laws had been passed limiting the size to only 320 pairs of fighters, reportedly in response to the Spartacus revolt of 73–71 BC. In later years, however, he staged yet more extravagant games, owned his own gladiator school in Campania, erected new wooden seating in the Forum Romanum and staged major battle re-enactments with hundreds of fighters (one with ships on a specially dug artificial lake, as described by Suetonius; Suetonius, *Caesar*, 39; Köhne & Egwigleben, 2000, 16).

By the time of Augustus, important *munera* were still held in the Forum; in his *Res Gestae* (22) he boasted of gladiatorial games held three times in his own name, and five times for his sons and grandsons, with 10,000 men taking part. He also described displays of athletes, wild beast hunts (where 3,500 animals were killed) and a naval battle (again on a specially dug lake), with 3,000 fighters, not including the slaves at the oars (Köhne & Egwigleben, 2000, 19). His grandson Caligula also had a great passion for the games, particularly the chariot races (described by Suetonius; *Caligula*, 56), reportedly performing as a gladiator (training as a *Thraex*), charioteer, dancer and singer (*ibid.*, 21).

Just a few years later, the games had increased in popularity to such an extent that the Forum was no longer large enough, with Nero having to build a wooden amphitheatre on the Campus Martius, although this was subsequently destroyed in the great fire of AD 64 (*ibid.*, 24). Vespasian therefore ordered the building of a new stone amphitheatre on the site of the lake at the centre of the gardens of Nero's palace, the 'Golden House', or *domus aurea*. This new amphitheatre, the Colosseum, opened in AD 80 (the year after his death) but was not fully completed until after the death of his son Titus (AD 79–81), under his second son Domitian (AD 81–96) (*ibid.*, 24).

Gladiatorial entertainments remained popular until the fifth century AD, when they were finally abolished (banned by the Emperor Honorius in AD 404), although the wild beast hunt events (*venationes*) continued until the sixth century AD (Jacobelli, 2003, 6; Köhne & Egwigleben, 2000, 30).

THE GAMES

Initially these funerary games had been held in the tomb of the deceased himself (the name for the combatant, the *bustuarius*, literally meaning 'tomb fighter', from *bustum*, 'tomb'). Servius, however, reported that it had once been 'the custom to put captives to death at the graves of strong men, which later seemed a bit cruel, so it was decided to have gladiators fight at the tombs' (Futrell, 1997, 34). Therefore, with the rise of the tradition for *munera* leading to greater and more elaborate spectacles, and involving trained combatants, purpose-built arenas appeared throughout the Empire to accommodate them. Wisdom (2001, 12) reported at least 186 known amphitheatre sites, with potentially a further eighty-six, the most famous of these being the Colosseum in Rome. Wisdom (2001, 4) reported that Christian martyrs had been executed at the Colosseum under the orders of the emperors, including Nero, who reportedly used the method of *crematio* (burning the victim in pitch-covered cloth).

Wisdom (2001, 5) reported that Romans had a different concept to modern civilisation and culture, and so did not see gladiatorial combat as being brutal or barbaric. Instead, bloodthirsty displays of death were viewed as acceptable public entertainment, serving to state the power of Rome and its intolerance of anyone who did not embrace its ideals (opposing barbarians, prisoners of war and criminals), who would be executed during the games. He cited Seneca, who wrote that 'the purpose of executing criminals in public is that they serve as a warning to all, and because in life they did not wish to be useful citizens, certainly the state benefits by their death'. The displays could involve thousands of criminals, prisoners of war, or bought slaves, re-enacting past military victories to show Roman superiority. These allowed the condemned the final opportunity to display the Roman moral value of *virtus*, or virtue, to achieve an honourable 'Roman' death. Other displays would involve single pairs of 'armoured fighting men', or gladiators (*Hoplomachi*), fighting with the Roman short sword, or *gladius*.

The games would not only include mass battles and single combat; the entertainment could also be augmented by the exotic spectacle of staged animal hunts (*venatio*). Here highly dangerous animals (for example lions, tigers, bears, etc.) would be displayed by a performer, or hunter (the *venator*) and enticed to perform 'tricks' (such as the hunter riding a camel while leading lions on a leash, placing his arm in the lion's mouth, and making an elephant walk a tightrope; Seneca *Ep.* 85.41). Alternately they would be despatched by a specialist gladiator, known as a '*bestiarii*', or 'beast fighter', the resulting exotic meat then making its way into the Roman diet (Wisdom, 2001, 11; Fig. 99).

Not all gladiators were criminals, prisoners or slaves; many (perhaps 20 per cent of combatants) were volunteer professional participants, more usually from the poorer classes, drawn to the games by the potential for fame, wealth of winnings and the offer of 'favours' from rich Roman lady admirers. Most fighters, however, would be acquired from the slave markets to live and train in gladiator schools ('*ludi gladiatori*'), in groups known as '*familia gladiatoria*', trained and managed by the '*lanista*' and the '*doctores*'. The *lanista* featured very low on the social scale, despite his wealth, being regarded in status as comparable to that of a pimp (*leno*), or procurer of prostitutes. He may often have been a retired successful gladiator himself (a *rudiarius*). One *lanista*, attempting to improve his social status, described himself as '*negotiator familiae gladiatoriae*', or the 'business manager of a gladiatorial troupe' (Wisdom, 2001, 15).

Fig. 99. *Bestiarius* relief. (Artwork by J. R. Travis)

In addition to the harsh discipline and intense combat practice, under the instruction of fight trainers ('*doctores*'), the gladiator's health and fitness would be maintained by strict diet, and the attention of medics and masseurs (*unctores*), as they were an expensive asset into which the *lanista* had made a substantial investment. For this reason, the gladiators would normally only use wooden weapons when not participating in paid combats, the wooden sword being known as a *rudis* (this also being used as a reward of honour for surviving, successful gladiators, who would then be known as a *rudiarius*, the award then qualifying the holder to either retire from combat, or to join the ranks of managers, trainers and referees).

Whereas most *lanistae* purchased and assembled their own teams of gladiators, hired out to wealthy clients (*editors*), from the reign of Domitian (AD 51–96), four state-owned Imperial schools were set up (the *ludi Magnus*; *Gallicus*; *Dacias*; and *Matutinus*, the latter specialising in training for *bestiarii*), with some teams owned by wealthy nobles and trained by itinerant *lanistae* and *doctores* (Jacobelli, 2003, 19; Wisdom, 2001, 20).

Whereas the criminal combatants (*noxii*) of the mass battles were usually sent to their demise unarmoured and sometimes unarmed, the gladiators of the *familiae* would be provided with a range of arms and armour. Whether in mass battles or single combat, the primary function of the combatant was to provide entertainment, and so to prolong the confrontation and not to provide a quick death for their opponent. The armour and equipment therefore was designed to provide the maximum protection that would maintain the safety of that expensive commodity, the combatant; and to make the spectacle of the fight visually exciting to the audience (in some cases by artificially disadvantaging them with inbuilt limitations to their assemblage; overly heavy armour, reduced visibility, less effective weaponry, etc.), but without obscuring too much of the musculature of the body for the wealthy ladies in the audience. Finds of gladiator equipment and graffiti (both images of fighters and 'messages' from admirers and supporters) have been found at Pompeii, buried under ash of the AD 79 eruption.

The gladiator's armour fell into a range of common styles, to provide the impression of a number of set fighter personalities, some of which were traditionally paired protagonists, their armour, helmets, shields and weaponry reflecting these supposed 'identities', often portraying the ethnicity of previous enemies of Rome (obviously, as some 'enemy' nations later became 'friendly allies', some of these 'identities' would fall from use, or were modified to reflect new opponents).

Among these early enemy 'identities', later phased out as 'allies', were the Samnites (an early type of heavily armed fighter, named after the Italic people of Campania with whom the Romans were at war between 326 and 291 BC), the *Gallus* and the *Crupellarii* (less obviously, representative of the Gallic nations). The Samnite gladiator, who disappeared in the Early Imperial period, later to be renamed as the *Murmillo*, had been equipped with the distinctive long rectangular shield (*scutum*), short sword, a greave on the left leg and a plumed helmet. The *Crupellarius* (another heavily armed fighter, probably impeded by the weight of his equipment), was described by Tacitus (*Ann*, 3.43.46), as a Gallic-style trainee, slave gladiators equipped 'after the national fashion' of *Gallia Lugdunensis* under Julius Sacrovir during the Aeduian revolt of AD 21 against Rome, 'encased in the continuous shell of iron usual in the country'. Tacitus further described how their armour was so heavy that it had to be hacked off (Köhne & Egwigleben, 2000, 63).

At the outset of gladiatorial contests, and throughout the Republican period, gladiators and military alike were similarly equipped, although with some combatants representing distinct ethnic groups, their equipment visually reflecting those 'origins', as previously discussed. Köhne & Egwigleben (2000, 37) believed that some of these first gladiators were possibly captured warriors fighting in their own armour. This changed, however, following the reforms of Augustus, with gladiators being divided into 'identities', under categories based on arms, armour and fighting styles (by this time the Roman military assemblage itself had become more homogenised in style, much of their equipment being commissioned and provided by the state).

TYPES OF GLADIATOR

The six main 'identities' or gladiator types encountered, from the Imperial period onwards, were the *Thraex*, the *Murmillo*, the *Hoplomachus*, the *Provocator*, the *Retiarius* and the *Secutor* (Wisdom, 2001, 29–32). However, this list is not definitive, as there may be other more specialist types of which we know nothing, and there is the possibility of some duplication in categories, with some fighters being known under different names. For example, it has been suggested that the *Hoplomachus* and the *Murmillo* may be the same, although there appear to be sufficient differences between them, to be able to list them as two distinct types (Jacobelli, 2003, 7). Furthermore, while some categories exist over lengthy periods, their equipment showing some developmental changes through time, other categories appearing in the early periods disappear altogether (for example, the Samnite and Gallic fighters), being replaced with new styles of gladiator. Other types of gladiator included the *Essedarius*, the *Sagittarius*, the *Bestiarius*, and those with an entirely entertainment purpose (the *Paegniarius* and the *Andabatae*) (Wisdom, 201, 41).

All types of gladiator wore visored helmets, to protect their head, throat and neck, except the *Retiarius* (first appearing in the first century AD), who fought bare-headed. Their arms and legs were protected by padded, quilted wraps, *manica* and greaves; their bodies were left unprotected, except for the *Provocatores*, who wore small breastplates. They were usually bare-footed, as it was better for working on sand; and their clothing (with the exception of the *Eques*, who wore tunics), was always the draped loincloth (*subligaculum*), with a broad metal belt (*balteus*). The belt followed an old southern Italian tradition, formed from a long strip of bronze, leather-lined, fastened by hooks (Köhne & Egwigleben, 2000, 35). Examples of these early Samnite belt plates can be seen in the British Museum (GR1856.12–26.665; Fig. 100), and they are frequent finds in Samnite tombs, also appearing in Campanian and Lucanian vase and tomb paintings dating to the time when the area was occupied by Oscan tribes.

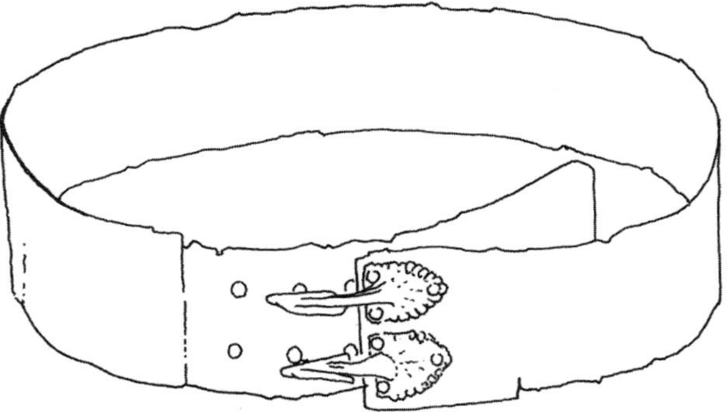

Fig. 100. Samnite belt plates from the British Museum (GR1856.12–26.665): frequent finds in Samnite tombs, and also seen in Campanian and Lucanian vase and tomb paintings (from the time when the area was occupied by Oscan tribes). These are ancestral to the later metal belt plates worn by Gladiators. (Artwork by J. R. Travis).

The Samnis *(Samnite)*

The Samnite is the oldest known gladiator type. Livy (9.40) tells how, in 309 BC, the Samnite people were defeated in war with the Romans. The Campanians, another Italic people allied to the Romans against the Samnites, reportedly 'claimed' some of the Samnite equipment discarded on the battlefield, using it to equip gladiators in the style of their old enemy, and naming these fighters as Samnites (Jacobelli, 2003, 7).

These gladiators were heavily armoured, their left, leading leg protected by leather covering (sometimes topped by an additional metal greave), armed with a short, straight-bladed sword (or *gladius*), and carrying the distinctive Samnite long rectangular shield (the *scutum*). Their helmets were fitted with a visor and a crest, and were decorated with feathers (*galea*). An example of a Samnite warrior in his traditional armour assemblage can be seen on a red-figure amphora dating to the fourth century BC, now in Naples Museo Archeologico Nazionale (Jacobelli, 7, fig. 1).

After Augustus' reforms, the Samnite people were no longer enemies but allies, so it was no longer appropriate for them to be represented in this way; the category of gladiator therefore disappeared from use and was replaced by *Secutor* and the *Hoplomachus* (or possibly the *Murmillo*). Also disappearing around the same time, and presumably for the same reasons, were gladiators equipped to represent Gallic warriors (*Gallus*), reminiscent of combatants in the now finished Gallic Wars, who were now considered to be 'allies'.

*The Thracian (*Thraex, *plural* Thraeces*)*

Like the earlier 'Samnites' and 'Gauls', the 'Thracian' gladiator gets his name from the warriors of Thrace (now modern-day Bulgaria), with whom the Romans had previously been at war (during the war against Mithridates). Unlike the two former types, however, the Thracian continued to appear after the Augustan reforms. He is usually depicted paired against a *Murmillo*, a *Hoplomachus* or another Thracian (Junkelmann 2000a, 51–57; Fig. 101).

In common with most other gladiators, the Thracian fought bare-chested, with a broad belt (*balteus*) above a loincloth (*subligaculum*), the latter formed from a large, folded triangle of cloth (with one side edge across his back, the two corners brought around the waist to tie at the front, and the point brought up between the legs, to tuck behind the front knot). His armour (similar to that of the *Hoplomachi* and *Murmillo*) included a small, strongly convex, square-shaped shield (*parmula*), *manica* (arm band) on his right, sword arm, and a pair of thigh-length leg protectors, or greaves (these often decorated up to the knee, with substantial quilted fabric padding beneath). His weapon was usually a short sword with either a curved or angled blade (the *sica* or *falx*, approximately 34 cm in length). He

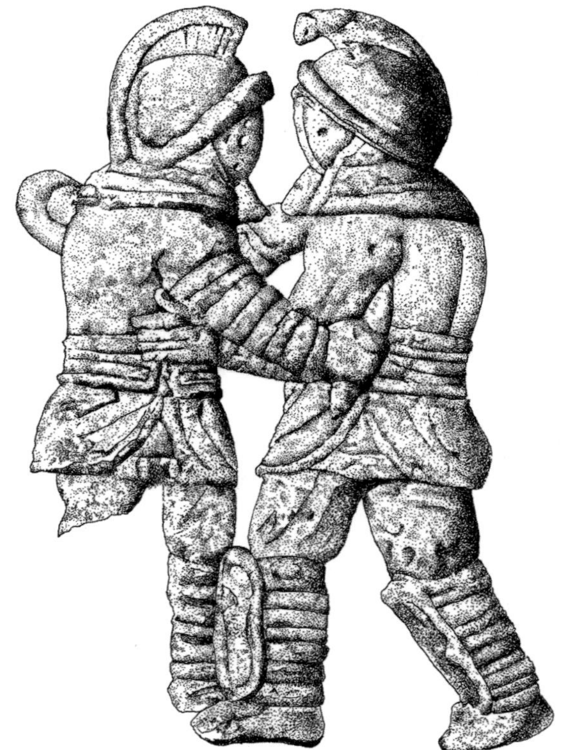

Fig. 101. *Murmillo* vs Thracian relief, marble, dating to third century AD, possibly part of a parapet from Ephesus. From Antikensammlung, Staatliche Museen zu Berlin (from Köhne & Egwigleben, 2000, 57, fig. 55). An inscription names the two gladiators as Asteropaios (probably a *Murmillo*) and Drakon (the *Thraex*, who is being defeated). (Artwork by J. R. Travis)

wore a distinctive broad-rimmed helmet, enclosing the full head. It was visored and topped by a tall crest, decorated with a griffin head, and adorned with feathers (one such first-century AD Thracian helmet was found in the gladiator barracks at Pompeii, in the Museo Archeologico Nazionale di Napoli; Jacobelli, 2003, 10, fig. 6; Fig. 102).

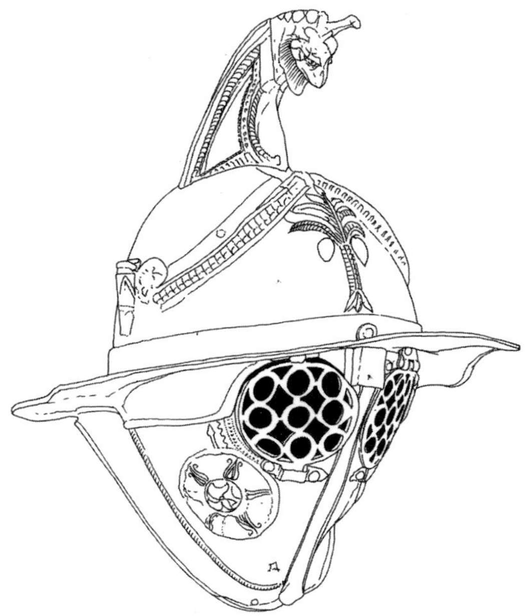

Fig. 102. Thracian helmet, bronze, first century AD, found in the gladiator barracks at Pompeii, now in Museo Archeologico Nazionale di Napoli (from Köhne & Egwigleben, 2000, 54, fig. 47). (Artwork by J. R. Travis)

Although the early *Thraex* wore an Attic crested helmet, the fully developed standard Thracian helmet (*galea*) was easily recognised by its distinctive stylised, sculptured griffin at the front peak of its crest. The griffin was the companion of Nemesis, the goddess of fate, avenging figure of judgement (Köhne & Egwigleben, 2000, 52). Wisdom (2001, 30) cited Junkelmann's reconstruction experiments which suggested that these helmets would have weighed between 3.3 and 6.8 kg compared to the much lighter legionary helmet (estimated at 2 kg), although noting that they would have only been worn for the duration of ten- to fifteen-minute bouts, rather than all day. The Thracian helmets usually bore an elaborate crest, with Wisdom (2001, 30) reporting several *Murmillo* helmets from Pompeii (both Thracian and *Murmillo* helmets being structurally similar) also seen with feathered side plumes. He also reported an example from Herculaneum (although for a *Murmillo*) fitted with small rings on either side of the crest for these *crista* (plumes of exotic feathers, possibly ostrich, in wooden mounts, held by leather thongs). *Thraeces* do not, however, appear to have used horsehair plumes (Köhne & Egwigleben, 2000, 52).

An example of a helmet with these side feathered plumes can be seen on a bronze sculpture of a Thracian gladiator at the British Museum. Similarly, another sculpture, also from the British Museum, depicts a Thracian holding a small shield and curved short sword. On both of these examples, the helmet brim appears to sweep down in a curved V shape from the centre front, appearing integral to the bowl (Wisdom, 2001, 13).

Two examples of bronze Thracian helmets dating to the first century AD were found in the Pompeii gladiator barracks, one of which can be seen in the Museo Archeologico Nazionale di Napoli (Köhne & Egwigleben, 2000, 41, 45, 54 figs 23 & 47, Fig. 102), with another in Castel Sant'Angelo, Rome.

The helmet bowls were beaten from a single piece of bronze sheet, flaring out at the edge, with a horizontal 'brim'. This was not integral to the bowl, but separately formed, applied and soldered into place (the brim edge rolled for extra strength). Two face plates, hinged in front of the ears, meet at the centre front to enclose the face completely. The jawline (the lower edges of the cheek pieces) flared out into a flange, to deflect blows away from the throat and neck. The eyeholes were reasonably large, covered with a round, bronze grate to protect the wearer's eyes, each formed of one large ring containing nine smaller rings fused together, providing good ventilation and forward vision but less than ideal side vision (Wisdom, 2001, 29). These could then unclip and hinge upwards.

Lateral transverse plates on each side under the brim, running from the back of the cheek piece to the eye grate, covered and protected the cheek piece hinges. The join between the cheek/visor halves was covered by a narrow strip of bronze, soldered to one side to form an overlap. At the top of the visor, the left side fitted under a clip on the right, and clipped into the brow. The lower chin was then perforated with holes for internal ties.

The helmet was decorated with embossed motifs, with a 'palm of victory' over the forehead; and crossed lances and the round shields (of *parma equestris* type) on the visor, below the eyeholes (this despite it being a Thracian, and not an *eques*, helmet). The bowl was further decorated with a raised, inverted V shape on the forehead (above the 'palm of victory'), which curved around to above the ears, ending in curled volutes at the sides, just in front of two raised and embossed plume tubes for feathers.

A tall crest rose in a crescent-shaped curve from the back of the bowl, hooking over at the front, where it terminated in a solid, moulded griffin head. A removable plume of large feathers could then have been fixed to the top of the crest. Köhne & Egwigleben (2000, 41) suggested that the surface of the helmet must originally have been partly tin-plated to emphasise the embossed features, contrasting the gold colour of the bronze with the silver.

The Murmillo *(or* Myrmillo*)*

The *Murmillo*, or *Myrmillo* (derived from the Greek word for a marine fish, the *Mormylos*), was a heavily armoured gladiator, normally clothed and equipped in similar fashion to a Thracian. On first consideration, he would have seemed to be a natural opponent for the *Retiarius* (the net fighter), both having the apparent marine theme, although in most depictions the *Murmillo* is shown paired against the Thracian, or less commonly against the *Hoplomachus* (the *Retiarius* always paired against the *Secutor*, the latter otherwise known as the *Contraretiarius*). At times, the *Murmillo* has been equated with the *Hoplomachus* or the *Samnis* (the latter no longer appearing after the Augustan period, by which time the Samnites were allies of Rome), but it is possible that he may have descended from the *Samnis* (Köhne & Egwigleben, 2000, 48).

As with the similarly equipped Thracian and *Hoplomachus*, the *Murmillo* fought bare-chested, wearing only the *subligaculum* (loincloth) and *balteus*, very thick padded wrappings on the tops of his feet and ankles; his heavily padded right, sword arm and leading left leg were protected by a *manica* and a short leg/ankle guard (greave) respectively. Five of these short greaves (which usually weigh approximately 1 kg) were found at Herculaneum and Pompeii, where they were initially mistaken for armbands (Jacobelli, 2003, 14, fig. 11). Another highly decorated example is in Berlin, with a matching helmet (Köhne & Egwigleben, 2000, 49). He was armed with a Thracian-style sword or a standard military short sword, or *gladius* (64–81 cm long), and carried a tall, oblong curved shield (*scutum*), of average size 100 cm by 65–70 cm, with either a long *spina* or a round *umbo*, resembling the legionary shield. His weapon was the short sword (*gladius*). The total weight of his arms and armour was around 16–18 kg, including shield, making him a heavyweight fighter.

His helmet, however, was distinctive, differing from that of the Thracian, being constructed with a slightly different design, with a visor and a tall, angular crest, which may have been adorned with horsehair or feathers, with single feathers in side sockets. Whereas the Thracian helmet was provided with a crest, that of the *Murmillo* had a very large three-dimensional dorsal fin, presumably to represent a fish (Wisdom, 2001, 30).

Helmets identified as belonging to a *Murmillo* have been found at both Herculaneum and Pompeii, which were similar in construction to that of a Thracian (one example from Pompeii, dating to the first century AD, now in the British Museum, carries a relief bust of Hercules in the centre of the forehead; Jacobelli, 2003, 15, fig. 12; Fig. 103). Another example, from Berlin, however, is more elaborate, constructed of polished bronze and decorated with an all-over silver-and-gold two-toned pattern to give the appearance from a distance of shimmering fish scales (Wisdom, 2001, 30). A similarly decorated greave was also found, possibly intended to accompany the helmet.

The *Murmillo* never fought other *Murmillones*, and is usually depicted paired with a *Thraex*, but can occasionally be seen fighting against the similarly equipped *Hoplomachus* (Junkelmann 2000a, 48–51). A depiction of a *Murmillo* fighting a *Hoplomachus* can be seen on a marble relief from Pompeii, dating to AD 20–50, in Museo Archeologico Nazionale di Napoli (Köhne & Egwigleben, 2000, 56, fig. 51; Fig. 104). Jacobelli (2003, 8, fig. 3) described the figure as wearing on both legs 'horizontal bandages over the thighs' (which he also described as being on his bare-legged opponent). However, these appear to be too substantial to be 'bandages', but seem to protrude and overlap downwards. This would suggest that rather than layers of fabric, these may be some form of segmented thigh 'cuisse' either of leather or of metal plate (as in the *lorica segmentata* body armour, or like the segmented arm/leg protector found at Newstead; Curle, 1911, plate XXIII). These would have been constructed to overlap downwards (as appears to be the case on the relief), in order to deflect a sword strike away from the body. Similarly constructed segmented arm protectors (*manica*) can also be seen on both the *Murmillo*'s and his opponent's right, sword arms, although on the *Murmillo* this is damaged, only the top couple of segments remaining.

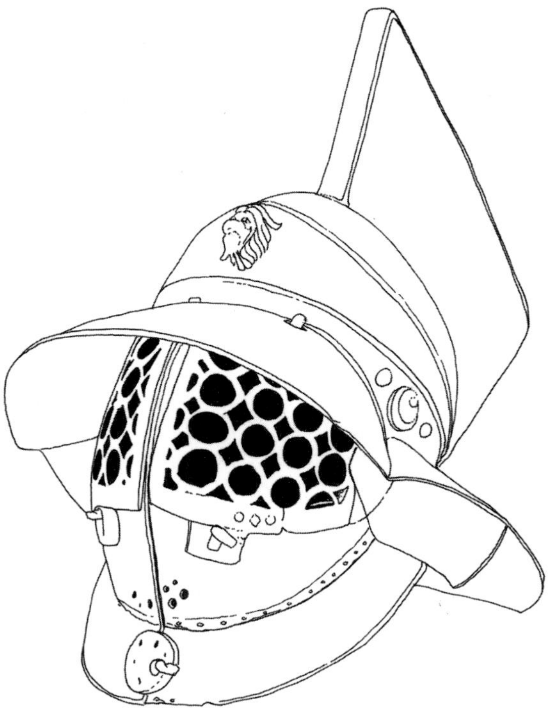

Fig. 103. *Murmillo* helmet, bronze, first century AD, from Pompeii, now in British Museum (from Köhne & Egwigleben, 2000, 42, fig. 24). (Artwork by J. R. Travis)

An image from the Zliten mosaic, AD 200, depicts three pairs of gladiators: a disarmed and surrendering *Retiarius* and his *Secutor* opponent; a *Thraex* and a *Murmillo*; a *Hoplomachus* and *Murmillo* (the latter of whom is signalling his surrender); and the referee (Köhne & Egwigleben, 2000, 41, fig. 50).

Further images of *Murmillones* can be seen on graffiti from the entry corridor to the theatre complex at Pompeii; in one depiction two gladiators can be seen, one figure with sword and small shield but the other armed and shielded as a *Murmillo* (although, less typically, carrying a trident – a weapon almost always only used by the *Retiarius*).

Another graffiti from Pompeii depicts a named trainee (*tirone*) *Murmillo*, identified as Mattilius, defeating, in only his second fight, Lucius Raecius Felix, an experienced Thracian gladiator reputedly with many previous victories (Wisdom, 2001, 30).

The Hoplomachus

The *Hoplomachus* (or Greek-style 'armed fighter') is usually depicted matched against the *Murmillo* or the Thracian, and may have developed out of the earlier Samnite type.

He was usually depicted wearing a broad belt (*balteus*) above his triangular loincloth (*subligaculum*), and heavily padded, quilted upper-leg defences. In all other ways he looked very similar to the Thracian, similarly equipped with high leg padding and a pair of full-length greaves, further padding and *manica* on his sword arm (of segmented or scale construction) and armed with the standard short, straight sword (*gladius*), spear and very small, round shield. His helmet was plain, with wide, upturned brim, feathered crest and a pair of single-feathered side plumes.

An image of a *Hoplomachus* fighting a *Murmillo*, dating to AD 20–50, can be seen on a marble relief from Pompeii, now in Museo Archeologico Nazionale di Napoli (Jacobelli, 2003, 8, fig. 3; Köhne & Egwigleben, 2000, 56, fig. 51; Fig. 104). The figure is armed with a short, straight sword (although the small, round shield cannot be seen) and wears a segmented arm protector (*manica*) on his right, sword arm and short ankle greaves, decorated with a swirling design. His helmet is decorated with an inverted V shape embossed on the forehead, terminating on the sides of the head with curling volutes.

Fig. 104. *Murmillo* vs *Hoplomachus* relief, marble, AD 20–50, in Museo Archeologico Nazionale di Napoli (from Köhne & Egwigleben, 2000, 56, fig. 51). (Artwork by J. R. Travis)

The Retiarius

The *Retiarius* ('net fighter') developed in the early Augustan period. He was the lightest-equipped of all gladiators (the total weight of his arms and armour being around 2–3 kg), in a style intended to reflect a fisherman. He was armed with a trident and net, in which he attempted to trap his opponent, whom he would then 'finish off' with a short sword or dagger carried in his belt.

He fought bare-chested and un-helmeted, wearing only a loincloth (*subligaculum*) formed from a large, elaborately draped triangular piece of cloth, topped by a wide metal belt (*balteus*). He was equipped with only the minimum of protective armour: padded lower legs and left arm (this being unlike all other gladiators, who wore their protection on the right, their sword arm); and a segmented metal arm protector (*manica*). Also unique to the *Retiarius* was a high metal shoulder plate (*galerus*) worn above the *manica*, tied to the left shoulder by leather straps passing across his body and right shoulder, fastened by a buckle on his chest. This was formed from a rectangular plate of bronze, shaped to the shoulder and raised at the edges by 12 to 13 cm to protect the bare head and neck (Wisdom, 2001, 31).

Three different specimens of *galerus* have been found in the *quadriportus* of the theatres at Pompeii (varying in size from 30 to 35 cm, weighing approximately 1 kg): one decorated with raised marine symbols (anchor, crab, dolphin, oar, etc.), another with a relief of Hercules' head and some cupids, and the last one with an engraving of a *Retiarius*' weapons, the words 'RET/SECUND' (indicating that it had belonged to a *Retiarius*, second rank) and the victory symbols of a palm and crown (Jacobelli, 2003, 13; Fig. 105).

Apart from a small dagger (*pugio*) with which to finish of his defeated opponent, his only weapon was his trident (around 1.6 m long) and, tied to his wrist, a net of wide, round mesh (the '*Rete*'), 3 m in diameter, weighted with lead around the perimeter, with which he could lash, trip or ensnare his opponent. He held the folded net in his right hand and cast it underarm; his trident and long dagger he held in his left hand (Köhne & Egwigleben, 2000, 60).

Although Junkelmann (2000a, 59–61) reported that *Retiarii* sometimes also fought *Murmillones*, his more common opponent was the *Secutor*. The *Retiarius* was more lightly equipped, and therefore more mobile, to better ensnare his opponent while avoiding his weapon; the *Secutor*, on the other hand, traded strength of armour against mobility and visibility, the tiny eyeholes of his helmet being specifically designed to minimise injury from the prongs of the trident (Wisdom, 2001, 39). Another variation to the normal combat may be a *Retiarius* facing two *Secutores* at the same time. Less commonly, there also existed a couple of variants of *Retiarii*: the *Laquearius* (who fought with a lasso, or *laqueus*, instead of a net); and the *Retiarius tunicatus*, an effeminate and even less socially acceptable class of gladiator, who wore tunics rather than fighting bare-chested (Junkelmann, 2000a, 63; Cerutti & Richardson, 110, 589–594).

Visual representations of *Retiarii* include a funerary relief (from the Museum of London), dating to the third century AD, of a *Retiarius* armed with a trident and dagger (although his net is not shown) and bearing a shoulder guard (*galerus*) on his left arm. He is bare-chested, wearing a loincloth (*subligaculum*) and broad belt (*balteus*), and un-helmeted, with a headband tied around his hair (Köhne & Egwigleben, 2000, 58, fig. 56; Fig. 106).

Further visual depictions include a bronze figurine from the British Museum dating to between the first and second centuries AD (Wisdom, 2001, 32). He is bare-chested, wearing a *subligaculum* and *balteus*, a *manica* and *galerus* on his left arm and holding a long-handled trident, although its prongs are now missing, as is his net (Köhne & Egwigleben, 2000, 59, fig. 57; Fig. 107). Another image comes from a relief on the Colchester vase, where a *Retiarius* (named as 'Valentinus') is depicted losing to a *Secutor* ('Memnon'). The *Retiarius*, wearing just arm padding and a *galerus*, carries a legionary-style rectangular shield (*scutum*), his arm raised ready to strike. His opponent, the helmeted *Secutor*, can be seen to be more substantially equipped: padded on the legs and one arm, wearing greaves (Wisdom, 2001, 23).

Fig. 105. *Retiarius* shoulder guard (*galea*). (Artwork by J. R. Travis)

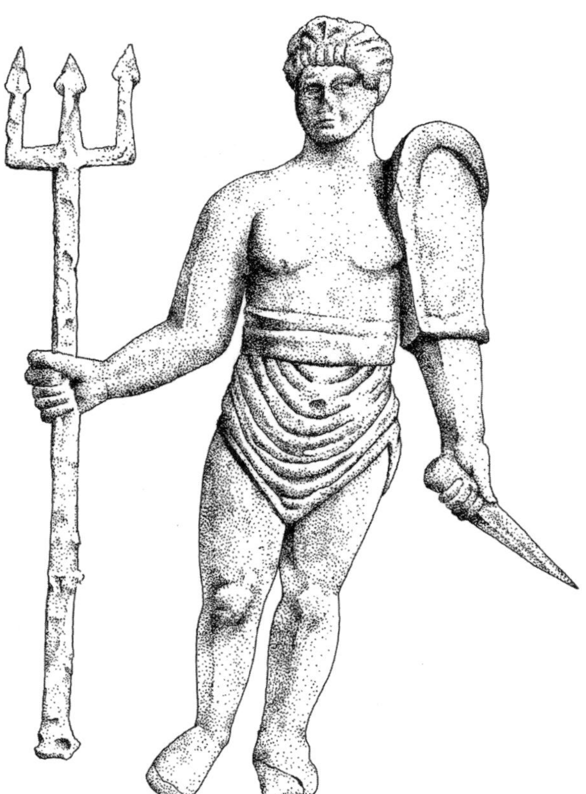

Fig. 106. *Retiarius* funerary relief, third century AD, marble, in Museum of London (from Köhne & Egwigleben, 2000, 58, fig. 56). It shows a *Retiarius* armed with trident and small dagger, wearing *galerus*, shoulder protection, but without his net. (Artwork by J. R. Travis)

The Secutor

The *Secutor* was a variant of the *Murmillo*, and similarly equipped. He usually fought against the *Retiarius* (the net fighter), and was sometimes known by the alternate name of *Contraretiarius* (cii.vi.631). As with most other gladiator types, the *Secutor* ('pursuer') fought bare-chested, his only body protection being his heavy belt (*balteus*) and quilted padding to lower legs and right, sword arm, these further augmented by a single metal arm protector (*manica*) and single or paired greaves (for either both or left legs). His usual weapons were the short sword (*gladius*) and the legionary-style rectangular shield (*scutum*).

Although frequently depicted paired against the more lightly armoured *Retiarius* (as seen on the Colchester vase), he did not fight with such a weighted advantage as would immediately appear, his vision being greatly restricted by his heavily enclosed helmet. The *Secutor*'s helmet was close-fitting, the face completely closed by the visor, with only small eyeholes (just 35 mm); the bowl, with narrow-bladed, finlike crest, was round and smooth so that the *Retiarius*' net would slide off (Junkelmann 2000a, 40–41 & 61–63; Fig. 108). Köhne & Egwigleben (2000, 61) also suggested that his appearance was designed to look like a fish, suiting the role as opponent to the fisherman, '*Retiarius*'.

The helmet was fitted with deep cheek pieces that covered the ears (limiting the hearing of the wearer), fastening down the centre front and tied at the chin, fully enclosing the face. The cheek pieces flared out sharply along the jawline into a wide flange, to deflect blows away from the neck and throat. The rear of the bowl dropped down to cover the occipital area, where, level with the cheek piece flanges, it also flared out into a matching integral neck guard. The wearer had to fight at close quarters due to the reduced visibility of his helmet, while (in a circular argument), this was necessary in order to protect his eyes from the

Fig. 107. *Retiarius* figurine. (Artwork by J. R. Travis)

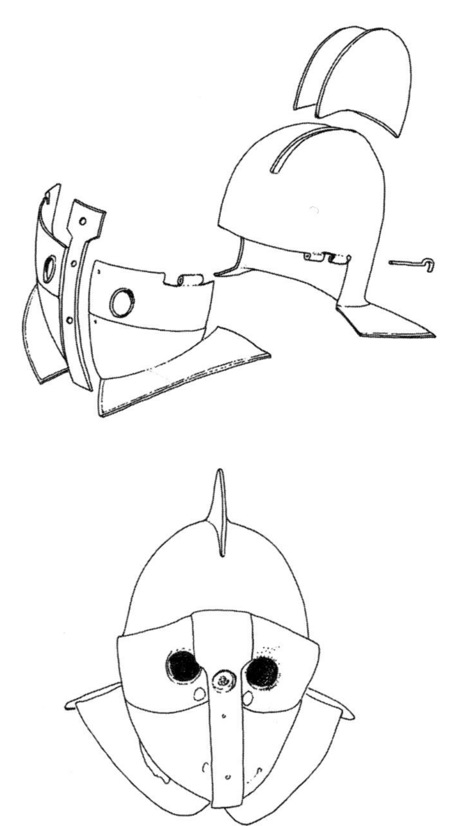

Fig. 108. *Secutor* helmet from Pompeii. (Artwork by J. R. Travis)

thin prongs of his opponent's trident (Wisdom, 2001, 39). He also needed to move in close to his opponent quickly, as the heavy armour and reduced ventilation in his helmet made him tire quicker than the lightly equipped, more mobile *Retiarius*.

A depiction of a *Secutor* can be seen on a fourth-century AD mosaic where the figure can be seen carrying a sword, a long, rectangular shield and wearing a metal leg protector, or greave (Madrid Museo Archeologico; Jacobelli, 2003, 10, fig. 7).

A bronze statuette of a *Secutor* from Arles, dating to the second century AD, from Musée de l'Arles Antique, has been made with a removable helmet, which flips up to expose the face of the gladiator underneath (Jacobelli, 2003, 12, fig. 8; Köhne & Egwigleben, 2000, 62, fig. 62; Fig. 109). The figure is bare-chested, a greave on his lower left leg and a *manica* on his right, sword arm, armed with a short sword. He stands behind a legionary-style rectangular shield. His helmet is close-fitting, with very small eyeholes, a central seam visible on the visor, and it has been fitted with a small, low crest. In reality these helmets would have hinged out sideways from the seam, however, rather than flipping upwards, but this must not have been feasible on such a small figurine.

Another image of a *Secutor* helmet can be seen on a bronze finial (a decorative terminal), dating from first to third century AD, from the British Museum, showing the smooth, close-fitting, brimless helmet, with small eyeholes, small crest and wide, flaring flanges at the jaw edge of cheek pieces and neck guard, a large central seam emphasising the two halves of the visor/cheek pieces (Köhne & Egwigleben, 2000, 61, fig. 61; Fig. 110).

Fig. 109. Bronze statuette of a *Secutor* from Arles, dating to second century AD, from Musée de l'Arles Antique, made with a removable helmet, which flips up to expose the face of the gladiator underneath (from Jacobelli, 2003, 12, fig. 8). (Artwork by J. R. Travis)

Fig. 110. Finial in the form of a *Secutor* helmet, first to third century AD, bronze, from British Museum. (Artwork by J. R. Travis)

The Provocator

The *Provocator* (the 'challenger') is mentioned by Cicero (*pro Sestio*, 64) although little is known about him, apart from that he only appears to have fought against other *Provocatores* (Junkelmann 2000a, 37 & 57–59). He was a middleweight fighter (his full arms and armour assemblage weighing approximately 14–15 kg), armed legionary style, with a short, straight-bladed sword (*gladius*) and a large, curved, legionary-style rectangular shield, or '*scutum*' (with either a long, central *spina*, or metal boss), and wore a visored helmet similar to those of the Thracian and *Hoplomachus* but without a crest or brim (Köhne & Egwigleben, 2000, 54). In the earlier years of the Empire, his helmet was similar to that of the *Secutor*, although this later changed to a more bulbous design, as seen on a grave relief from Smyrna, in Turkey.

As with all other gladiators, he wore a triangular loincloth (*subligaculum*), with a metal belt (*balteus*), and some additional protection from *manica*; he also wore a half-length greave on his left leg (Jacobelli, 2003, 17). Köhne & Egwigleben (2000, 54), suggested that his shield may be smaller than that used by the *Murmillo*, as his greaves appeared to be longer (relating the length of greaves necessary to cover the area of leg remaining exposed).

Unlike other gladiators, the *Provocator* did not fight bare-chested. Instead he was provided with a retro-style small breastplate (*cardiophylax*), fastened by straps across the back, a type of body armour worn by the majority of Roman soldiers of the Republican period (those not sufficiently wealthy to afford the mail cuirass, *lorica hamata*). The breastplate was rectangular in shape in the earlier periods, often with a semi-circular 'cusp' cut away at the neck, but in the Imperial period became crescent-shaped.

An early *Provocator* can be seen on a marble tomb relief from the Tiber, of Augustan date, dating to 30–10 BC (Museo Nazionale Romano alla Terme di Diocleziano, Rome). It shows three gladiators (the fourth one is missing, with only his knee remaining). It depicts (to the left of the relief) two *Provocatores* fighting, shields raised. They wear early-style helmets of Weisenau type (Imperial Gallic), a type used by the army. The helmet is open-faced with a wide, horizontal neck guard, broad cheek guards, 'eyebrow' decoration on the forehead, feathered side plumes, but no crest or plume (Köhne & Egwigleben, 2000, 38–39, 21; Fig. 111).

Both figures can be seen wearing the small, rectangular breastplates – with curved cut-out for neck, and decorated with a gorgon's head – held by leather straps passing under the arms and over shoulders, crossing the centre back, and fastened by buckle (the rear view being visible on the fighter to the right, the one on left providing the front view). They also wear *manica*, greaves on their left legs and a blunted, oval-shaped early legionary shield with a *spina* down the middle. In addition, they are armed with a short, straight *gladius* (Köhne & Egwigleben, 2000, 38–39, fig. 21; Jacobelli, 2003, 16, fig. 13). The other gladiator on the relief was identified by Köhne & Egwigleben (2000, 37) as a *Thraex*, with his opponent, the one with only his leg remaining, being probably a *Murmillo*, from his shorter rectangular shield.

There is an additional image in the central group on the Pompeii monument, dating to AD 20–50 (Museo Archeologico Nazionale di Napoli) with a pair of *Provocatores*, one with a breastplate decorated with a gorgon's head (Köhne & Egwigleben, 2000, 55). A further relief, dating from third century AD, in Antikensammlung, Staatliche Museen zu Berlin, depicts a *Provocator* in a late form of his equipment (Fig. 112). He wears a crescent-shaped breastplate and carries a rectangular shield (legionary style). His helmet is a later version, with closed face, its bowl reaching down over the back of the neck and at the sides, with a broad, downward-slanting neck guard. His face is covered with a visor made in two halves, closing down the centre middle, perforated with a series of holes to represent the grill over the eyes (Köhne & Egwigleben, 2000, 57, fig. 55).

Fig. 111. Early *Provocatores* on a marble tomb relief from the Tiber, of Augustan date, dating to 30–10 BC (Museo Nazionale Romano alla Terme di Diocleziano, Rome; from Köhne & Egwigleben, 2000, 39, fig. 21). (Artwork by J. R. Travis)

The remains of a helmet found at Hawkedon in Surrey, dating to the first century AD (now in the British Museum), has been described by Köhne & Egwigleben (2000, 45, fig. 28; Fig. 113) as 'one of the best pieces of evidence for gladiator combat in Roman Britain', and has been interpreted by Junkelmann (2000c, 116) as probably belonging to a *Provocator*. Although it is bronze, it still retains the remains of tinning on the surface, suggesting that it would have had a 'shiny' appearance (possibly a two-tone effect, of silver-coloured tin, contrasting with the golden coloured bronze). Although it is now damaged, having lost its visor, a reconstruction has been proposed using existing rivet holes to suggest its original appearance as being similar to one of the Pompeii helmets (Junkelmann, 2000c, 116, fig. 3; Fig. 114). The bowl steps down at the sides of the face, to double its depth at its wide neck guard. The front edge, across the bowl, appears to have two curved 'cut aways' above the eyes, curving down to a point above the nose, where two disc-shaped grills would have been attached, with the two cheek piece parts of the visor below (Köhne & Egwigleben, 2000, 45, fig. 28)

A further sculpture which has been interpreted as possibly depicting a gladiator is that from Alba Iulia (Coulston, 1995, 13–17). On the sculpture, the figure is depicted as wearing a form of *lorica segmentata*, but with his *segmentata* girdle plates appearing to be combined with small, rectangular chest plates (as seen with scale and mail shirts), along with what seems to be a separate scale coif. There has been much discussion as to whether the sculpture may depict either a gladiator or legionary (it also being probable that the *lorica segmentata* was not universally worn by all legionaries, but used only for heavily armoured troops with specialist skills, for specific purposes, such as for siege situations). As it is known that the *Provocator* was deliberately styled in legionary fashion, if the figure is indeed a gladiator, the *Provocator* would appear to be the obvious interpretation. However, the *Provocator* is generally perceived to be a middleweight combatant, equipped

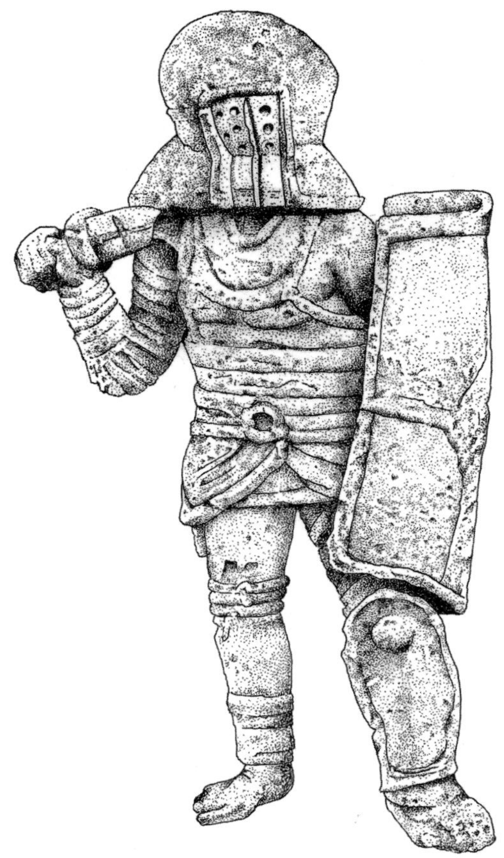

Fig. 112. Late-period *Provocator stela*, marble, dating to third century AD, from Antikensammlung, Staatliche Museen zu Berlin (from Köhne & Egwigleben, 2000, 57, fig. 54). (Artwork by J. R. Travis)

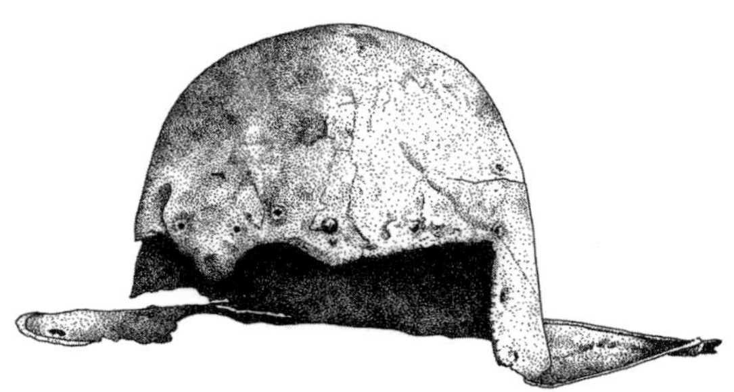

Fig. 113. Gladiator helmet, bronze with traces of tinning, first century AD, from Hawkedon, Suffolk, now in British Museum (from Köhne & Egwigleben, 2000, 45, fig. 28). (Artwork by J. R. Travis)

to represent the normal, lightly equipped legionary, wearing usually only a small chest protector (*cardiophylax*), whereas the Alba Iulia figure is very heavily armoured, which then suggests that there may have been a heavyweight version of this combatant, equipped to represent the heavily armoured specialist legionary troops, who may have been known as *Provocatores* or some other, unknown name.

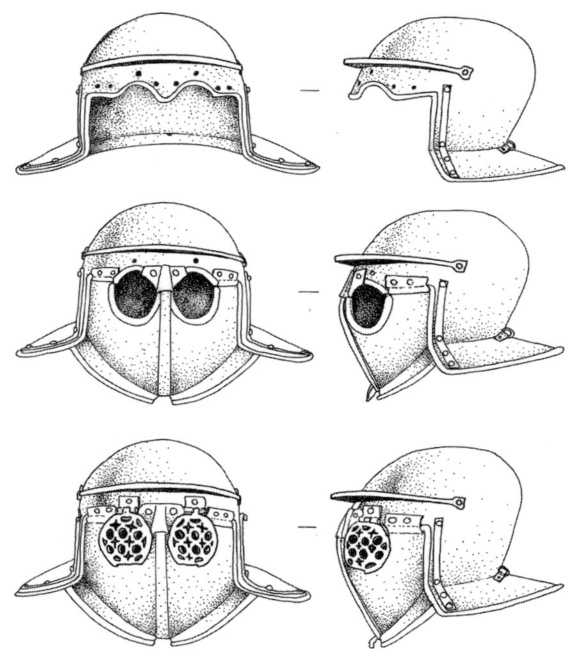

Fig. 114. Reconstruction of the gladiator helmet found at Hawkedon, Suffolk, interpreted by Junkelmann as being for a *Provocator* (from Junkelmann, 2000c, 116, fig. 3). (Artwork by J. R. Travis)

OTHER LESS COMMON GLADIATOR TYPES

Other less usual types of gladiator included those associated with specific weapon types (such as the *Arbelas*, the *Dimachaerus*, the *Laquearius* and the *Scissores*), those with specific purposes (such as the *Essedarius*, the *Equites*, the *Sagittarius* and the *Cestus*) and those with an entirely entertainment purpose (the *Paegniarius* and the *Andabatae*).

The Dimachaerus, Arbelas, Laquearius *and* Scissores

The *Dimachaerus* (from the Greek 'bearing two knives') fought with two swords, one in each hand, whereas the combatant known as a *Scissor* (plural *Scissores*) was equipped with a double-bladed short sword that resembled a pair of open scissors, possibly used to trap his opponents' weapon (although Junkelmann proposed that this may have been hardened steel tube encasing the forearm, with a semi-circular blade attached to the capped-off end; Junkelmann, 2000b, 63). Similarly, the name of the *Arbelas* refers to a distinctive crescent-shaped knife seen in images of these gladiators fighting against *Retiarii*, deriving from the *Arbelai*, a crescent-shaped shoemaker's knife, used to cut leather, although it is possible that this may be the same as the *Scissor*. Another less frequently seen gladiator was the aforementioned *Laquearius*, who should really be considered as a type of *Retiarius*, although fighting with a lasso (*laqueus* meaning 'noose') instead of a net (Köhne & Egwigleben, 2000, 63).

The Essedarius, Eques *and* Sagittarius

The *Essedaria* (charioteers), who fought from a chariot (the name taken from the Latin word for a Celtic war chariot, *essedum*), were possibly first brought to Rome from Britain by Julius Caesar. They appear as arena fighters in many inscriptions after the first century AD, and may have been used against wild beasts, as in one mosaic depiction from Augusta Treverorum (Trier in Germany) of an *Essedarius* fighting against a panther (Wisdom, 2001, 41).

Associated with mass battle re-enactments rather than individual combat, the *Sagittarii* were mounted archers, wearing Eastern-style pointed helmets and scale armour and using oriental reflex bows. They would shoot across the arena during re-enacted 'battle' combats, although this potentially endangered the audience (Wisdom, 2001, 41; Köhne & Egwigleben, 2000, 63).

The *Eques* (pl. *Equites*, or horsemen) is usually depicted on foot, at the point of finishing the fight. He only ever fought other *Eques*, and was never seen paired against any other types of fighter. He did not fight bare-chested, in early periods wearing scale armour (*squamata*) and later wearing a tunic. He usually wore a brimmed helmet without crest, carried a medium-sized round shield (the *parma equestris*) and did not wear greaves (Köhne & Egwigleben, 2000, 37).

Although not a gladiator in the conventional sense, the *Cestus* was a fist fighter or boxer who fought without body armour, armed only with the *cestus*, a cross between a boxing glove and a knuckleduster. Two further 'entertainers' associated with gladiatorial combat, although more in the way of 'joke' gladiators, were the *Paegniarius* and the *Andabatae*. The *Andabatae* wore a helmet with no eyeholes, being herded towards the fight for the amusement of the crowd and not forming part of the true gladiatorial contest.

Similarly, the *Paegniarius* was more of a 'warmup' entertainer than gladiator, provided to get the audience 'in the mood', but not engaging in any serious combat, instead fighting with fake wooden weapons, often to musical accompaniment during breaks. He had neither a helmet nor a shield, but wore heavy padding on his lower legs and head.

THE DEVELOPMENT OF GLADIATOR HELMETS

In the early years, helmets had been of late Hellenic type, combining elements of the Boeotian helmet (with broad folded and curved brim) and the Attic helmet (with forehead peak curving back to lateral volutes, broad cheek guards and a metal crest, although the latter was not always present). However, reliefs show similar helmets worn by the army at this period, with little difference between gladiator and military equipment in general. An example of this early type of helmet was found in southern Italy, now at Hamburg Museum für Kunst und Gewerbe, dating to the Augustan period, which Köhne & Egwigleben (2000, 36, fig. 18) suggested may be military or gladiator. It is bronze, with a very wide brim, widening to the back where it appears to flare outwards at 90° to the edge. On the forehead it has been decorated with an embossed inverted V shape, curving down to above the ears where it terminates in a large, round volute.

A substantial amount (75 per cent) of all known gladiator equipment comes from the Pompeii gladiator barracks (excavated in 1766 to 1767, so not particularly well recorded and with some finds now lost). Some of that equipment was given to Napoleon Bonaparte in 1802 and is now in the Louvre, or in the National Archaeological Museum in Naples. These finds included fifteen helmets, six short greaves, one medium-length greave, one small, round shield and several fragments (Köhne & Egwigleben, 2000, 38). Obviously, from its context, all finds would have been items of equipment in use contemporaneously in the first century AD, some possibly not absolutely new from the workshop (with some visual evidence from frescos and public graffiti), but none would have dated to after the eruption, so could not provide any evidence to later developmental progression.

Most of the Pompeii helmet shapes display 'classic' traits, traceable back to Boeotian and Attic helmets of the Late Republic. Most of the helmets were 'brimmed', with two brim types evident: the earliest examples have flat, wide brims and the later ones have brims curving up over the forehead. This was then transitional to a third type, not found at Pompeii, therefore dating to after the eruption (an example of this later type can be seen in Berlin), whereby there is no real brim, but the curve above the visor extends down vertically, to fully frame the grating 'like blinkers'. The bowl drops down vertically over the neck at the rear, ending in a broad neck guard, and meeting the 'blinkers' at the sides. An example of this type of helmet can be seen on a bronze figurine from the British Museum, dating to the first or second century AD, although it is not clear whether it was intended to depict a *Murmillo* or a *Thraex* (Köhne & Egwigleben, 2000, 43, fig. 25).

At the same time that the brim shape was developing, the visor similarly went through changes, into two movable hinged halves. The wide cheek pieces, initially seen on the early helmets, widened further to fully enclose the face, their two halves meeting in the middle, hinged at the sides to open outwards, closing with a small overlap (this formed by the addition of a soldered strip on one half, covering the small gap where the two plates came together). Narrow extensions at the top of the plates fitted into a slot at the centre top of the forehead, whereas at the lower end, chinstraps threaded through internal eyelets and tied the two halves closed. The lower jaw edges of the visor were turned outward, forming a projecting rim or flange, to protect the neck and throat. At the point where the brim met the visor, transverse plates on each side covered and protected the hinges. The visor halves would therefore not have fully opened, prevented by these transverse plates, so would have only partly opened at the chin, just enough so that the helmet could be removed, the top extensions remaining in their slot (Köhne & Egwigleben, 2000, 43).

In the earliest forms, gladiator helmets only had small, round eyeholes, similar to those on the *Secutor* helmets (although perhaps not quite as small). However, by the time these developed in to the type 1 helmets found at Pompeii, their visors had evolved to have 8 cm-diameter openings, covered by removable disc-shaped gratings (as seen on the Thracian helmet depicted in Fig. 102). Later, by the time of the Pompeii deposition, the type 2 helmets (with the curved brims) had evolved further, with a larger, rectangular horizontal grating now covering the full upper half of the visor (replacing the round holes with the disc-shaped grates). The two halves were now joined by a flexible peg and socket, the peg-shaped extension at the top fitting into a slot in the brim, fastened by a pin, with the peg at the lower chin position pushed into a horizontal groove (as seen on the *Murmillo* helmet; Köhne & Egwigleben, 2000, 42, fig. 24; Fig. 103). In the later type 3 Berlin helmet the visor closure is similar, although the grating is much higher, covering almost all of the visor area.

All nine of the Pompeii brimmed helmets have high crests soldered to the apex, and all have sockets at the side for feather adornments. From the pictorial evidence, these then fit into two categories of gladiator: the *Murmillo* and the *Thraex* (Köhne & Egwigleben, 2000, 44).

There were six *Murmillo* helmets found at Pompeii. On these, the crest is tall, rising vertically from the back of the neck, then arching over at 90° at its highest point, running in a straight line horizontally forward, then sharply down towards the front of the bowl. The crest is also rather wider than those on the other helmet types (Köhne & Egwigleben, 2000, 42, fig. 24; Fig. 103). Three of the helmets found belonged to *Thraeces*. These also had tall crests (although thinner than those of the *Murmillones*), curving forward in a crescent shape, with a moulded figure in the shape of a griffin fixed to the front point (Köhne & Egwigleben, 2000, 41 & 54, figs 23; & 47; Fig. 102).

The *Secutor* helmet, in contrast, differs from those for the *Murmillo* and *Thraex*, with no brim and no crest (Fig. 108). Instead it was specially designed to minimise the chance of entanglement in the *Retiarius*' net, with a close-fitting bowl, a narrow, downward-sloping neck guard at the back, and a low, rounded, crescent-shaped crest, fitted directly to the top. It also had much smaller eyeholes (around 3 cm diameter), to prevent penetration by the trident points (Köhne & Egwigleben, 2000, 44).

PARADE ARMOUR

Köhne & Egwigleben (2000, 38) discussed the possibility of parade armour. They noted that eleven of the fifteen helmets from Pompeii had been 'lavishly' embossed with ornamental and figural decoration. These had been previously identified as being parade armour, for use in pre-contest processions (*pompa*) but not for actual combat. This argument was based on the assumptions that the equipment was too expensive to risk damage; that decorated surfaces would not be strong enough to withstand impact; that there were no traces of combat damage on them; and that they would be too heavy to wear in a fight.

Köhne & Egwigleben (*ibid.*), however, suggested that as *munera* were all about display, they would use 'lavish' equipment; and if damaged, the cost of replacement would be minimal when compared to the overall costs of the games. Further, they suggested that an embossed bowl was actually stronger, not weaker, than a smooth one. To support the latter view, they observed that bowls were made of sheet bronze between 1 and 3 mm thick (average 1.5 mm), the visor grating slightly thicker (averaging 1.8 mm), with all edges faced in metal, with weights of complete helmets between 3.3 and 6.8 kg. In comparison, military helmets were only 1 mm thickness, so considerably weaker than the gladiator equivalent, and weighing half as much, although Köhne & Egwigleben (*ibid.*, 40) noted that the gladiator was not wearing his helmet all day, but only for ten- or fifteen-minute bouts, and without the rest of the full kit of a soldier. They considered that, had the gladiator helmets been only for parade use, they would have used thinner sheet metal, which would have been easier to emboss with decoration. Furthermore, gladiator weapons were not intended for heavy cut and thrust, but were only light slashing swords (useful only against unarmoured bodies or for stabbing).

Experimental testing of reconstructed helmets had found that those of thickness of the originals would have been resistant to denting, which may explain lack of apparent combat damage (with the exception of one *Provocator* helmet, which they noted had a crescent-shaped piece of bronze riveted to the bowl, in an apparent repair). Also, they noted as an exception that the *Secutor* would have to face the *Retiarius*' trident, which could inflict considerable damage. For this reason, they suggested that the *Secutor* helmets were made considerably thicker than those of other gladiators (also being made smoother, without crest or decoration where the trident or the net would slide off; Köhne & Egwigleben, *ibid.*, 40). Furthermore, the *Secutor* helmet was made to completely cover the face, apart from two small eyeholes, 3 cm diameter, to prevent the prongs of the trident penetrating. In conclusion they cited the imagery from the Pompeian tomb reliefs (for example Köhne & Egwigleben, 48, fig. 34), which show embossing on greaves and helmets, suggesting that decorative equipment would be used for fighting, and not just for parade purposes.

<table>
<tr><th>Find location</th><th>(Br)
(Ir)</th><th>Date</th><th>Additional info (inc. curent location, if known)</th></tr>
<tr><td>Hawkedon, Surrey</td><td>Ir</td><td>1st C AD</td><td>Provocator. In British Museum</td></tr>
<tr><td rowspan="5">Pompeii (gladiator barracks)</td><td rowspan="10">Br</td><td rowspan="10">1st half of 1st AD</td><td>Thracian. In Museo Nazionale, Napoli (I).</td></tr>
<tr><td>Thracian. In Castel Sant 'Angelo, Rome</td></tr>
<tr><td>Thracian additional : a total of 3 Thracian helmets were found at the Pompeii barracks.</td></tr>
<tr><td>Murmillo. Relief of Hercules on forehead. In British Museum</td></tr>
<tr><td>Murmillo. With all over silver/gold 2-tone fish scale effect. Found with matching greave. In Berlin</td></tr>
<tr><td>Pompeii (gladiator barracks). 4 additional Murmillo helmets</td><td>4 additional Murmillo helmets: a total of 6 Murmillo helmets were found at the Pompeii barracks.</td></tr>
<tr><td>Pompeii (gladiator barracks)</td><td>Secutor</td></tr>
<tr><td>Pompeii (gladiator barracks). 5 additional helmets</td><td>5 additional helmets: 15 helmets in total were found at the Pompeii barracks.</td></tr>
<tr><td>Nijmegen (NL)</td><td>Fragments of dome and brim. Rijksmuseum van Oudheden, Leiden (NL)</td></tr>
<tr><td>Xanten (D)</td><td>Left part of face guard. Rheinisches Landesmuseum, Bonn (D)</td></tr>
</table>

Table 7. List of known gladiator helmets.

XI

FITTINGS: CHEEK PIECES, CRESTS AND HELMET LININGS

CHEEK PIECES (*BUCCULAE*)

When discussing the origin of cheek pieces on Roman helmets, it is necessary to consider traditions deriving from periods of Greek and later Celtic influences on their armour assemblage. Cheek pieces are known on helmets of classical origins (and indeed earlier into pre-classical Mycenaean periods), from both archaeological contexts and from sculptural and artistic representations.

The Dendra helmet, for example, found near Mycenae (dating to around 1500–1400 BC), is not fully fashioned in bronze (only the cheek pieces), with the bowl formed of laced boar tusks laced on leather thongs (Warry, 1980, 12; Figs 8 & 9). The deep bronze cheek pieces, however, do display some similarities to later Greek Corinthian and Illyrian helmets, and much later Roman examples, suggesting a continuance of stylistic influence (Fig. 19).

By the fifth century BC, two close-fitting bronze helmets were in use by Greek hoplites: the Corinthian and the Illyrian (Figs 22–26). The former covered most of the face, with nasal protection and cheeks that wrap around towards the mouth, whereas the latter was more open-faced, with long cheek pieces (although not wrapping around the face) and without nasal protection. These were higher-value and higher-status helmets, however, the less wealthy using a cheaper, mass-produced helmet: the Pylos type (Warry, 1980, 44, fig. 8). The lower-status Pylos helmet had no cheek pieces, attaching to the head by leather strap ties. This may have been the forerunner of the later Negau bell helmet used by the lower ranks of Samnite and Etruscan forces in the fourth century BC (Warry, 1980, 103; Figs 15 & 28) and possibly even the Celtic (and eventual Roman) Montefortino, and is similar to those worn on the *Certosa Situla* (Fig. 20; Zotti, 2006). Again, these simply shaped, lower-status helmets were not provided with cheek pieces.

As time progressed, both Corinthian and Illyrian styles developed along similar lines, with the introduction of a cranial ridge (for increased ventilation and better impact absorption), ear cut-outs on the sides for improved hearing and cheek pieces elongated further (to protect the mouth and throat), these wrapping further around towards the mouth in the Corinthian style (Fig. 24). A further, more open variant of the Corinthian style of helmet, the Chalcidian (Figs 27–28), later developed into the Attic style used by the Romans into the Imperial period. This also had the cranial ridge, small nasal protection (although this tended to disappear through time as it impeded vision), long, rounded cheek pieces and cut-away ears for improved hearing (Fig. 25; Warry, 1980, 44). These extra-long cheek pieces enabled the wearer to push the helmet up on to the top of his head when not in use, allowing greater ventilation and visibility, the extended cheek pieces acting as a visor to shield the eyes. A corruption of this feature can be seen continuing into the Roman period in the Etrusco-Corinthian style of helmets worn by officer and cavalry, whereby the helmet is provided with a 'face' on the upper visor part of the helmet (Fig. 30a). These helmets were also fitted with additional cheek pieces, indicating that, in these cases, the helmet was intended to be worn in this fashion at all times (Russell-Robinson, 1975, 137, pls 413–416).

Following the reforms of the Athenian general Iphicrates in the fourth century BC, the 'Thracian' type of helmet was introduced, although the form did not come from Thrace; the name derives from the shape (Anglim *et al.*, 2002, 30), echoing the shape of the hats worn by Thracian peltasts in its bowl. It could be worn without cheek pieces, but could similarly have very long, pointed cheek pieces. In one style these cheek pieces joined at the chin and were decorated to look like a beard, producing a 'face helmet' similar to later Roman cavalry styles (Fig. 29c).

Montefortino helmets were in use from the late third century BC Punic Wars to the first half of the first century AD. Their origins may go back to the conical helmets of Knossos, around 1400 BC (these have similar cheek pieces, but with no neck guard). The known origin of the Montefortino is Celtic, appearing in Italy from the time of the invasion in the late fifth/early fourth century BC by Gallic tribes. The cheek pieces are formed of very thick metal, worked into a projecting lip on the outer face; a hinge is then formed by turning down the top face on the upper edge, and securing this in place with three to four rivets. The centre of the rolled edge was then cut away to fit into the matching half inside the helmet rim (Russell-Robinson, 1975, 11).

The chinstrap would have been fastened with hooks, or button terminals riveted to the inside of the cheek pieces. Inside the neck guard at the centre back, a folded bronze strip was riveted in place, holding two D-shaped rings. Russell-Robinson (1975, 14) believed that these rings not only served for hanging the helmet when not in use (as can be seen on some of the figures on Trajan's Column), but also formed a third anchor point for fastening the closure strap. The narrow strap would then pass through the D-rings at the nape of the neck, passing under the jawline towards the front (to help stop the helmet from slipping, or being dislodged by a blow), crossing at the chin and anchoring over the projecting button studs. This exact same method of closure can be seen on the helmet worn on a sculpture of King Pyrrhus of Epirus, although the helmet depicted in that instance was not of Montefortino type (Russell-Robinson, 1975, 14; Fig. 1).

Of the sixty-one examples of Iberian Montefortino helmets studied by Quesada Sanz, almost half (49 per cent) came from indigenous, often funerary contexts, dating to the end of the third, through to the second century BC (Quesada Sanz, 1997, 155). These he believes to have been of Italic origin, used in either the Hannibalic/Punic Wars by soldiers of both Roman and Carthaginian sides, or dating from the early Roman conquest (Quesada Sanz, 1997, 162). However, helmets do not appear to feature widely in grave contexts, for which Quesada Sanz offers two possible reasons. He proposes either that the majority of helmets at that time could have been made of organic materials, or that their use was not universal, featuring more as imported status/wealth symbols. However, he points out that some rich burials are found without helmets, where others are found in apparent low-status burials. He suggested that these may represent the property of returning Carthaginian mercenary or allied forces, included into burials as booty, or as Carthaginian 'issue' (Quesada Sanz, 1997, 163), citing Polybius and Livy, both of whom report that Hannibal issued looted Roman weapons to his troops after battles at Trasimene and Cannae (Polybius, 3.87.3; 3.114.1; 18.28.9; Livy, 28.46.4). Several helmets were also found from Villaricos in Almeria, the location of an important coastal recruiting centre for Punic mercenaries.

These early Montefortino helmets, where used by the original Celtic cultures, consist of just the basic conical bowl, with decorative or plain crest knob and small neck guard, but without cheek pieces, being secured to the head by simple straps. The introduction of cheek pieces appears to be attributable to the Romans, incorporating long-standing features from pre-existing helmet types, although these, as suggested by Russell-Robinson, may be traced back to Bronze Age Minoan/Mycenaean cultures, or even earlier (Russell-Robinson, 1975, 13).

In his study of Iberian helmets, Quesada Sanz notes a lack of cheek pieces in those helmets from the non-Roman, indigenous burial contexts, with the view that, in the case of ex-Roman 'booty', these may have been 'discarded' as 'inconvenient or useless'. This suggests that, even after the Roman introduction of cheek pieces, Celtic/non-Roman users continued with a deliberate preference to the contrary (Quesada Sanz, 1997, 155).

Although the presence or lack of cheek pieces may help to differentiate Roman and non-Roman use, Russell-Robinson also identified six variants (A to F) within the Montefortino typology, based on the helmet bowl and neck guard shapes, which he used to suggest a developmental progression (Figs 34–35). Even within this framework, however, the basic features remained constant, with little to differentiate at first glance until the much later examples.

Cheek pieces do not always survive with their helmets, so it is not always possible to determine the exact shape for each helmet type. However, usually the rear edge of the plate can be seen to follow the curvature of the jaw, and the front edge is 'cusped', or indented, on line with the eyes and mouth. This would have provided maximum protection for the cheekbones without obscuring the eyes and mouth of the wearer. On some examples this 'cusping' is slight, whereas on others it may be very exaggerated, as can be seen on the cheek piece from the Museo Stibbert, Florence, and on the helmet in Castel Sant'Angelo, Rome (Russell-Robinson, 1975, 17, fig. 20 & plate 5).

By the time of the development of the Montefortino type F, with its wide neck guards and applied brow reinforcements, cheek pieces had evolved further. No longer just flat across the top edge, they were now narrowed by indenting 'cusps' on both the front and rear faces – the rear cusp perhaps being added with the intention of improving the hearing of the wearer by exposing the ears (the helmet now sitting lower on the wearer's head than previously). The cusping on the front face had also become more extreme, with the cheekbone protective area squared off for maximum coverage (Russell-Robinson, 1975, 22). One example of this type from Cremona, which was found in the River Po, possibly associated with the Civil War battle of AD 69, Russell-Robinson believed showed signs of having been produced by an Italic workshop (Russell-Robinson, 1975, 22, fig. 30, plate 34).

However, Coolus-type helmets (in use from the third century BC to the first century AD; Figs 36–38) coexist alongside the Montefortino helmets for many years. One example of a Coolus type C helmet, from Schweiz Landesmuseum, Zurich, dating from late first century BC to early first century AD (inscribed with the name of its owner, '*P. Cavidus Felix C(enturia) C(aius) Petroni*'), was fortunate to have both of its cheek pieces remaining. These have deeply indented cups on the front edge, the leading edge squared at the cheekbone (as on the Cremona example previously), but with a wide, flat top edge, no cut-away for ears and the rear edge just gently curved all the way down to the jaw (Russell-Robinson, 1975, 28).

Further shape changes can be seen by the time of Coolus type E (dating to the first half of the first century AD), as seen on the Russell-Robinson reconstruction of an example found in the Thames at Kew (Russell-Robinson, 1975, 32, plate 56). On this cheek piece the basic shape is not unlike that on the Montefortino type F described above: narrowed at the top edge, cusping on the front and back edge (for the ear) and squaring over the cheekbone. However, the panel is no longer a simple flat plate, with the central part of the plate raised, crescent-shaped lower relief at the 'cuspings' and a wide strip of lower relief following the rear jaw edge. This jaw-edge strip is then shaped into an outwardly curved flange, presumably to deflect blows away from the neck. This shaping would still allow the cheek piece to fit snugly against the wearer's face, but would allow better air circulation within the helmet. The raised panel would also permit a 'crumple zone' in the event of a strike, absorbing some of the impact and minimising injury to the wearer (Russell-Robinson, 1975, 32).

By the time of the introduction of the Agen/Port early iron helmets (dating to the first half of the first century BC, with examples found during excavations by Napoleon III of the Gallic stronghold of Alesia, which had been besieged by Julius Caesar in 52 BC; Fig. 39), some cheek pieces were found that had been decorated with a series of raised bosses, some decorative and some functional (the use of decorative bosses in this manner being a feature common to helmets of Gallic/Celtic origin, including non-Roman Montefortino examples). Some Agen/Port cheek pieces, however (for example Russell-Robinson, 1975, 42, pls 91, 92, 94 & 95), are similar to those found on Coolus type E, as described above, with a raised central panel. Of note however, is that on these the fastening stud/button is no longer placed at the front chin point, being set further back at the apex of the curve to the jawline.

Plate 1. Early Roman (Etruscan influence) 'hoplite' soldier of early fourth century BC (of Class I in the Servian system), wearing bronze Chalcidian-type helmet (which shows Greek influence); bronze cuirass tied at the shoulders; leg protectors (greaves); carrying small, round *hoplon* shield. (Artwork by J. R. Travis)

Plate 2. Samnite warrior of early fourth century BC, wearing triple-disc cuirass, carrying long rectangular shield (*scutum*) and projectile weapons (javelin and prototype *pila*). (Artwork by J. R. Travis)

Plate 3. Republican legionary (*Triarius*), from the start of the Second Punic Wars (218–201 BC), wearing bronze Montefortino helmet; long, sleeveless mail cuirass with shoulder doubling; leather armguard (*manica*) and bronze leg protectors (greaves); carrying an early form of Roman short sword (*gladius*); and long, curved oval Gallic-style shield. (Artwork by J. R. Travis)

Plate 4. Auxiliary cavalryman of Imperial period, wearing mail cuirass and 'Sports' masked face helmet, carrying oval cavalry shield. (Artwork by J. R. Travis)

Plate 5. First-century standard bearer (*vexillarius*), carrying small, round parade shield. (Artwork by J. R. Travis)

Plate 6. Centurian of the first century AD, Imperial period, wearing an Imperial Gallic helmet with transverse crest, denoting his centurion rank. He also wears a mail cuirass (*lorica hamata*), *phalerae*, leather *pteruges* and leg greaves. (Artwork by J. R. Travis)

Plate 7. Syrian archer, as depicted on Trajan's Column, wearing ankle-length flowing tunic, short mail cuirass and Eastern-style conical helmet. Tunic colour unknown, but depicted in green, based on conjectural interpretation of Hamian archer *stele* from Housesteads Fort, Hadrian's Wall. (Artwork by J. R. Travis)

Plate 8. Late Empire centurion of fourth century AD, wearing thick woollen over-tunic over mail shirt. Geometric symbol on tunic hem is a symbol of centurion rank. His iron helmet is of Spangenhelm type (similar to that found from Der-el-Medineh, Egypt). He carries a wide oval shield, of gently convex shape, its decoration based on an image from the *Notitia Dignitatum*. (Artwork by J. R. Travis)

Plate 9. Legionary from marine unit from first century AD, wearing Attic-style helmet, blue tunic and padded linen armour, carrying transitional semi-rectangular *scutum* with curved sides (painted blue and decorated with dolphins and Neptune's trident to denote marine unit). (Artwork by J. R. Travis)

Plate 10. Gladiator combat depicting a pair of *Provocatores*, the loser unhelmeted, awaiting his fate from the audience, the victor wearing a first-century AD type 1 helmet, as found at Pompeii, with round eye grills, brimless, with small neck guard, decorated with two side feathers. (Artwork by J. R. Travis)

Plate 11. Gladiator combat depicting a *Murmillo* and a Thracian, wearing first-century AD helmets as found at Pompeii. (Artwork by J. R. Travis)

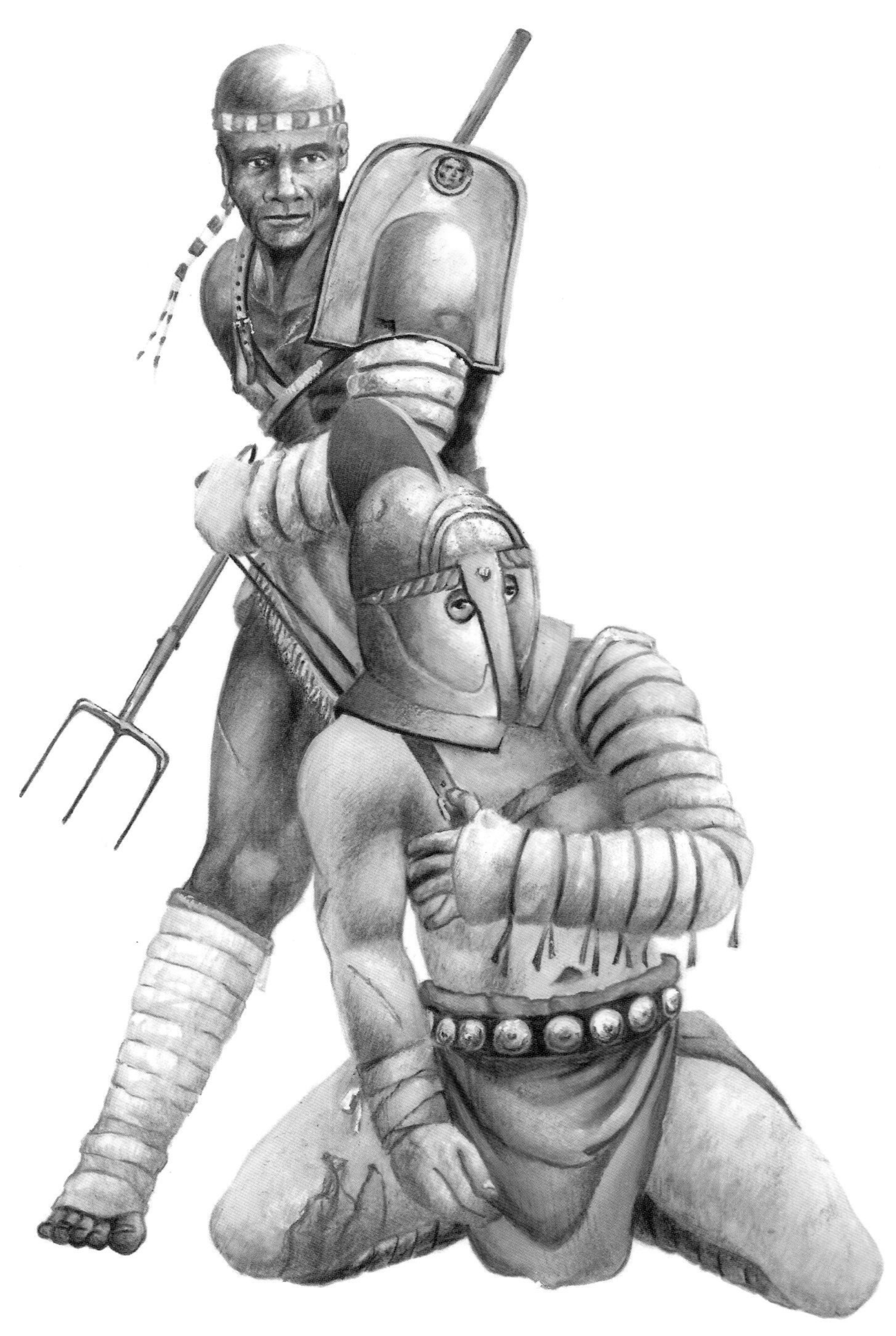

Plate 12. Gladiator combat depicting a *Secutor* against a *Retiarius* (unhelmeted). The *Secutor* is wearing a first-century AD helmet, as found at Pompeii. (Artwork by J. R. Travis)

Above left: Plate 13. Celtic re-enactor and author Will Llawerch portraying Iron Age/Celtic warrior wearing Montefortino helmet and Celtic-style mail with 'cape' shoulder doubling. (Photograph by H. Travis)

Above right: Plate 14. Reconstruction of Coolus type E helmet. (Photograph by J. R. Travis)

Right: Plate 15. Reconstruction of Imperial Gallic type A helmet. (Photograph by permission of D. Flockton Photography)

Above left: Plate 16. Reconstruction of Imperial Gallic type G helmet. (Photograph by permission of D. Flockton Photography)

Above right: Plate 17. Reconstruction of Imperial Gallic type H helmet. (Photograph by permission of D. Flockton Photography)

Left: Plate 18. Reconstruction of Imperial Gallic type J helmet. (Photograph by permission of D. Flockton Photography)

Above left: Plate 19. Reconstruction of Imperial Italic type C helmet. (Photograph by permission of D. Flockton Photography)

Above right: Plate 20. Re-enactor portraying an auxiliary soldier of the Imperial period, first to second century AD (a member of second cohort of Tungrians), wearing mail cuirass (*lorica hamata*) with shoulder doubling closed by serpentine-style closure hooks, and helmet of Imperial Italic type D (as dated by H. Russell-Robinson to *c.* AD 83). (Photograph by J. R. Travis)

Right: Plate 21. Re-enactor portraying an Imperial legionary of the late first century AD, wearing a helmet of Imperial Italic type G ('Hebron'). (Photograph by H. Travis)

Above left: Plate 22. Re-enactor portraying an officer (*optio*) wearing a reconstruction of an Imperial Italic type C helmet, decorated with a crest of contrasting red-and-black horsehair. (Photograph by permission of D. Flockton Photography)

Above right: Plate 23. Re-enactor portraying a standard bearer (*signifier*) wearing a reconstruction of an Imperial Italic type C helmet, covered by a wolf skin. (Photograph by permission of D. Flockton Photography)

Left: Plate 24. Re-enactor portraying a standard bearer (*signifier*) wearing a reconstruction of an Imperial Gallic type H helmet, covered by a bear skin. (Photograph by H. Travis)

In addition to his categorisation of helmet types, Russell-Robinson also categorised thirty types of cheek piece in use on Coolus, Imperial Gallic and Imperial Italic helmets, listing these along with their find locations (Russell-Robinson, 1975, 78–81):

Types 1, 3, and 4 (Fig. 115) he used for Coolus (bronze) helmets, dating from the Augustan period (Coolus type C) through to the second and third quarters of the first century AD (Coolus types F and G);
Types 2 and 5 through to 16 (Figs 115 & 116) he assigned to Imperial Gallic helmets (types A to I: Augustan to early second century AD); and
Types 17 to 30, he assigned to Imperial Italic (types C to E: third quarter of first century AD to late first century AD; Figs 116 & 117).

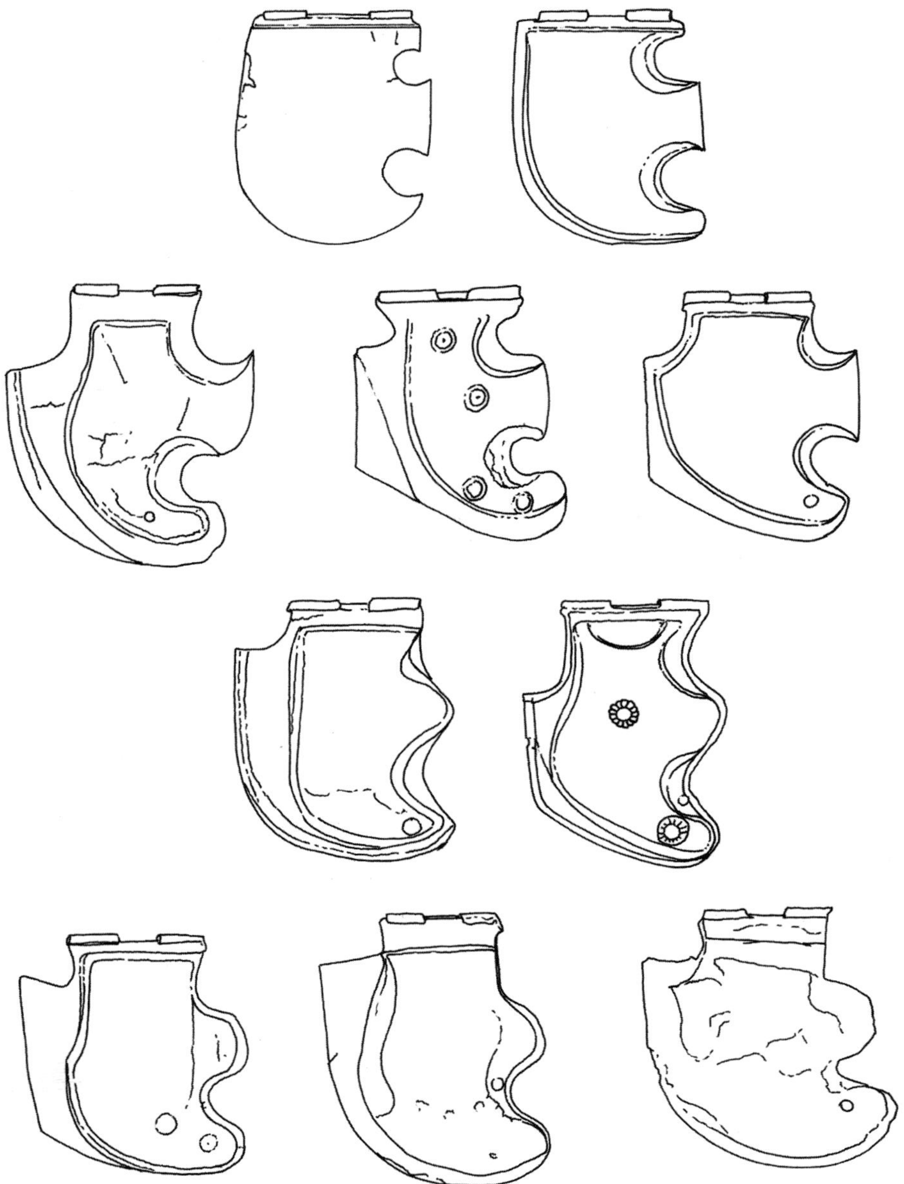

Fig. 115. Cheek pieces (types 1–10) (from Russell-Robinson, 1975). (Artwork by J. R. Travis)

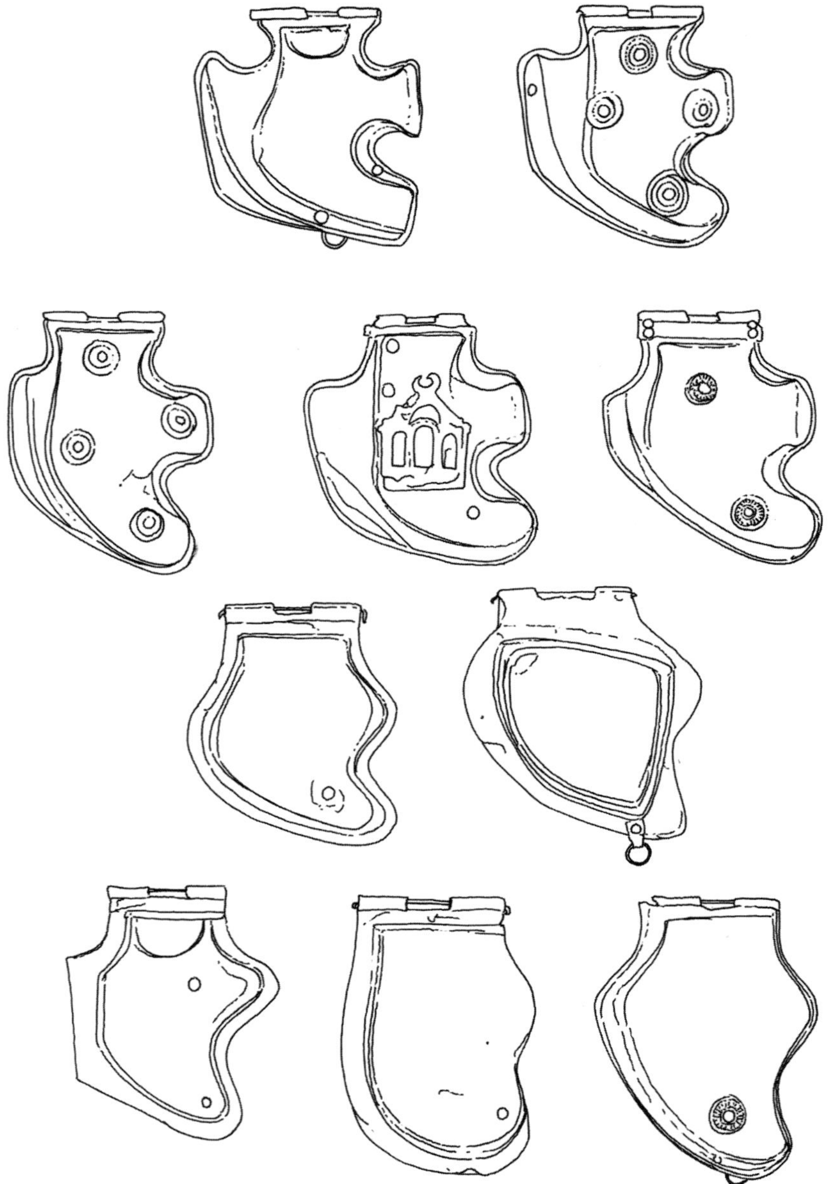

Fig. 116. Cheek pieces (types 11–20) (from Russell-Robinson, 1975). (Artwork by J. R. Travis)

However, there is little (other than find location linking perhaps to possible legion identity) to justify his assignment to these types. All that can be seen is that the earliest (type 1) is wide, flat and undecorated, with deep frontal cusping and gently rounded jawline, with squaring at the cheekbone. By type 2 there is a raising to the central panel, and by type 3 an additional rear cusping for the ear and an out-turning at the jaw edge. By types 4 and 5, the squaring at the cheekbone becomes less sharply defined, rounding off the edges.

On types 5, 7, 8, 10, 12 and 16, Gallic-style decorative bosses appear supporting rivets (mostly decorative, with no particular function). On some there are four bosses (7 and 8); on others three bosses (5, 12); and yet others only two (10 and 16). On some (types 9, 11, 13, 14 and 15) rivets are present, but are not accompanied by decorative bosses). In addition,

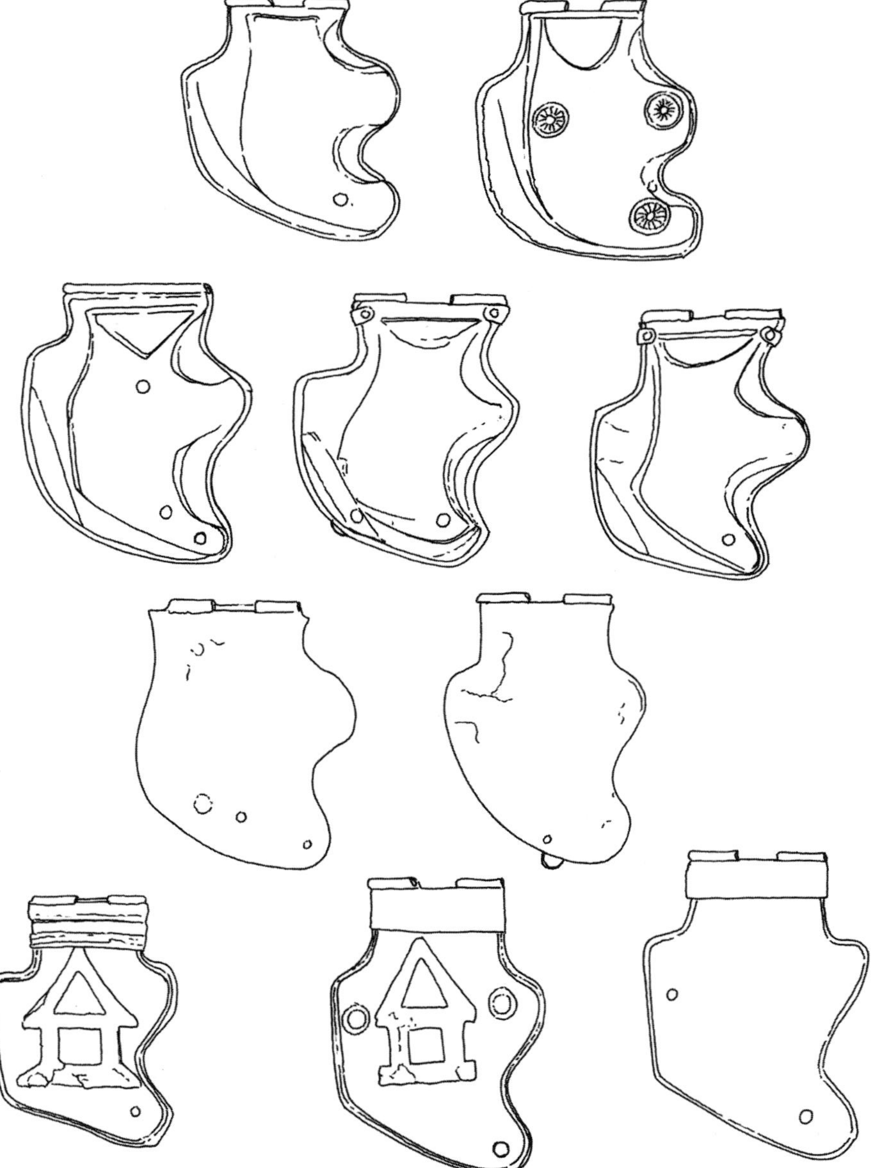

Fig. 117. Cheek pieces (types 21–30) (from Russell-Robinson, 1975). (Artwork by J. R. Travis)

type 9 bears a raised stylised image of a temple structure, which is similar to those seen on Russell-Robinson's type 28 and 29, although these latter he designated as being Imperial Italic.

The Imperial Gallic type A had similarly shaped cheek pieces to that on the Coolus type D example from Schaan (this had no cusping for the ears, and conical stud fastenings), and these similarities suggest a similar Augustan dating. The Imperial Gallic type B, however, was not found associated with any cheek pieces, but Russell-Robinson (1975, 51) suggested that these should have been provided with ear cusping 'cut-aways' and throat flanges (the type 5 cheek pieces in his typology).

By the time of the Imperial Gallic type C helmet, the cheek pieces had developed deep cusping to expose the ear, with the rear edge now angular (with an out-turned flange) and an embossed semi-circular area below the hinge. The front edge, between the eye and mouth cusps, was also slightly curved and outwardly flanged. In addition, the previous button stud fastenings were now replaced by tying rings riveted in the centre bottom edge, closure now being achieved using a tied length of thong, rather than a wider crossed strap.

The Imperial Gallic type D cheek piece, although lacking the embossed semi-circular area below the hinge, presents further cheek-piece developments; the forward edge is more rounded, and there is the addition of decorative embossed bronze bosses set with domed coral studs. One of these was placed at the hinge and three more lower down, one of the latter covering the rivet securing the chin tie rings (this being the only one with any particular functional purpose).

Whereas the Imperial Gallic type E was similar to the previous type D, the type F was of a much plainer design, with embossing only on the jawline and on a horizontal rib below the hinge, the chin tie ring being the only rivet covered by a silver and enamel boss, but with the addition of an outward-turning throat flange. By the time of the Imperial Gallic type G, the cheek piece was fully developed with outward-turning neck flanges, bronze edge bindings and three of the ornamental bosses which Russell-Robinson (1975, 56) regarded as being a feature of Gallic workmanship.

The Imperial Italic cheek pieces (types 17 to 30) show many similarities to the previous Imperial Gallic types, although with a softer, more rounded profile to the cheekbone area and lacking the outward-turning neck/throat flanges. Types 17, 18, 19, 20 and 23 do present a quite sharp edge to the ear cusp, with types 18 and 23 then having a straight rear face, from this sharp ear cusp corner leading down to another sharp corner at the jaw edge.

Overall, however, while all thirty of the cheek pieces presented by Russell-Robinson in his typology are different from each other (Russell-Robinson, 1975, 78–81), there is little that could be taken as diagnostic of either an Italic or Gallic origin, save perhaps for those with the Gallic decorative rosettes (and not all of those examples designated by Russell-Robinson as Gallic had these rosettes, although one example designated as Imperial Italic also had a supposedly Gallic rosette). What we may be seeing within this wide-ranging typology could instead simply be representative of the broadly similar work of many different craftsmen and *fabricae*. Furthermore, while Russell-Robinson's typology may be too wide-ranging in the number of categories identified, it is also perhaps not wide-ranging enough with regard to timespan and helmet types, restricting itself purely to Coolus, Imperial Gallic and Imperial Italic helmets (mostly dating from the first century AD, with just a tiny dip into the late first century BC and the early second century AD). It does not even include the early Montefortino and Agen/Port helmets described in his own previous chapters, which would have aided in his arguments for origins of influence, and does not extend to the contemporary auxiliary and cavalry helmets, or to those of the later Empire.

Auxiliary helmets can be seen on many monumental sculptures, such as the Arch of Septimus Severus, the Column of Marcus Aurelius, Trajan's Column, etc., where they show a variety of shapes, many of which have never been found in the archaeological record (although this is perhaps because these never existed in reality, being the invention of artistic licence). For example, helmets are seen on the Column of Marcus Aurelius, which had been fitted with a large round loop on the top of the bowl. The only versions of this helmet type which were found in the past subsequently turned out to be poor-quality modern copies, made with the intention of defrauding unknowledgeable and naive collectors. These sculptural representations of helmets also have another common factor in that their cheek pieces are always shown to be excessively small and narrow, presumably so as not to obscure the features of the wearers.

In contrast to this sculptural view, and also to the examples of helmets identified as being of 'legionary' origin, auxiliary cavalry helmet cheek pieces were even more substantial than those for infantry use, with those of auxiliary cavalry type F (for example from Konighofen, Strasbourg Museum) being very wide, with out-turned jaw edges, but without 'cut-aways' for the ears (Russell-Robinson, 1975, 92).

On auxiliary cavalry type C (early second century AD) cheek pieces had been very simplistic, but by type D they had become wider and shaped to fit upwards into the ear arch 'cut-away' on the bowl, the jaw edge beginning to have a small out-turning. By type E this jawline out-turned flange was becoming much more substantial (matched also by the development of widely out-turned neck guard). These features (cheek piece shaped to fully enclose the ear; jawline flange out-turned) continued on later auxiliary cavalry types, up to type H (late second to early third century AD). Some type H bronze examples even (for example those from Theilenhofen and another from South Shields; Fig. 118) were very highly decorated, with pounced decoration and applied borders (Russell-Robinson, 1975, 103).

On cavalry sports helmets, cheek pieces evolved from those decorated to look like a face when closed (as had been seen, for example, of the fourth-to-third-century BC Negau-type helmets, where cheek pieces formed an almost fully covered bearded face, with only the eyes exposed; one example from Etruria is in the Vatican Museum). By cavalry sports types F, G and H, the shapes of cheek pieces had evolved further, to leave just a small part of the face (eyes and mouth) exposed when closed, this later evolving yet further to be replaced with full-face masks.

Fig. 118. Bronze left-cheek piece, with engraved decoration, from an auxiliary cavalry helmet, dating to the second to early third century AD. Found in the River Tyne at South Shields, it is now in Newcastle University Museum. The decoration shows one of the *Dioscuri* with his horse, picked out in white dots. His brother possibly featured on the opposite cheek. Below the figure a dolphin can also be seen. (Artwork by J. R. Travis)

CRESTS

As described in previous chapters, Roman helmets evolved through influences from numerous directions; mostly from classical Greek influences arriving through trade and migration, spreading from the sixth century BC, firstly into other Italic states (such as Etruscan, Samnite and coastal areas) and later diffusing into Roman use.

One marked difference between these Greek predecessors and their later Roman counterparts lies in the style of crests and manner of attachment. The Greek style of crest was made of horsehair set in a solid wooden base, similar to a brush, fixed directly to the helmet along the crown and allowed to flow freely down the back, although it is not clear whether either of these were removable or permanently fixed in place (Spartan warriors, however, are depicted with transverse crests, similar to those on later Roman centurion's helmets; Warry, 1980, 52). Russell-Robinson (1975, 140) cites similar crests on Assyrian and Urartian helmets of the eighth to seventh centuries BC. In the Italian copies, both the low-level and the raised-stem mounted crests were used (a feature that appears to originate in the Italian variations of these Greek styles by the Etruscans and Samnites; Warry, 1980,

109), with the latter being particularly seen on bell-shaped Italic and Etruro-Corinthian helmets (for example, one Corinthian helmet, no. 2828 from the British Museum, fitted with a rectangular tube for a wooden crest box stem), which Russell-Robinson (*ibid.*) saw as ancestral to those on the later Imperial Gallic and Italic types.

The helmets in use by the Etruscans included the more open Corinthian variant, the Chalcidian, adopted from the Greeks, combining it with their own style of long crest attached to the centre of the helmet. At the same time, they also embraced the local Italian fashion for a bell-shaped, conical helmet, the Negau, optionally combined with a crest that was raised lengthwise or transverse. Although Warry (1980, 109) attributes this style of helmet to an Italian origin, it does bear marked similarities to the Greek Pylos type. Like its Greek counterpart, it could be simply tied with leather thongs, or could be combined with large cheek pieces, in one variant embossed to resemble a mask, as with the Greek Thracian (Fig. 27; Warry, 1980, 109).

The Samnites were similarly influenced by Greek colonies in the southern parts of the Italian peninsula, using both the Attic style (derived from the Chalcidian) and one combining features of the Attic and the Thracian, the Thraco-Attic, with hinged cheeks and curved peak. These could be combined with the Samnite's own style of upright feathers, wings and raised crests (Figs 29 & 31; Warry, 1980, 106). Some combinations of these feathered Attic helmets can be seen depicted in use by Samnite cavalry on a fourth-century tomb at Paestum (Russell-Robinson, 1975, 141, figs 148, 149).

The other major area of influence was Gallic/Celtic, through invasions in the fourth century BC, bringing in Celtic-style mail cuirasses, long oval shields, Montefortino helmets and a change to manipular fighting formations. Both of these cultural traditions, Graeco/Italic and Gallic/Celtic, brought with them a history of helmet adornment, from embossed decoration to painted helmet bowls, feathers, plumes and crests.

As described earlier, plume tubes appear to be an Italic fashion, always appearing on Attic-type helmets (one method of attachment can be seen on a shaped bar with a feather tube at each end and a central crest support in the middle, reportedly from an Attic-style helmet, from the British Museum; Russell-Robinson, 1975, 141, fig. 146), although less commonly on Montefortino helmets. However, one example of a type E Montefortino helmet was recovered from the Rhine at Mainz, dating to the first half of the first century AD, with tubes for feathers on each side of the brow band (Russell-Robinson, 1975, 23, plate 33). Similar feather tubes were also found on a Coolus type G helmet from Drusenheim, Hagenau, dating to the third quarter of the first century AD (Russell-Robinson, 1975, 29, pls 84–87). Whereas many of these feather tubes are welded or riveted directly to the sides of the helmets, another method of attachment can be seen on a shaped bar with a feather tube at each end and a central crest support in the middle, reportedly from an Attic-style helmet, from the British Museum (Russell-Robinson, 1975, 141, fig. 146).

From the first century AD plume tubes for side feathers were combined with crests, which Russell-Robinson (1975, 141) believed may have been used as a distinction for some cohorts or centuries of men, possibly using different-coloured feathers for different sections. Although tubes were also found on Imperial Gallic types F and I, their use appeared to have become less popular by the second half of the first century AD. Representations of side feathers can be seen on some grave *stelae*, including on the Coolus-type helmet of Caius Castricus of *legio II Adiutrix pia Fidelis* from Budapest (Russell-Robinson, 1975, plate 470); and on that of the standard bearer Flavinius of the *Ala Petriana*, from Hexham Abbey, which shows two large feathers on the right side of the crest (Russell-Robinson, 1975, plate 307). Plume tubes are also occasional finds on cavalry sports helmets, as, for example, on the iron helmet from Newstead (Fig. 82).

Traditionally, the Greek-type arched crests would have been formed from black, white or red-brown naturally coloured horsehair. Russell-Robinson (1975, 140) believed that other colours would have been unlikely due to the difficulty in dying oily fibres. Feathers, similarly, may have been naturally self-coloured, although it is possible to dye feathers to a wide range of shades. It is interesting here to note that reconstructed cavalry helmets are frequently provided with yellow-feathered plumes. However, it has also been noted on many occasions that modern horses appear to have an avid dislike for the colour yellow, resulting in several Roman cavalry re-enactors becoming unexpectedly and rapidly acquainted with the ground. It would therefore appear to be an odd choice of colour, although no doubt the horses could be trained to lose their aversion.

Despite the classical tradition for crests, the Montefortino and later Coolus helmets (type D onwards) of the Late Republican and Early Imperial period were instead provided with simple horsehair tails or plumes, attached to the central knob. These were then inserted into a hole drilled into the knob (or, in later Coolus helmets, into a slot drilled through the knob and secured by a pin through a small horizontal hole). These plumes can be seen on a number of sculptural reliefs, such as the Altar of Ahenobarbus (Fig. 5), the Arch of Orange (Fig. 120) and the late first-century BC *Julii* Monument at St Remy de Provence (also on the latter, an additional form of crest can be seen, formed of a fan shape of feathers). A similar helmet with horsehair plume can be seen on a tomb painting of a Galatian mercenary dating to the third or second century BC from Sidon Archaeological Museum, Istanbul, and another worn by a soldier from Pompeii on a mural of a magistrate's court dating to the first century AD (Russell-Robinson, 1975, 17, figs 17 and 18). Also on the funerary *stela* of Caius Valerius Crispus, of *legio VIII Augusta*, dating from the beginning of the first century AD, the figure can be seen wearing a helmet topped by what appears to be a flowing horsehair plume (Fig. 121).

Fig. 119. *Stela* of Caius of *legio II Adiutrix*, who is depicted wearing mail cuirass and a helmet decorated with a central crest and feathered side plumes, his hand resting on his long oval 'legionary' shield. (Artwork by J. R. Travis)

Fig. 120. Legionary from the Arch of Orange, his shield design attributed to the *legio II Augusta*. (Artwork by J. R. Travis)

Whereas Montefortino and Coolus helmets are provided with a knob at their apex, sometimes slotted for the attachment of plumes, with the appearance of the iron helmets (initially the Port/Agen and later the Imperial Gallic and Italic types), fittings change to removable solid, brush-like crests (Fig. 122), although the earliest form of Imperial Gallic was not provided with any crest attachment. However, the ancestors of these type of crests can be seen much earlier, as previously described on the classical Greek helmets (Figs 19, 22 & 27) and also on the early Gallic iron helmets. For example, the Gundestrup cauldron (Copenhagen) carries an embossed image of a Celtic horseman wearing a crested helmet, which appears to be a rigid, semi-circular 'brush', raised from the helmet bowl on a single crest pillar (*ibid*, 141, fig. 147). A similarly shaped crest, with fixed crest box supported on a single column riveted to the apex of the bowl, was seen on a seventh- or sixth-century BC Italian helmet from the British Museum (*ibid.*, 140, fig. 144), and a similar fixed column can be seen on a mid-first-century BC Agen helmet from the well on the Plateau de l'Ermitage, Agen, Lot-et-Garonne.

Fig. 121. Caius Valerius Crispus, of *legio VIII Augusta*, from the beginning of the first century AD. (Artwork by J. R. Travis)

On the Imperial Gallic helmets, the crest-supporting 'stem' was formed from a single piece of bronze divided at the head and bent into a squared U-shape with curled terminals. At the opposite, base end it was then bent at a right angle to form the 'foot'. A rectangular bronze plate was then riveted

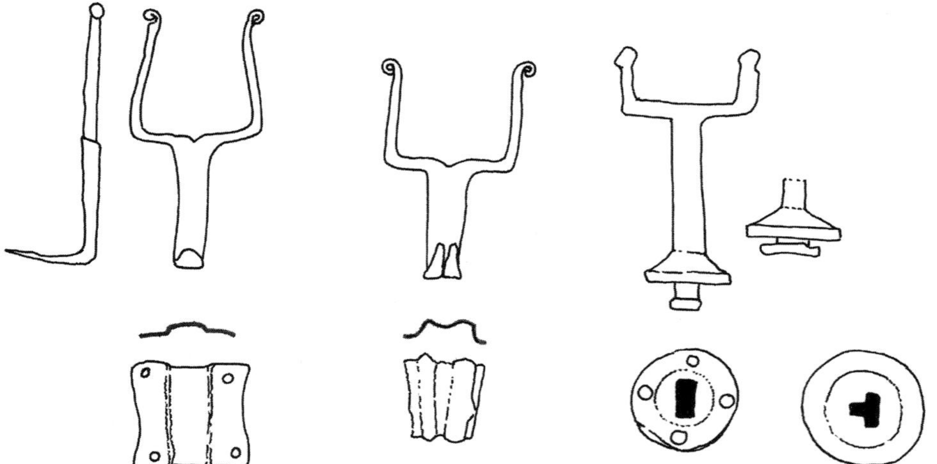

Fig. 122. Crest holder types (from Russell-Robinson, 1975). (Artwork by J. R. Travis)

at each corner to the apex of the helmet bowl. This plate was then raised from front to back (into either one or two grooves) to accept the right-angled 'foot' of the crest-supporting stem. On earlier examples the stem 'foot' was broader and divided into two (for double-grooved base plates), but on later examples the 'foot' was narrower, again with a split, but with both parts inserted into a single groove (the two parts then pressing outwards on the groove to form a firmer grip). The crescent-shaped crest box, curved to the shape of the helmet, would then sit in the U shape of the support, front to back, tied at the rear to an anchoring hook or ring riveted to the back of the helmet bowl (Fig. 122).

The Imperial Italic helmets (and Imperial Gallic types F and I) had a slightly different method of attachment (known as the 'twist-on' method), being provided with a circular plate with a raised slotted centre. Instead of the right-angled 'foot', the corresponding crest supports for these helmets had a circular base plate, with a T-shaped stud underneath. This stud was then inserted into the slotted plate and secured with a half-turn. A slight variation on this type of support can also be seen on an example from Rheingönheim which had been provided with an additional central spike in the U-shaped holder, to insert into a corresponding hole in the crest box for extra anchorage. Another variation can be seen on the Imperial Italic type D helmet, where the helmet slot was also T-shaped, so that the stud would only need to be inserted and pushed forward, rather than twisting.

The wooden crest box itself was formed from a crescent shaped block of wood, drilled with numerous holes for the insertion of bundles of horse hair glued in place, similar in construction to a hair brush. An example of such a crest box was found at Vindolanda.

Although the above crests, as described, would normally be aligned from front to back, there is sculptural and literary evidence to suggest that centurion crests may have been transversal, aligned from left to right, as a symbol of office. Vegetius (65 & 71) reports that centurions (*centenarii*) could be recognised by their men from their different crests, and that their crests were 'placed transversely' ('*transversis Cassidum Cristis*') and 'ornamented with silver'. Further evidence can be seen on grave *stelae*, for example those of two centurions (T. Calidius Severus from Carnuntum and Marcus Petronius Classicus from St Veit bei Pettau) who were depicted with transverse crests (although that of the former being horsehair and raised on a central support, whereas that of the latter appears fixed directly to the bowl and is formed of very large feathers; Russell-Robinson, 1975, figs 150 & 151).

Further images of crests can be seen on a number of sculptural reliefs which do not fully appear to reflect the archaeological evidence of actual helmet finds: the Arch of Severus, AD 203; the Basilica Aemilia, 14 BC; the Praetorian relief, early second century AD; the Triumphal relief of Trajan, now part of the Arch of Constantine, AD 113; and Trajan's Column, AD 113 (Russell-Robinson, 1975, figs 152 to 157). On all of these images the helmets appear to have short curved crest boxes fixed directly to the helmet bowl, with no raised supports, all being shown to be on archaic-style Attic helmets. However, in addition to all other reservations as to the accuracy of many monumental sculptures (as opposed to the cruder but more accurately represented grave *stelae*), also of consideration may be that this style of low crests would be more stable and easier to represent in high sculptural relief than would those on narrow, raised stems, as these would be more likely to snap off, either during sculpture or during subsequent years.

HELMET LININGS

Although many actual examples of Roman helmets are known, spanning the entire range of use through the Republican and Imperial periods, many in remarkably good condition, archaeological evidence for any form of lining or removable under-cap is poor, due to the unlikely survival of such flimsy textiles under most conditions. It is most probable that helmets would have been worn with either fixed linings or removable caps of some sort, to improve fit, give added comfort (particularly for those owners who were no longer blessed by nature's padding – hair), and also to provide additional impact absorption.

Some helmets, particularly in the later composite forms and in the case of the cavalry sports type A, are provided with holes around the edges, which would have probably served for the attachment of fixed linings, of textile, leather or fleece. Evidence for removable caps is known from the fourth-century AD writings of Ammianus Marcellinus, who refers to a removable, pill-box-shaped cap known as the '*pileus*' (19.8.8), the cap being used on this occasion to soak up water in a makeshift attempt to access the contents of a deep well.

However, the only known example of a cap, suggested to be an 'arming cap' for under the helmet, comes from Dura Europos (James 2004, 108, Fig. 51). This one-piece hat of felt and wool is not a pill-box-shaped '*pileus*', as described by Ammianus, but resembles more a Phrygian-style cap, with long ear tabs. James (2004, 109) interprets this as being a protective liner, the pointed top folded over and flattened for under the helmet, with pile added to the side tabs to fit under the cheek pieces, the padding serving to 'absorb sweat, minimise chafing and to dissipate blows'.

Although this particular cap was found in levels with context datable to the fall of Dura, its shape being consistent with helmets of that time, there is every probability that helmets of preceding eras would similarly have been worn with under-caps, although shaped to fit contemporary helmets.

Cheek Piece Type	Helmet Category (C)oolus (Imp)(G)allic (Imp)(I)talic (Aux)(I)nf	Helmet Type	Material (Br)onze (Ir)on	Date	Location
1	C	C	Br	Augustan	Liechtenstein
2	Imp G	A	Ir		Nijmegen
3	C	E	Br	1st 1/2 of 1st C AD	Thames at Kew
4		F & G		2nd & 3rd 1/4 of 1st C AD	Hod Hill
5	Imp G	B	Ir	1st 1/4 of 1st C AD	Mainz
6		C			River Kupa
7		D		2nd 1/4 of 1st C AD	Rhine at Mainz
8		E			Idria near Baca
9		nk			Nijmegen
10		F			Besançon
11					Hod Hill
12		G		3rd 1/4 of 1st C AD	Rhine at Mainz
13		I	Br	2nd 1/2 of 1st C AD	Nijmegen
14				Late 1st C AD	Leiden
15					Caerleon
16		J	Ir	Early 2nd C AD	Brigetio
17	Imp I	C	Br	3rd 1/4 of 1st C AD	Cremona
18					
19				2nd 1/2 of 1st C AD	Nijmegen
20					
21		n/k			
22			Ir	Before AD85	Richborough
23				2nd 1/2 of 1st C AD	Carnuntum
24			Br		
25		B	Ir	2nd 1/4 of 1st C AD	Klakanji
26	Aux I	nk	Br	1st C AD	Büderich
27		B		2nd 1/2 of 1st C AD	Rhine at Mainz
28	Imp I	D	Ir		
29					
30		E		Late 1st C AD	Hofheim

Table 8. Cheek pieces – description of H. Russell-Robinson typologies.

Find location	(Br) (Ir)	Additional info (inc. curent location, if known)
IJzendoorn (NL)	Br	Right piece. Rijksmuseum van Oudheden, Leiden (NL)
Nijmegen (NL) (?)		Right piece. Rijksmuseum G.M. Kam, now Museum het Valkhof, Nijmegen (NL)
Nijmegen (NL)		Right piece. Rijksmuseum G.M. Kam, now Museum het Valkhof, Nijmegen (NL)
		Similar to a Valkenburg (NL) cheek guard. Right piece. Instituut voor Oude Geschiedenis en Archeologie, R. K. Universiteit Nijmegen (NL)
		Pair. Rijksmuseum G.M. Kam, now Museum het Valkhof, Nijmegen (NL)
		Left piece. Rijksmuseum G.M. Kam, now Museum het Valkhof, Nijmegen (NL)
		Right piece. Rijksmuseum van Oudheden, Leiden (NL)
Unknown location	Brass	Cavalry helmet, Guisborough/Theilenhofen (?) type. Left piece, fragmentary. remains of tinning. Axel Guttmann Collection
		Early Imperial. Right piece. Axel Guttmann Collection
	Br	Montefortino-Cremona type. Pair. Tinned. Axel Guttmann Collection
	Brass	Pseudo-attic cavalry helmet. Right piece, fragmentary. Axel Guttmann Collection
		Special Weisenau type. Pair. partially tinned. Iron rivets. Axel Guttmann Collection
	Br	Weisenau-Mainz type. Right piece. Axel Guttmann Collection
Vechten (NL)	Ir	Left piece. bronze rim. Rijksmuseum van Oudheden, Leiden (NL)
Venlo (NL)	Ir & Br	Right piece. temple decration and rim. Rijksmuseum G.M. Kam, now Museum het Valkhof, Nijmegen (NL)
Xanten (D)	Br	Right piece. partially tinned. Rheinisches Landesmuseum, Bonn (D)

Table 9. List of known cheek pieces.

XII

CONSTRUCTION

MATERIALS

Any discussion of helmet constructional methods has first to consider the materials used and their different properties. While many of the helmets from the Imperial period onwards described above were made from iron, those from the earlier periods were for the most part made from copper alloy. When these are then described in archaeological reports, or catalogues of private collections, they may also be described as bronze or brass, not necessarily based on any metallographic analysis. This is understandable in that both metals would present with similar brown/green patina in their oxidised post-excavation condition. However, both of these metals differ, not only aesthetically in their original colour but also in their chemical properties.

Copper is a particularly soft metal. It is easy to shape, and is ideal for the manufacture of rivets, which will require periodical removal for maintenance, but would not be resilient enough to withstand sustained attack. By alloying copper with other elements, a much harder, more resilient metal is produced. In some copper deposits, levels of arsenic occur naturally, producing a slightly harder metal than purer deposits. In the early Bronze Age (around the third millennium BC), these properties were noted and metals augmented by the deliberate addition of arsenic producing arsenical bronzes (Champion *et al.*, 1984, 198). In the later Bronze Age, with less harmful side effects, bronzes were also produced using antimony, and from the later periods (around 1800 BC), 'true' bronzes were produced using tin, improving casting and producing a harder metal, although in some regions, such as Iberia and Italy, these new processes were not adopted until the later Bronze Age, around 1200 BC (*ibid.*, 226). Bronzes are generally of a reddish-brown colour and are much harder than copper, although this makes them more brittle and they may have a tendency towards breakage. Some areas rich in mineral deposits, such as Britain, appear to lead the way in metallurgical innovation and in trading with those less developed. Trade in preformed bronze bar ingots from the second millennium BC and trade in scrap for reuse from the tenth century BC can be evidenced from shipwrecks transporting scrap materials from France to Britain (Figs 123 & 124; Champion *et al.*, 1984, 289). Further metallurgical innovation can also be seen in Britain and northern France around this time with the addition of 7–10 per cent of lead to copper-tin bronze, which made the mix easier to pour, producing fewer casting failures and consequently increasing output/reducing fuel overheads (*ibid.*). In later periods metals were produced with up to 30 per cent lead to increase malleability and improve casting, although this was traded against slight reduction in hardness.

During the Roman period copper was also alloyed with zinc, producing a golden-yellow-coloured metal which we would describe as brass and which the Romans referred to as '*oricalchum*'. This metal, although harder than pure copper, would not have been quite as hard as bronze but may have been preferred because of its 'golden' colour, initially used for currency production (Pliny, *Hist. Nat.*, 34.4), and would also have a pleasing effect for applied decoration. With the melting down of old articles for recycling, this definition blurs between copper-tin and copper-zinc alloys, with some artefacts including both. Both bronze and brass seem to have been used for the manufacture of copper alloy helmets, generally those from the earlier, Republican period being of bronze, with the appearance of brass

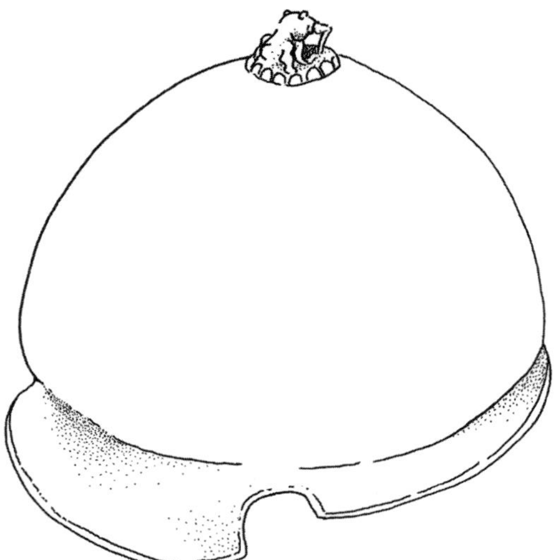

Fig. 123. Etruscan bronze helmet dated to fourth or third century BC, from Les Sorres shipwreck, dated to second century BC (from Izquierdo & Solias Aris, 2000). (Artwork by J. R. Travis)

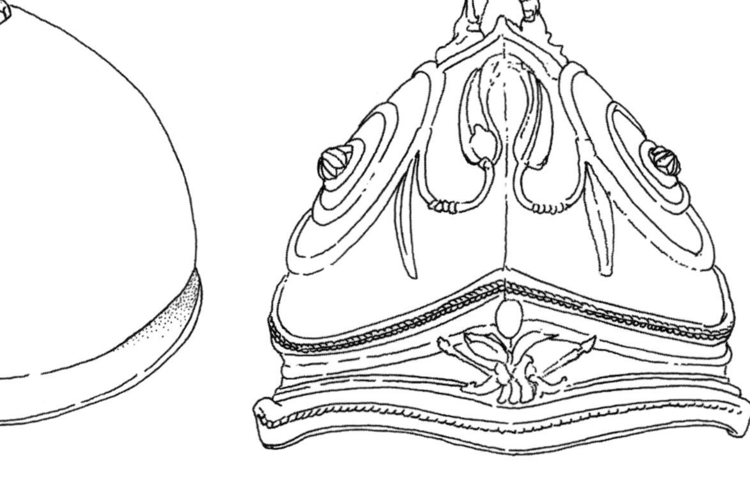

Fig. 124. Etruscan bronze helmet dated to fifth century BC, from Les Sorres shipwreck, dated to second century BC (from Izquierdo & Solias Aris, 2000). (Artwork by J. R. Travis)

(*oricalchum*) introduced around the times of the increased production following the Marian and Augustan reforms.

There is no evidence that the zinc was added to the mixture in its pure form (which was not produced until the sixteenth century, with development of distillation processes). Instead it would probably have been introduced as an oxide, possibly produced as a by-product of processing other metallic ores such as lead, silver, iron and copper, or as found in naturally occurring 'earthy' compounds such as calamine. Literary references to these 'earthy' compounds are known from Aristotle ('a certain type of earth'), Theophrastus ('a peculiar earth', 'mixed with copper', with the 'ability to enhance the beauty of copper' which he refers to as '*cadmeia*'), and Pliny (who describes absorption of '*cadmeia*'; Aristotle, *On Marvellous Things Heard*, 62.835a; Theophrastus, *De Lapidibus*, 49; Pliny, *Hist. Nat.*, 34.4).

It would be convenient to suggest that the introduction of brass for helmets rather than bronze was due to its properties being better suited to mass-production methods, but both metals can be produced with varying levels of hardness and malleability, so this cannot be the only reason. It could be that the choice of metal was influenced by preferred colour, although, again, this theory is weakened by evidence of traces of surface tinning on some helmets, which would then hide the underlying colour. It seems more probable that the choice of alloy may therefore have been dictated by the preferences and traditions of the individual craftsman, and the raw materials most plentiful to him, and may possibly be indicative of region of manufacture. It may also not be entire coincidence that the more widespread use of *oricalchum* appears to date from first movements into Britain, a country already well known for its mineral wealth, metal production, scrap recycling and trade, from the Bronze Age.

While mindful that these copper alloy helmets could be of bronze, brass or a mixture of both, as the properties are broadly similar, for ease of discussion of construction methods these will be referred to as bronze. There are a range of possible methods of manufacture that could have been in use, including hammering manually from sheet metal (either drawn down over a former, or beaten from the inside), casting in one piece or spinning on a lathe. Casting would not have been a suitable method of production for iron helmets, as this would have produced metal that was too brittle, resulting in helmets shattering in use. Similarly, spinning was not considered to be suitable for the production of iron helmets, according to

Paddock (1985, 147), as he considered Roman iron not to be of a consistent enough quality, with too many impurities, spinning only being used for bronze helmets. Although Paddock reports evidence of several bronze helmets produced by spinning as a result of attempts to increase production following reforms to the army, he suggested that this reverted to the traditional drawing-down process for iron helmets.

HAMMER SHAPING

To produce a helmet by hammer shaping, the process would start with a sheet of annealed metal roughly shaped to the end product. If metal were brought in from an outside source this would probably begin in the shape of a bar or 'pig'. However, if the entire process was being completed at one site, this may include the processing of mineral ore through smelting into a 'bloom' of iron, or casting into a bar of copper alloy. In any event, before the metal reached the skilled armourer's workshop it would have already undergone preliminary processing into sheet form, possibly through rolling, pressing or machine hammering, similar to in the spinning process.

There are then two methods that could be used to raise the bowl of the helmet. Firstly the metal could be hammered from the inside, rotating in concentric circles around the bowl, starting from the centre, working outwards, beginning with a large ball-ended hammer, similar to a modern cross-peen form. Once the shape has been roughly achieved, the process is repeated using smaller and smaller hammers, to remove visible hammer marks, finishing with a small, rounded, 'planishing' hammer. However, although it is possible to raise a bowl in this manner, it is difficult to maintain an even shape, deeper bowls are not easily achieved and the outer surface is often rough and uneven, requiring surface planishing to finish off. It is possible to produce reasonable results forming shield bosses in this way, although for helmets, where a larger object is being made, the alternative method of shaping by hammering the metal from the outer surface over a ball-shape was found to produce better-quality results.

To raise a helmet in this way, the armourer would use a variety of ball-headed stakes of different sizes. Firstly, in the case of Montefortino-type helmets, with raised-crest knobs, moulded integral with the bowl, the centre of the sheet is indented from the inner surface by hammering with a pointed rod. This raised point is then worked into the required shape, a process which requires a high level of craftsmanship, prior to any shaping of the helmet bowl itself. The annealed sheet is then hammered, again using a cross-peen type of hammer, over a ball shape of approximately similar profile to the end shape required, working around the bowl, spiralling downwards with overlapping blows, until the approximate shape is produced. Each of these concentric hammer blows would have produced small, dished markings. By repeating the process lightly, with smaller and smaller hammers, these dishing marks are gradually 'planished' away to leave a smooth surface. Finally, the surface is ground and polished to smooth it further, roughened edges are 'knocked back' to thicken and take off any sharpness, and engraved or embossed decoration, or applied fittings, are added. It had been thought that applied fittings were either riveted or soldered to the helmet body (and where rivets are visible this would be the case). However, recent restoration work on a decorated cavalry helmet from Xanten found that a wreath of decorative silver laurel leaves had been attached using a form of 'superglue', still holding strongly after almost 2,000 years, visible as threadlike strands when melted. Analysis suggests that this was made of a combination of bitumen, beef tallow and pitch (Paterson, 2007).

If the helmet is being produced from iron, it can be produced in one continuous process. However, copper alloy reacts differently to iron, the metal becoming brittle and work-hardened during the hammering process, the crystalline structure within the metal aligning, creating weak points where splits may occur. This will require frequent annealing or softening, by heating to high temperatures (to randomise the crystalline structure once more), and subsequent cooling (to set the structure), to prevent splitting.

CASTING

Although there is no direct evidence for producing an entire helmet by casting, the process is known to have been used for other artefacts, large and small, and so its potential must be considered. Both of the alternative methods of production, spinning or manual hammering, require first the cutting of a blank from sheet metal, which is then wasteful, producing cut-offs from the sheet, and labour intensive. Casting as an alternative would minimise waste and the need for prolonged hammering. It allows for ease of applied decoration, particularly for producing crest knobs or other applied external decoration. Rather than having to raise the central knob manually, then knock back and shape the raised area into complex shapes, which is labour intensive and requires a high level of craftsmanship, this could be achieved by casting, using the lost wax method. This method could be used to cast applied features, such as crest knobs, on to preformed bowls using techniques developed in the later Bronze Age to apply handles on vessels, hilts on to sword blades, etc. (Champion *et al.*, 1984, 285). Any resulting 'flashes' from the casting process would be cleaned up by the craftsman later and would not be immediately evident in high-quality items made for the individual, as was the case during the pre-Imperial periods.

Alternately, casting could also have been used to produce an entire helmet; again techniques for producing larger objects had been developed since the end of the second millennium. Although there is no direct evidence for this method, theoretically it could be achieved. Melting into a bowl of hot water, and allowing to cool while floating on surface can produce sheet wax of uniform thickness. This sheet wax could be moulded onto a 'former' of the basic bowl shape, and the crest knob moulded manually on to the centre. Additional wax filling tubes and vents to permit escape of gasses would also be applied to the model. Ribbed or cabled decoration at the rim edge could also be fashioned at this point, avoiding later work. The finished wax 'helmet' model could then be encased in clay (with more 'inclusions' than for normal pottery production, to permit higher temperatures), to form a casting mould with vents through to the surface. Once hardened, this would be lifted from the 'former' and the underside of the 'helmet' model similarly encased, to form one solid, complete mould. The mould would then be heated, the wax poured out and retained for future use. Molten bronze would then be poured into the filling tube, hot gasses being forced out of the other vents, until the mould was filled. The resulting casting, when cooled, would retain casting lugs at the points where these vents had been, which would need to be removed, along with any unwanted flashes, during the finishing process.

This method could only be used for small-scale production, but would allow detailed decoration, such as that seen on the bronze Etruscan Negau-style helmets from the Les Sorres shipwreck site (Figs 123 & 124), or some of the highly decorated Iberian Montefortino helmets. This method would only really be feasible for bronze helmets, however. If casting were to be used for iron helmets, the result would be brittle and not resistant to any applied force, shattering on attack. This could explain the preponderance for bronze helmets and the scarcity of iron helmets in the early periods, when mass production was not an issue. Bronze and other copper alloys have different properties to iron and require different treatment. Although iron lends itself more to forge shaping through hammering, similar treatment of bronze (or copper alloy) is more problematic, as it would require periodic and repeated reheating to anneal the metal to prevent splitting. This could form the basis for an argument in favour of casting rather than hammer shaping for copper alloy helmets, although the latter method was clearly also used.

To produce a helmet by casting would require a substantial amount of molten bronze, which would need either a particularly large crucible, or many small ones. Large crucibles would require a very efficient system of heating, to achieve a large quantity of molten metal in one single batch. It would be more sensible to use multiple pourings with small crucibles. All of these would need to be heated simultaneously, and poured in rapid succession, which would require the assistance of several co-workers. The process may leave signs on the metal where multiple pours met, where the molten metal meets partly solidified earlier pourings.

Different batches may contain a slightly different mixture of components in the alloy, some parts being harder, or more resistant to corrosion, and this may leave some areas more fragmentary than others.

As stated previously, there is no evidence for this method having being used in Republican- or Imperial-period helmets. No signs have been found of flashing, no evidence of joining between multiple pourings, and no remains of discarded moulds. Further, possible evidence of hammer marks, identified in some cases by Russell-Robinson, also suggested that erosion around the bowl may be due to thinning at this point during the hammering-out process, when the shape was being produced by beating out manually from a sheet. However, these problems with areas of thinning around the bowl, and the introduction of applied features possibly to combat this weakness, are later features, at the time also when crest knobs were either applied or non-existent. It is possible that, during the earlier periods, where crest knobs appear to be integral with the body of the helmet, casting may have offered a means to produce this effect, at least at lower levels of production. Lack of casting 'flash' in these cases could be simply a result of higher-quality finishing by craftsmen involved. In small-scale production it is possible to afford greater time to perfecting finish than in mass production. It is probably more likely that better workmanship would be seen in these cases as the individual purchasing a single item for his own personal use would be a more discerning customer than someone placing a mass order for a full legion at a time.

SPINNING

To produce a helmet by spinning, a sheet of metal would be punched at the centre to provide a locating point, and then set on a lathe between a wooden 'former' and a 'follower'. As the lathe rotated, the metal would be guided towards the 'former' using stroking motions, which produces concentric tooling marks. This central punch mark could be later hidden by the addition of an applied crest knob, and the concentric tooling marks may be later polished off in the finishing stages. Helmets produced in this way will tend to be round, with equal measurements on any axis, despite the human head not being that shape, whereas a helmet hammered out for an individual would be more naturalistically shaped.

As described above, Paddock suggested evidence for spinning could be seen on a number of Montefortino/Buggenum and Coolus helmets, suggesting that the process was introduced at a time of mass production, coinciding with the increased legion sizes and influx of lower-status citizen and non-citizen troops of the Marian and Augustan reforms. The process does require sheet bronze of a consistent gauge as a starting point, suggesting some pre-processing of the raw material. It is therefore unlikely that the helmet began in the armourer's workshop as a pig or bar. To arrive at a sheet of bronze of a consistent thickness it would be logical to assume that it may have been rolled, pressed or machine hammered in an earlier process. However, there has been no evidence for sheet metal transportation, although pigs and bars are known, which suggests that any such pre-processing would have been done in another workshop close to the armourer's workshop.

XIII

CONCLUSION

SUMMARY OF DEVELOPMENTAL PROGRESSION

The earliest head protection would probably have been fashioned from whatever resilient material was close to hand, although organic materials (wood, horn, etc.) do not survive as well as metallic ones. For example, simple copper alloy helmets are known from Ur dating to 2500 BC (Fig. 10; Fagan, 2004, 184), with a sculptural representation (the Vulture *Stela*) also at Ur, depicting soldiers in 'shield wall' formation, wearing similar helmets (Fagan, 2004, 85). Many features of helmet design which are seen copied in later Roman helmets can be first identified during the Hellenistic period, with the higher-status Illyrian and Corinthian styles of the seventh to fifth century BC (Figs 19 & 27) gradually improving cheek protection, bowl ventilation, overall visibility and hearing, to produce more open styles such as the Chalcidian (forerunner of the Attic form also seen in later Roman officer use; Warry, 1980, 44; Fig. 28). The longer cheek pieces of the later Corinthian styles permitted the wearer to push the helmet up on to the top of the head when not in use in a feature later mimicked on the Roman officer Etrusco-Corinthian helmet (with an imitation 'face' on top of the head; Russell-Robinson, 1975, 137; Fig. 30).

The basic hoplite equipment assembly in use in Hellenic regions was then adopted in the sixth century BC by a number of the Italic peoples, including the Romans, as depicted on the *Certosa Situla* (Fig. 20), although the Italic hoplite wore simpler-designed body armour, their equipment following the traditions of that particular region (Figs 11–15 & 21; Burns, 2003, 62–72). This earliest Roman army consisted of those who satisfied a property qualification that determined their level of equipment and status into five classes, with increasing levels of protection, in order of its importance and value (Livy, *Hist. of Rome*, 1.43), and who were responsible for the supply of their own equipment (Paddock, 1985, 143). Armour was privately owned, commissioned from craftsmen operating small-scale workshops, and probably handed down to later generations as high-value heirlooms.

By the end of the fourth century BC, a homogenisation of armour can be seen, with almost universal use of Samnite-style oval shields and the Celtic-style Montefortino helmets (although with some higher-status use of the Attic and Etrusco-Corinthian helmets for officer and cavalry use) probably due to its simplicity, ease and economy of manufacture, along with its non-contentious, 'neutral' lack of association with any particular Italic city-state (Burns, 2003, 73). At the start of the fourth century BC, the Samnite people wore a better-designed triple-disc cuirass, and close-fitting Attic-style helmets with feathered side plumes (Figs 29 & 31); they carried long, rectangular shields (*scuta*), fighting in more open formation, using projectile weapons (javelins and prototype *pila*). Each of their allied neighbours had their own, slightly different armour assemblage, reflecting their regional traditions and origins, with different styles of helmets, crests and plumes, and slightly different weaponry and body armour (Burns, 2003, 72; Figs 16–17 & 31). During this century, two developments can be seen. Firstly, the Romans witnessed the superior mail body armour and Montefortino helmet (with its simplicity and ease of manufacture) of the Gallic Celts at Allia in 386 BC (Livy, *Hist. of Rome*, 4.59; Burns, 2003, 70), and their wealthier members assimilated this into their own assemblage (Fig. 33). Secondly, they reorganised the structure of their army from the hoplite phalanx (ineffective against the open formation of the Samnites) into the more flexible manipular legions, abandoning the small *hoplon* shields (now obsolete) in favour of the Samnite-style long, oval *scuta*, which were more effective against projectile weapons (Burns, 2003, 70).

The Punic Wars of the third century BC again brought about further change. The Roman forces were volunteers, equipped from their own resources and recruited as required, requiring fresh training for each campaign. The Carthaginian opposition, however, were time-served mercenary troops, with the additional incentive of fighting for booty (Quesada Sanz, 1997, 155). By the Second Punic War, however, some Roman troops were similarly time-served, and the army had once more reorganised, forming a new light infantry with less armour. The number of legions was increased, annual selection of temporary conscripts was introduced, including men from the poorer classes, and volunteers were encouraged by a small allowance, to help man the new legions. These men still mostly equipped themselves from local craftsmen, their equipment reflecting regional and cultural differences (Paddock, 1985, 143).

The opposing Carthaginians were similarly equipped with Montefortino-type helmets and oval shields, re-kitting at established assembly points. Finds of helmets of similar date and perhaps similar style of workmanship may reflect the locations of these assembly points, either Roman or Carthaginian mercenary, several of the latter known from the Iberian peninsula (Quesada Sanz, 1997, 155, 162). It was around this time (mid- to late third century BC), that the Coolus (Mannheim) style of simply shaped bronze helmets (without crest knobs) also began to appear, these being of Gallic-Celtic origin, rather than the Italic-Celtic Montefortinos, and again may not always represent Roman use, although in both cases the presence of cheek pieces may be indicative of Roman ownership, the Celtic versions being worn with just simple ties instead (Russell-Robinson, 1975, 26).

The second century BC saw further revisions to the organisation and identity of the Roman army, with greater relaxation of recruitment restrictions, restructuring of the manipular legions into cohorts and some redesign of equipment (Campbell, 2000, 6). Many were unable to afford their own kit, which had to be supplied by the state, using mass-production 'factories' (probably state-owned), as the quantities required at short notice were outside of the capacity of the small-scale private workshops. Many innovations to improve rate of production at the expense of quality can be seen at this time, particularly in helmet construction (Paddock, 1985, 146). Helmets appear to be mass produced by 'spinning', poorly finished, with separately made crest knobs (or none at all) and with little or no decoration (Paddock, 1985, 146). With further relaxation of citizenship following the Social and Civil Wars of the early to mid-first century BC, the increase in number of legions to twelve, and increase in the level of payment to volunteers, quality reduced still further.

New equipment was also required to re-equip existing legions before and after conflicts. For example, Caesar in his Gallic Wars (*Bel. Gall.*) was known to have re-equipped his men using 'friendly' Gallic craftsmen, known for their skills in metalworking and armour production, hence the introduction of Gallic/Celtic features to the military assemblage at that time, seen in the introduction of iron Agen and Port styles of helmet (dating to the siege of Alesia in 52 BC; Russell-Robinson, 1975, 42; Fig. 39), and of the Gallic-style round iron and copper alloy shield bosses (also found from Alesia, Slovenia and Gaul; Feugère, 2002, 73). Although the exact locations of these Gallic 'state-owned' factories are unknown, it is suggested that these would be in regions known to be friendly to Caesar, in particular the Coolus district of Marne, close to the Rhine. Furthermore, Paddock (1985, 146) suggests that the innovation of 'spinning' may derive from a Greek tradition, reflecting also the activity of Italic workshops, introducing methods for high-capacity production from their own 'historic' traditions (with the possibility of 'spinning' features in mass-produced, bell-shaped Greek Pylos helmets of the fifth century BC).

Metallurgical analysis of copper alloy helmets also suggests further changes in production methods to increase supply, by speeding production and reducing failure rates, with a change from the use of the harder bronze (copper and tin) to the addition of zinc to produce the softer, more easily worked, golden-coloured *oricalchum* (Paddock, 185, 147). This change to metallic properties may again reflect the actions and influences of different workshops and craftsmen. Some of the regions newly being incorporated into Roman territories, or experiencing greater levels of Roman trade and influence had long-standing metalworking traditions and high mineral wealth, such as parts of Gaul, Germania and Britain. It is possible that the need for mineral wealth, to provide armour for increasing armies to then power further expansion into regions rich in these necessary minerals, was the basis for a self-generating cyclic process (which may in part explain subsequent expansion into Germania and Britain to access this mineral wealth, and which may here be seen reflected in helmet production). Paddock (1985, 145) then identified a break in production and possible stockpiling of equipment between the death of Caesar (in 44 BC) and the defeat of M. Antonius (in 31 BC), with Augustus introducing further reforms to the military and reducing the number of legions.

After a short period of relative peace, around the end of the first century BC and the start of the first century AD, production then recommenced with re-equipping of the legions in advance of the Germanic campaigns. Around this time, new features appear to have been introduced to the military assemblage, possibly in preparation for changing weaponry and tactics of the new opponents. During the Republican (and pre-Republican) period, Rome's enemies had been similarly equipped, using similar fighting styles and tactics. When confronted with different styles or equipment that proved more effective than their own, the Romans quickly assimilated and adapted the best features into their own assemblage and methodology (as witnessed in the movement towards long, oval *scuta*, projectile weapons and manipular formation fighting). Even the Carthaginian armies of the Punic Wars were seen to have been similarly equipped, as obviously would combatants of the Social and Civil Wars of the first century BC.

These non-Roman opponents now used a different weaponry and fighting style, using long slashing and hacking swords and axes in open-formation fighting, with combatants acting as individuals in guerrilla-style skirmishes, rather than as a solid body of men in regulated standing battles. Further, many of these conflicts were taking place in close and restricted woodland locations or in hilly regions, where the previous Roman strengths of block formations could not be applied and where opponents could use the opportunities for showering from above with heavy objects and projectiles.

To combat these new threats, helmet design (unchanged for centuries) can be seen to commence a developmental progression with the introduction of peaks and brow bands to strengthen the helmet bowl, stepping and lengthening of the occipital regions (with ridged 'crumple zones') to better protect the back of the head (and minimise dislodging), and gradual widening and sloping of neck guards (to protect the neck and shoulder areas, by deflecting slashing and hacking blows away from the body; Russell-Robinson, 1975, 26). At the same time, ear guards also began to appear (firstly by simple flanging out directly from the bowl, and later by addition of larger, applied ear guards), and cheek pieces are improved (with stronger hinges, more secure, close fastening and, on Gallic examples, with outwardly turned throat flanges).

This, then, was the atmosphere of innovation and changing armour design which coincides with the earliest appearance of the segmented plate armour usually associated with the typical Roman legionary of the first century AD, the *lorica segmentata*. Segmented plate arm and leg protection is known from contexts of Eastern peoples, as reflected in depictions of Sarmatian horsemen, although the trend in Roman armour assemblage towards the use of iron appears to derive from the influence of Gallic craftsmen. Armour types also continued to adapt and develop, probably again in answer to changing opposition as the boundaries of the Empire expanded.

Initially in the first century AD, body shape is seen to be greatly reduced, shortening to hip length and losing the additional shoulder doubling The reduced-size cuirasses would also have been quicker and cheaper to produce, which may have been a deciding factor at times of financial crisis, or where large bodies of men were required to be mobilised at short notice (possibly reflected in the poor-quality, mass-produced iron helmets of Imperial Italic type C, as found, for example, in the River Po at Cremona, associated with the Civil Wars of AD 69; Russell-Robinson, 1975, 67).

Again, perhaps in answer to changing tactics and weaponry (with actions in the East against slashing weapons delivered from horseback), the shape of both infantry and cavalry body armour changes once more. From the third century, mail and scale cuirasses are seen to lengthen, becoming looser-fitting and developing sleeves of varying lengths. Helmets at this time continue to adapt, developing still larger neck guards, ear guards and cheek pieces to protect against slashing attack from long cavalry swords; later still, strengthening crossbars were added to the helmet bowl to guard against overhead assault.

CLASSIFICATION

This helmet study initially arose out of an apparent confusion of two different methods of identification. One was a highly simplified Continental system based on the find locations of a few exemplars, and the other was devised by H. Russell-Robinson (1975), whereby known helmet finds were separated into a wide range of categories and subcategories based on his perceived origin of manufacture and developmental progression of component and decorative features. The problems with these dual systems derived from the overly simplistic nature of the Continental system, in that its categorisations were rather too bland for any accurate use, and the fact that the Russell-Robinson system was overly categorised, with the work formulating the categories too long out of print and virtually unobtainable.

To counter the gulf between these two systems, whereby some finds may have featured twice due to confusion of their descriptions, a list of all known helmets was commenced, identifying all entries under both systems for comparison. The starting point for this study was logically based on the Russell-Robinson work (1975), which defined his categorisation, matching these finds in subsequent works to their Continental typologies (the Russell-Robinson work being particularly heavily weighted towards helmets). However, once the research was underway, with the addition of subsequent finds and helmets in private collections, the list grew exponentially, particularly with information drawn from the internet and contributions from participation of enthusiasts on specialist internet forums (a research medium of which Russell-Robinson could not have made use in his lifetime). This constantly expanding and incomplete list is included as a gazetteer in Appendix IV, although it was only accurate at the date of compilation and will continue to expand as further examples come to light in the years to come.

What is immediately clear, however, from the material collated, is that there exists a wealth of helmets greatly in excess of those known to Russell-Robinson, many of which do not fit neatly into any of his defined categories. Criticisms of Russell-Robinson have been that his system has attempted to categorise helmets by his perceived view of place of origin, based on features which he identified as 'Italic' or 'Gallic' in origin. This led to a range of subcategories of helmets which were almost identical, their entry into separate categories being based on often almost indistinguishable, minor differences. If we were to follow this lead, then almost every one of the additional helmets on the list would differ slightly from Russell-Robinson's exemplars, meriting the addition of yet more subcategories. Clearly this would be counterproductive, but it serves to highlight the problem of an overemphasised reliance on categorisation and explains the preference of some for the Continental system. However, this great variety of styles and features does suggest that we should view helmet production in a different light.

If we had had the opportunity to view a body of Roman soldiers at any given time, it is probably unlikely that all would have been similarly equipped, although the general style of equipment may have been overall identifiably 'Roman'. Where a body of men had been equipped by the state at short notice (perhaps in the raising of a new legion, or re-equipping men following a campaign), with this equipment perhaps all sourced from one location or region (perhaps from state *fabricae*), then these men may have been similarly equipped.

However, within this unit there may also have existed men with equipment still serviceable from previous campaigns and passed down from previous owners, produced by different armourers at different workshops. Within this body of men there may also have been time-served soldiers who had invested some of their own savings from many years of service in the purchase of better-quality equipment purchased privately from independent craftsmen.

Although there does appear to be a general trend towards a developmental progression of certain features (such as a deepening of the occipital region, widening of the neck guards, elaboration of ear, cheek and throat protection, and the strengthening of helmet bowls, first with brow bands and peaks, and later with cross-strengthening bars), perhaps in answer to new enemies and new fighting techniques, we should also acknowledge a wide range of differences attributable to the work of different armourers and workshops. We would anticipate a wide range of styles associated with a large number of independent individual craftsmen during the earlier Republican period, when each soldier was required to source his own equipment prior to each campaign (although the reality shows a close similarity of styles, in the widespread adoption of the Montefortino helmet, albeit with individuality expressed in the quality of work and level of decoration).

With the transition towards Empire, the work of Paddock (1985) then suggested a movement towards mass production and possibly state-promoted, if not state-controlled, factory sites. The work of James (1988) in his study of the *fabricae* of the later Empire listed in the *Notitia Dignitatum* (Anon.) similarly suggested a number of specialist *fabricae* which may have had specific importance in helmet production. It would not, then, be unreasonable to anticipate a variety of stylistic features attributable to these workshops, in addition to those of individual craftsmen in private workshops who undoubtedly operated outside of the regular supply network, providing the better-quality bespoke items for private commissions.

APPENDIX I

THE ORIGINS AND DEVELOPMENT OF THE ROMAN ARMY

THE 'ANCIENT' PERIOD AND EMERGENCE OF THE REPUBLIC

The early period of Rome's history, from its almost mythical foundation by Romulus, supposedly on 21 April in 753 BC (or 748 BC according to Fabius Pictus), is not well documented, their known written history only commencing towards the end of the third century BC.

Initially Rome was only one of a number of frequently warring small communities of indigenous, Latin-speaking peoples of the Italic peninsula, sharing a common language, similar material culture and religion, and some common sanctuaries (Burns, 2003, 62–63; Rich, 2007, 8; Le Glay *et al.*, 2005, 1–7). Of these, their immediate neighbours were the *Sabines*, to the north-east; the *Aequi*, to the east; *Latium*, to the south; the *Volsci*, further south (Rich reported some controversy surrounding the first appearance of the *Volsci* in the Italic peninsula; traditionally they were already in the area during the 'Royal' period, but modern scholars propose an 'invasion' in the early fifth century BC, although there is no reference to support this in the classical sources; 2007, 10); and the *Hernici*, further south-east. Yet further south and into Sicily were Hellenised, former Greek colonies, which Polybius called '*Magna Graecia*', and Cicero described as 'the old Italian Greece, that used to be called Great', who funnelled Greek and Etruscan artistic and cultural influence into the Italic mainland through trading activities (Le Glay *et al.*, 2005, 14).

Their most immediate neighbour to the north (with Gallic tribes still further north), the Etruscans, were more technologically advanced (with systems of drainage and irrigation to improve crop yields; mining of tin, copper and iron; and craftsmen skilled in the production of tools and armaments, which display strong Greek stylistic influences), with a more highly developed political structure (which better fits the finer definitions of a 'state'). They had a patrician-led society, with rural plebeians and a huge servile class, split into a federation of twelve states, under the control of elected magistrates, but with the option to elect a single leader should events dictate the need. In contrast to their neighbours (who at that time were still living a simple, pastoral existence in village communities of small huts), they lived in cities with substantial stone buildings and temples, and public spaces. They used a different language but shared some similarities of culture and religion, with a pantheon of gods similar to that of the Greeks, and prototype to the later Roman (Le Glay *et al.*, 2005, 9).

The earliest habitation at Rome dates from around 1000 BC, developing gradually by the eighth century BC into a series of small clusters of huts on each of the seven hills (Le Glay *et al.*, 2005, 22). In March and October of each year, rituals marked the opening and closure of a campaign season of inter-community warfare throughout the Italic peninsula, which Rich (2007, 10) suggested were for the purpose of territorial expansion (although disputing their frequency), while Burns (2003, 62–63) described these as raids and skirmishes carried out by aristocratic warrior bands, fighting for personal glory and booty, in the best 'Homeric' tradition.

The Etruscans similarly appear to have embarked on a policy of expansionism, leading by the sixth century BC to Etruscan rule in Rome, possibly as a result of trade, intermarriage of dynasties or force. Traditionally the last three 'kings' of Rome were formed from this new 'Etruscan' dynasty (Tarquin the Elder, Servius Tullius and Tarquin the Proud, or Tarquinius Superbus), although their existence is disputed, their names possibly being no more than symbolic of an Etruscan presence, influence and domination. Le Glay *et al.* (2005, 24), however, suggested that this point in time should be better considered as the 'true foundation' of Rome, as the Etruscan influence stimulated a series of innovations (including improved water supply and drainage, substantial new public buildings and defensive walls).

Weapons and armour are found as grave goods throughout Italy from around 1000 BC (bronze armour and iron weapons), but as its use does not seem to be widespread, appearing to be mostly high-status and for display purposes, we cannot be sure how widely it was used, nor can we adduce any information about fighting styles or battle formations (Rich, 2007, 17). It is known that a new form of armour and battle formation was introduced in Greece from the eighth century BC (the hoplite phalanx of heavily armoured soldiers), and from around 650 BC similar panoplies are found in Etruscan contexts, with Rome and other Latin regions following soon after. The hoplite soldier was equipped with bronze helmet, cuirass and greaves covering his lower legs. He carried a spear (around 2.45 m long), a circular shield (around 90 cm diameter), known as a *hoplon*, and a short slashing or thrusting sword. They fought in close formation, each man protecting the right side of his neighbour, in rows between eight and forty men deep (Goldsworthy, 2003, 22).

However, Rich (2007, 18) cited Van Wees (2004) when he disputed that this new panoply would necessarily have led to a new style of fighting. Although in Greek use the phalanx line-up would have included men of all classes fighting together on an equal basis, aristocratic and middle-class, he believes that the same may not be the case in Etruria, where the society was dominated by an aristocratic elite (*gentes*). Citing hoplite equipment found alongside traditional Etruscan weapons, he suggests that the new equipment could have been adopted without necessarily also adopting the close-formation phalanx, continuing instead to fight in more flexible formations, but with a mixture of heavily and lightly armed troops.

THE EARLY REPUBLIC

The army in the earliest stages of the Republic was quite different to that at the time of its transition into Empire. As with any human-based system, it evolved over time, reflecting the evolution of the society that it protected. It was a citizen militia, recruited and organised along parallel lines to the political infrastructure, through the *Comitia centuriata* voting assembly, categorising the available manpower into classes according to wealth and ability to provide equipment (see Table 10).

The complexity of the initial incarnation of this 'Servian' system has been disputed. Livy (1.43) described a system of five classes of varying levels of equipment, which may represent its much later structure, whereas modern historians, including Keppie (1984, 17), suggest that its earliest form may have comprised one single *classis*. By the start of the ten-year war with *Veii* (406 BC), it is believed that the second and third classes of less wealthy men were added, when the army increased from 4,000 to 6,000 men, not all of whom could afford the full hoplite panoply. Keppie (1984, 18) suggests that the long Italic shield may have been introduced at this point to compensate for the reduced level of armour. Also around this time, the cavalry may have enlarged from six to eighteen centuries, with the state providing and maintaining horse and equipment for the less wealthy additional recruits (Keppie, 1984, 18).

The Gallic incursions at the end of the fourth century BC introduced the Roman army to an enemy fighting in more flexible, open formations against which their rigid phalanxes struggled. It is suggested that it was at this time, in answer to this open enemy battle formation, that the Romans introduced the looser, manipular formation, whereby the body of men was broken up into maniples (or 'handfuls'), a change which has been attributed to

Camillus, the commander noted for his success in both the *Veii* campaigns and in countering the Gallic threat (Keppie, 1984, 19).

During the course of the next fifty years, possibly in answer to some less than successful campaigns, gradually the smaller tactical units (maniples) became more widely used. At the same time some changes to the internal command structure were also evident. By 320 BC the army was split into two legions, with six military tribunes assigned three to each legion. By 311 BC, however, Livy (9.30.3) reports that military tribunes had increased to sixteen, with four to each of four legions (the army having therefore doubled in size), with two of the legions commanded by each of the two consuls (Forsythe, 2007, 24–42). Despite continued expansionist campaigns over the next 150 years (the *ager Romanus* expanding from 1902 sq. km in 338 BC to 26,805 sq. km by 264 BC) Polybius (6.19–29) reports that the size of the army remained steady at four legions.

In the new manipular formation, centuries of infantry, around sixty men in each, were organised into thirty blocks (or maniples) per legion, forming in battle three rows with gaps between (the *triplex acies*). At the rear, ten maniples containing one century each were formed of the *triarii*, the oldest and most experienced men. In front of these were two rows of ten maniples, two centuries in each – in the middle row the *principes* (men in their prime, aged twenty to thirty years), and at the front the *hastati*, drawn from the youngest men. All would wear the standard legionary kit of helmet, bronze cuirass and greaves. When deployed, the legion would be flanked by *alae*, or wings, of allied soldiers recruited from among the other Latin peoples, subdivided into cohorts of 400 to 600 men, along with two units of cavalry, one at each end. In front, in later periods, a row of *velites* provided a lightly armed protective screen, formed from those who could only afford the very least equipment (of helmet, shield and a bundle of light javelins) and those men too young to fight in the main line (Goldsworthy, 2003, 27; Campbell, 2000, 4; Polybius, 6.19–26; Russell-Robinson, 1975, 137). Keppie (1984, 33) linked the creation of these *velites* (or light 'skirmishers') around 211 BC (according to reports by Livy) to a reduction in minimum census requirement in 214 BC, which brought into the levy men who could only afford the bare minimum of equipment.

THE LATER REPUBLIC

With the prolonged campaigns of the Punic Wars and soldiers remaining in the army longer, the quality of manpower changed during the period. The longer-serving army became more efficient, better trained with improved tactics, but kept men away from their other livelihoods and family estates, so leading to dissent over the levy. Recruitment became difficult, as men who had already served were reluctant to participate in second campaigns.

After the Battle of Cannae against Hannibal in 216 BC a new army was needed at short notice, but there was neither manpower nor finances available to provide this. Polybius (6.23.15; 39.15) related how many of the men in the five classes (*assidui*) could no longer equip themselves. Years of continuous campaigns had drained resources, with some of the lower classes (impoverished and dispossessed of their land to the benefit of the more wealthy) now unable to meet the property requirements, decreasing the numbers eligible for military service.

To meet this shortfall, changes were instigated lowering the age of recruits and offering citizenship to slaves willing to volunteer (Cottrell, 1992, 153). New fiscal policies were introduced to equip this new army unable to supply their own kit, along with reuse of weapons and armour taken as 'spoils of war' stored on temple walls (Cary & Scullard, 1979, 130).

A progression of political and social reforms were introduced in the following years, to address problems of discipline and training within the legions and to increase numbers of citizens eligible for service, some with varying levels of success. It was therefore an understandable progression to the later reforms credited to Gaius Marius in 107 BC, in answer to the demands of the Jugurthine War, whereby he called for additional volunteers from the *capite censi* (who would be equipped at the state's expense), in addition to many time-served veterans (Scullard, 1970, 52–9).

While the Jugurthine problem was being resolved in North Africa, a new problem arose on the northern frontier, with threatened incursions by Celtic tribes, the *Cimbri* and the *Teutones*. Once these threats from Gallic/Celtic incursions were resolved, the whole of the Italian peninsula came under Roman control. The divisions between Latin and Roman citizen then became less defined, with many Italian communities wanting equality and full citizenship rights, leading to the subsequent Social War of 91–87 BC, and the Senate eventually conceding citizenship to all states south of the River Po which had remained loyal (Campbell, 2000, 7; Keppie, 1984, 62).

In addition to modifications to equipment, improved training, discipline and morale (introducing gladiator-style training, and use of the silver eagle standard, or *aquila*, as a rallying symbol; Pliny, *Hist. Nat.*, 10.16), and requiring the soldiers to carry most of their own equipment (leading to the description of *muli Mariani*, or 'Marius' Mules'), Marius was credited with initiating a change to cohortal formation, although similar formations had been tested by his predecessors. Polybius (11.23.1; 11.33.1) related that the new cohort system had been first used by Scipio in Spain during the Hannibalic War (at the Battle of Ilipa, in 206 BC), and Livy reports its later use during the war in Spain, in 210–195 BC. Aemilius Paulus is also credited with having used a more flexible variant of the standard maniples at the Battle of Pydna in 168 BC, breaking the rigid three battle lines into little squares (Cary & Scullard, 1979, 159).

The pre-Marian army had been formed into legions of around 4,000 men, organised into centuries of sixty men, forming three battle lines (the *triplex acies*), split into maniples (blocks of 120 men, or two centuries; Russell-Robinson, 1975, 137; Caesar, *Bell. Gall*, 1.24.2). It has been proposed that Marius restructured this system, replacing the maniples with the more flexible cohorts, ten per legion, each divided into six centuries of eighty men (a cohort being made up of three maniples of two centuries each), with each century commanded by a centurion, or *pilus prior* (the first cohort being larger than the others). Overall, with the inclusion of legionary cavalry, the legion would then have consisted of over 5,000 men (Campbell, 2000, 6).

As a consequence of the Social War (91–87 BC), whereby many Italian communities achieved equality and full citizenship rights, the *alae sociorum* ceased to exist. Recruits were now drawn from all Italy (all now being citizens and therefore entitled to legionary status). Many of those left homeless by the wars were recruited into the army (which from this point never numbered less than fourteen legions), with their equipment costs by necessity being borne by the treasury (Keppie, 1984, 69). In their place, auxiliary 'specialist' forces came to be provided by client kings. For example, Balearic slingers and Cretan archers and, by the first century, Numidian, Spanish and Gallic units replaced the Roman and Italian cavalry. However, organised, permanent, reliable auxiliaries were not found until the Imperial period (Cagniart, 2007, 88).

Whereas in the earliest periods the Roman army was raised afresh for each annual campaign season, by the later Republican period it served an entirely different function. Keppie (1984, 77) suggested that two separate functions can be identified, describing two distinct types of army: 'standing' and 'emergency'. The 'standing' army served for long periods as garrisons in the provinces, whereas the 'emergency' army was levied for a specific campaign (as with the earliest armies), at the end of which its men would be released with accumulated 'booty' and possibly additional rewards. The number of legions (and of course the number of men serving within them) fluctuated over time. By the time of the First Punic War there were still only four to five legions, but these were beginning to be retained in service (and so retaining their identification numbering), not being disbanded at the end of the season. By the Second Punic War, fourteen more legions were added: seven in 217 BC and a further seven in 216 BC. This increased further to twenty legions by 203 BC, reducing to sixteen legions by the end of the war in 201 BC, and further reduced to six legions for peacetime (Keppie, 1984, 97–100).

By the late Republican period, legions were using identifying numbers ranging from I to XVIII. Of these, numbers I to IV were still allocated to the consuls. However, with the exception of these consular legions, a system of clockwise numbering appears to have been used for the remaining legions, V for the legion in Spain, VII, VIII, IX, X in Transalpine and Cisalpine Gaul, with higher numbers for Macedonia and the East, and XVIII in Cilicia, in 56–54 BC (Keppie, 1984, 97–100).

TRANSITION TO EMPIRE – CHANGES TO THE LEGIONS UNDER THE TRIUMVIRATES

The First Triumvirate of Pompey the Great, Crassus and Julius Caesar, formed in 59 BC, under pressure to reward time-served army veterans with land, led to a restructuring and a further increase in the legions (Keppie, 1984, 71; Broadhead, 2007, 157–160).

With Crassus campaigning in Parthia, Pompey in Spain and Caesar in Gaul, existing legions were divided between them, the identification numbering becoming more complicated following Caesar's Gallic Wars and subsequent Civil Wars. In 58 BC, as proconsul in Gaul, Caesar had four legions under his command (VII to X). To these he added a further four (XI to XIV) to fight the *Helvetii* and the *Belgae* of north-eastern Gaul, adding another (XV) in 53 BC, leaving him in control of nine legions (Keppie, 1984, 97–100).

After the death of Crassus in 52 BC, a breakdown between Pompey and Caesar led to the Civil Wars from 50 BC, when Caesar famously crossed the Rubicon with *legio* XIII, increasing his army to twelve legions the following year (Keppie, 1984, 97–100). Caesar then continued to raise more legions, adding numbers up to XXX (the latter at Mutina), including his famous *legio* V *Alaudae*, the 'Larks', levied in Cisalpine Gaul. The 'Larks' were unusual in that they were the first legion to be formed from men born outside Italy. Caesar had formed a militia of twenty-two cohorts from the native population of Transalpina in late 52 BC to defend its northern borders. These, Keppie (1984, 98) proposed, then formed the basis of the V *Alaudae*, the legion then being supplemented by yearly drafts from Cisalpina.

By the Battle of Pharsalus in 48 BC, Caesar raised yet more legions (four new numbers, I to IV, as these traditionally were commanded by the consul) and others, bringing the full sequence (I to XXXIII) under his command. After the battle, further regrouping of Pompey's surviving troops added numbers XXXIV to XXXVII (Keppie, 1984, 103–106).

Between 47 and 44 BC, legions VI to XIV were retired from service as time-served (six years' service being expected at that time), but after Caesar's death in 44 BC some of these were reformed. On Caesar's death, Rome's (and Caesar's) wealth was controlled by Mark Antony. However, Caesar had made his nephew, G. Octavius (Octavian, born 63 BC), his protégé and his heir. Initially the two rivals campaigned against each other, but then joined forces against Caesar's assassins, forming a second triumvirate with Lepidus (Lepidus in the east, Octavian in the west, and Antony in the south/Egypt), Antony forming an alliance with Cleopatra during his campaigns to Egypt. To provide manpower for these campaigns, Keppie (1984, 132–5) reported that Octavian reformed Caesar's 'retired' legions, VII and VIII; in Campania, V *Alaudae* was regrouped by Antony, and legions VI and X were re-established by Lepidus. The fate of the remaining legions that had been disbanded (from VI to XIV) remains hazy. Keppie (*ibid.*) suggested that some may have been with Antony (including XII *Antiqua*), but others may not have been reformed at all (e.g. XI, XII and XIV).

As with the previous Triumvirate, however, relations soon broke down, Antony depriving Lepidus of his provinces (accusing him of collusion with an enemy, Sextus Pompey). With division between Antony and Octavian, the remaining legions were not immediately renumbered after Philippi (42 BC), but later many time-served men were released, and, while Antony retained some of Caesar's old legions (including V *Alaudae*, VI *Ferrata*, X *Equestris*, XII *Fulminata*, and III *Gallica*), Octavian regrouped the remainder into eleven legions, adding further legions between 42–32 BC to fill out numbers. Some legion numbers therefore came to be duplicated with those commanded by Antony (new V *Macedonica*, VI *Victrix* and X *Fretensis*; Keppie, 1984, 132–5).

After Actium, the victorious Octavius (now renamed Augustus) then 'retired' 100,000 men from the disbanded legions (who were all set up with gratuities and land provided by the state, in veteran colonies either in Italy or in the provinces), adding the Antony legions to his own, keeping their existing numbers (with duplications). These were then identified by 'names', some legions being given the name *Gemina* (twin), for example the X *Gemina*. Retaining eighteen legions, he then added eight more (in AD 6) and another two (in AD 9), leaving a total of twenty-eight legions, although legions XVII to XIX were lost on the lower Rhine in AD 9 and were not replaced, these being the three 'lost' legions of Varus (Keppie, 1984, 132–5).

THE *AUXILIA*

Following Caesar's model, Augustus formed more permanent auxiliary units of specialist troops to support the legions. These comprised cavalry, archers, slingers and specialist light infantry troops. The majority of these units were formed up under the command of their own chieftains. They wore native dress, used their own indigenous equipment, and fought using their own specialist weaponry.

However, following a number of rebellions by auxiliary troops – including the Pannonian Revolt, AD 6–9; the German revolt of the *Cherusci* under the command of Arminius, AD 9; the Thracian revolt of AD 46 (Luttwark, 1999, 13–20); and particularly the rebellion of Batavians under the command of Julius Civilis, AD 69 (Cary & Scullard, 1979, 418–19, 509) – all auxiliary units were disbanded shortly after the time of Nero. They were then reformed, no longer under the command of their own chieftains but to be commanded by a Roman tribune, aided by two prefects, and equipped with Roman-style equipment (helmets and mail or scale cuirasses). The specialist troops (such as the archers) retained their own native weaponry (where it was without Roman equivalent), but the infantry were equipped with a Roman-style short sword and spear (*gladius* and *hasta*), and the cavalry equipped with Roman-style lance or spear (*hasta*), along with either the long cavalry sword (*spatha*) or the alternate 'Spanish' sword, the *falcatta* (Webster, 1998, 141–55).

The overall identity of these troops had also changed over time by the second century AD. Initially these had been non-Roman, provincial troops of distinct ethnic origins. However, with units based away from their homeland, and fresh recruitment to the units made in other provinces, their ethnic identity became diluted. Some individuals were given citizenship on retirement (their sons then joining the units later with citizen status). There were also incidences of citizens choosing to join these units to serve as auxiliaries, rather than as legionaries. Furthermore, some whole units had been granted citizenship en masse as recognition of actions on campaign, as for example with the *cohors* I *Lepidiana equitata civium Romanorum* (Gilliver, 2007, 194).

The changes to the regular auxiliary units also forced the Roman army to introduce different types of auxiliary support, which Gilliver (2007, 195) described as the 'irregular' ethnic units of *numeri* and *nationes* (the most famous of these being the Palmyrian archers, used for the first time in Judea in AD 70–71; Southern, 1988, 89–92). Again, these were native troops, fighting in their own clothing with their own specialist weapons, their lower commanding officers drawn from their own chieftains but with an overall commander who was Roman. They differed from the standard auxiliary units in that they were units of non-Romans, often supplied by 'client' leaders, whose service was 'given' for short periods to an individual, their 'patron'. Their loyalty, therefore, was not primarily to Rome but to this individual 'patron' commanding the army.

Class	Property (asses)	Equipment	Centuries		
			Juniores	Seniores	Total
I	100,000	Helmet, round shield, greaves, cuirass, spear, sword	40	40	80
II	75,000	Helmet, oblong shield, greaves, spear, sword	10	10	20
III	50,000	Helmet, oblong shield, spear, sword	10	10	20
IV	25,000	(Oblong shield in Livy), spear, javelin	10	10	20
V	11,000	Sling, stones, (javelin)	15	15	30
Infantry total					170

Table 10. The infantry in the Servian system.

APPENDIX II

EQUIPMENT AND *FABRICAE*

THE EVOLUTION OF THE EQUIPMENT PANOPLY

There are numerous examples throughout the history of the Roman army whereby the valued qualities of an enemy's equipment and tactics were observed, then assimilated into their own, in order to use these against them. Rawlings (2007, 54), however, considered this to be part of a more complex process of military interaction and interchange throughout Italy and the Mediterranean, as evidenced in tomb paintings and pottery decoration.

In the fourth century BC the most common military equipment used was the 'hoplite panoply', although with some regional variation, adapted to local conditions and preferences. These were not exclusively used in hoplite battle formation, but were combined with the use of large thrusting, stabbing blades and light throwing javelins, which may indicate the use of more open formations (Rawlings, 2007, 45–62). By the fourth and third centuries BC some experimental use of '*proto-pila*' has been proposed, although Rawlings (*ibid.*) acknowledged the possibility that the standard second-century BC *pilum* may have developed from observation of equipment used by third-century BC Spanish and Celtiberian Carthaginian mercenaries.

It may have also been about this time that the round shield was phased out in favour of the long, oval *scutum* (as added protection for those soldiers equipped with less armour), with lighter javelins replacing the heavy lance (Feugère, 2002, 38). Diodorus (23.2) also considered the principle change of this period to be the introduction of the oval shield (*scutum*), which had been popular with the Gauls of northern Italy and is also seen on southern Italian vase and tomb paintings as an alternative to the hoplite circular shield.

Diodorus (23.2) at this time attributed a change from phalanx to manipular formation, although modern sources disagree on when this change was made. Rawlings (2007, 55), for example, considered the transition to be gradual, with the *triarii* of the second century BC still operating in a similar way to the hoplite phalanx. He also observed that Hellenistic armies of the later fourth century BC were beginning to use oval shields (known as *thyreos*), with groups of infantry called *thyreaphoroi* described in the third century by Plutarch (*Philip*, 9.1–2), who told of third-century BC Achaeans using *thyreos* and light spears. However, these were easily forced back and scattered in close-quarter melees, apparently because they still used the new equipment with the old phalanx formation, rather than in more flexible maniples.

In contrast, Rawlings (2007, 57) saw the Roman soldier's oath (*coniuriato*) not to flee or break ranks as indicative of their use of more flexible battle formation, rather than the rigid phalanx battle order, citing Livy (22.38.2–5), who noted the exemption for soldiers to leave their lines in order to 'to recover or fetch a weapon, save a friend or strike an enemy'. This would then permit troops fighting in small units to break lines periodically to collect scattered javelins for reuse, for example as described by Livy (10. 29.6) at the Battle of Sentium against the Gauls (Rawlings, 2007, 57).

Livy (8.8.9–13) also described the use of manipular formation in 338 BC, although this is not the same as Polybius' description from the second century BC, but indicates only the third line of troops (*triarii*) used javelins (*hastae*). Hoyos (2007, 69) interpreted this to suggest that the remaining two lines of heavy infantry must therefore have used *pilum* and *gladius*. Both Livy (31.34.4) and Polybius (6.23.6) described a 'Spanish' short sword which may have been the *gladius*, noting that both pieces of equipment and manipular array were in standard use by Polybius' accounts of battles against the Gauls in 225 and 223 BC (Polybius, 2.30.8, 33.4.6).

Polybius further described the differences of equipment used at that time by the different ranks within the battle formation, denoting the different functions served. For example, the *velites* were equipped with sword, javelin and a small, round shield (*parma*), better suited to light skirmish actions. The *hastatae* and *principes*, in contrast, used the oval *scutum* and *gladius*, along with two *pila* (one heavy and one light). Keppie (1984, 35) considered the *gladius* may have been adopted from Spanish auxiliaries serving with Hannibal, who conversely had also adopted Roman equipment and assimilated Roman fighting techniques for his own troops.

Less wealthy soldiers at this time would have worn a simple plate strapped to the chest, although the older, more experienced and wealthier men would have worn more substantial protection, possibly by this time a mail cuirass, or *lorica hamata* (as described by Polybius; 6. 23). This could perhaps have been combined with shoulder doubling for added protection, as seen on the Altar of Ahenobarbus (Fig. 5), although this example dates to the first century BC. This tradition appears to have been adopted from Gallic tribes of northern Italy, along with the tradition for Montefortino-type helmets (Burns, 2003, 71).

In contrast to the Roman military system, the opposing Carthaginians at this time did not use armies of temporary citizen militia. Their army was made up of contingents who owed loyalty to a particular commander, but who did not always cooperate readily with different leaders, leading on occasions to 'infighting', according to Polybius. They were professional soldiers, hired as mercenaries, of varying nationalities, originating from Africa and parts of Europe, including Libyan heavy cavalry, Numidian light cavalry and infantry from Spain and Gallic tribes of northern Italy. Their equipment would in many respects be similar to that of the Romans, the mail cuirasses appearing to be of Gallic origin, as are the Montefortino helmets. Both armour types originated from regions known to have supplied Carthaginian mercenaries, as well as their equipment, as suggested by finds of Montefortino-type helmets from Villaricos, in Almeria, which was reputedly an important recruiting centre for Punic generals (Quesada Sanz, 1997, 155).

Polybius, in describing the recruitment process of the Roman army, related that all eligible men of military age (seventeen to forty-six years) were normally called to the Capitol in Rome, from whom the best candidates (*dilectus*) were selected. These recruits were then dismissed to arm themselves and regroup elsewhere. Paddock suggested that the recruits would therefore either equip themselves prior to departure, or close to this assembly point, possibly being buried with these arms after their eventual return home years later. He cited as evidence helmets found from fourth- and third-century BC grave contexts in Perugia, Etruria, which he believed to be the location of a manufacturing centre (Paddock, 1985, 143).

With the change to the cohortal system, the spear fell out of general use (as less suited to the cohort formation), being replaced with a more standardised weapon assemblage of javelin (*pilum*), short sword (*gladius hispaniensis*) and dagger (*pugio*):

The *pilum* was designed to penetrate an opponent's shield, then break or bend so that it could not be thrown back;

The *gladius* was a short (30-inch or 75 cm) slashing sword, with its weight balanced at one-third from its tip;

The *pugio* was a short dagger, carried on the belt, which appears to have served a more utilitarian purpose than for combat (in re-enactment contexts being found to present more danger to the bearer than an opponent, from its tendency to 'accidentally' fall out with alarming regularity, with the result that many 'owners' have them permanently fixed into their sheaths);

The helmet (*casis*) provided unobstructed vision and hearing, permitting the wearer to see or hear orders (by *signa* or *cornu* respectively);

The *scutum* was a curved, oval shield formed from two or three layers of plywood, with covering of calfskin, 4 feet by 2.5 feet (120 cm by 75 cm) as an average size, with bronze or iron edge binding, central spine (*spina*) and an iron or copper alloy boss (*umbo*).

Polybius (6.39.15) related that it became necessary for the state to buy equipment for the poorer *assidui*, who were now admitted following further relaxations of the property requirements. The soldiers did not receive this equipment free of charge, however, but were required to reimburse the state for its cost in instalments deducted from their *stipendium*. In 123 BC, Gaius Gracchus tried to make it illegal to make deductions for food, clothes or equipment (Plutarch, *C. Gracchus*, 5.1), but was unsuccessful and the deductions continued, as described by Tacitus in AD 14 (*Ann.* 1.17.6). Livy related how this equipment was originally sourced from private manufacturers (22.57.11), with a further reference provided by Cicero (*Rab. Perd.*, 20), to state-owned armouries and arsenals in 100 BC.

Marius instituted an overall revision of military equipment, standardising and improving armour and weapons, ensuring that all men received mail armour, a standard sword and long javelin (*pilum*). He is also credited with the redesign of the *pilum*. Unchanged for centuries, it was now designed to bend on impact to prevent reuse by an enemy. Marius designed a wooden peg to secure the head to the shaft, which would then snap on impact. The *pilum* could still not be reused by an enemy during the course of a battle, but could later be retrieved after the conflict and quickly repaired by replacement of the wooden peg (Scullard, 1970, 58–9; Campbell, 2000, 6).

Although Marius' reforms may have had a positive effect on the organisation and efficiency of the army, the same cannot be said for the quality of its equipment. While the individual soldier had provided his own equipment, and while membership of the army was restricted to the more affluent members of society, the quality of their equipment remained high, in that they could afford the work of trained craftsmen, producing individual pieces to order. With the admittance of the poorer classes, who had to be equipped by the state, along with the necessity to have to kit out large numbers of men at short notice, quality suffered with the economies of bulk buying. This is particularly noticeable in the helmets produced at this time, with the known examples crudely formed, with minimal decoration, and even on occasions not fully finished off, or left rough from the raising process, not all of the surface hammer marks being planished off (Paddock, 1985, 144).

This decline in quality became more marked in the ensuing Social War of 91–87 BC and the subsequent Civil Wars, the former event providing more potential recruits, with the relaxation of citizenship to include those from all neighbouring Italian states south of the River Po (Campbell, 2000, 7).

In 49 BC, Caesar increased his army to twelve legions. Where previously soldiers had been paid barely sufficient to cover the cost of food, he doubled their pay, encouraging a greater volume of volunteer 'professional' soldiers from the lower social classes. With the death of Caesar in 44 BC, until Octavian's defeat of Mark Antony in 31 BC, military growth slowed. Existing equipment appears to have been stockpiled or remained in service for long periods, and demand fell for new equipment, with little evidence for the recycling or manufacture of new goods and with few innovations introduced to the equipment assemblage. The 'retiring' 100,000 men from the disbanded legions were all set up with gratuities and land provided by the state, in veteran colonies either in Italy or in the provinces, setting a precedent for army retirement policies (Scullard, 1970, 216).

The next major reorganisation of the army by Augustus, with his reforms of 27 BC, finally changed the 'Republican' army into the 'Imperial' army. Membership of the army was no longer seen as a disruption, instead becoming a career of choice, with citizens serving a minimum of sixteen years. The primary purpose of the army had changed, however; it was not employed in the great wars of conquest, as during the Republic, but in low-profit police actions in defence of the Empire. When production recommenced, evidence of new methods of mass production began to appear, such as spinning of helmets (Paddock, 1985, 148).

With the Augustan reforms, the Roman army became a true 'professional' army for the new Empire. Any future changes to equipment and fighting methods were event-driven in response to changing enemies and their chosen weapon types.

THE MANUFACTURE AND PRODUCTION OF ROMAN MILITARY EQUIPMENT FROM PRIVATE COMMISSIONS TO STATE ARMOURIES (*FABRICAE*)

Up until the later stages of the Republican period, armour was commissioned by the individual. This was then sourced from independent craftsmen, who operated from small-scale workshops, following their own traditional designs. As the boundaries of property ownership relaxed and less wealthy individuals increasingly participated in military duties, they were unable to meet the full cost of armour and weaponry provision personally (Polybius, 6.39.15). The state was therefore required initially to meet that expense, although recouping some of the cost later through deductions to the *stipendium* (Livy, 22.57.11, relating that equipment was originally sourced from private manufacturers). It would seem reasonable, therefore, that in order to kit out large numbers of these poorer *assidui* the state would commission equipment in larger quantities than could be supplied by the smaller independent workshops, which may then have required the establishment of larger dedicated arms factories (*fabricae*), with Cicero (*Rab. Perd.*, 20), referring to state-owned armouries and arsenals in 100 BC.

The location of these large arms factories, and how they were supplied, manned and operated, has been the subject of much discussion (with particular recognition to the works of Bishop, 1985, for the early period of the Principate, and to James, 1988, for the later Empire). No precise locations, however, have been absolutely identified, although some speculative sites have been proposed, based on building types and proximity to artefacts, such as tools and waste materials, as well as the limited epigraphic, literary and sub-literary evidence for the later periods.

Bishop (1985) described his perception of the 'legionary' *fabricae* of the Principate of the early first century AD. These he saw as firmly controlled by the military (as opposed to the later *fabricae*, controlled by the state, as described by James, 1988, 257–331). Although describing the organisational and command structures of the first century AD, Bishop uses as a source Vegetius' *De Rei Militari* (dating from the fourth century AD) and a fragment by Tarruntenus Paternus in Justinian's *Digest* (from the end of the second century AD). Vegetius, however, had made use of earlier sources, including Iulius Frontinus and Cornelius Celsus (both from the first century AD), and the latter of these used Cato (dating from the Republican period). Their views on the organisational and command structures may therefore at times be inaccurate, reflecting earlier or later periods. Vegetius related that the officer in overall charge would have held the position of *praefectus castrorum* (or *quaestor* in the Republican period), with the individual workshops controlled by an *optio fabricae*.

Bishop also made use of the sub-literary sources of writing tablets from Vindolanda, and a papyrus from Berlin, which describes the numbers of men employed in a 'legionary' *fabrica* on a single day (100 at the former and 340 at the latter), with a breakdown of their status. This would appear to have consisted of a core group of skilled workers and specialist craftsmen (*immunes*), with unskilled labour supplied by the soldiers (*cohortales)*, associated civilians and a group of possible slaves. Both of these *fabricae* appear to have been involved in general armour and weapon production; the German site producing *spathae*, two types of shield, iron plates (possibly for use in segmented armour or helmets), bows and catapult fittings; whereas at Vindolanda, mention is made of *gladiarii*, *fabri* and *scutarii* (Bishop, 1985, 3).

Although there are no positively identified *fabricae*, Bishop (1985, 7) cites the possible first- and second-century AD locations of Haltern, Hofheim, Valkenburg, Oberstimm, Inchtuthil, Wiesbaden and Vindolanda, where similarities of buildings (of a series of small rooms, arranged around a central courtyard), have been seen, often with an associated water supply and occasionally with proximity to evidence of hearths. In some instances these distinctive building types have been identified within a fort itself, but on other occasions appear within dedicated walled 'industrial' enclosures, often annexed to a fort (or within an otherwise 'civilian' town, such as at Corbridge, and as more recently found on the outskirts of the settlement at Vindolanda, presumably where industrial activity could be kept under direct military supervision.

Further secondary evidence of manufacture/repair workshops may come from waste materials (metal, crucibles, wood, bone or leather), or possible evidence of recycling, as in the case of a quantity of nails and iron tyres from Inchtuthil. Bishop (1985, 9) suggested that many of these *fabricae* may have practised a high level of repair/recycling in addition to manufacture, repairing damaged items where possible and recycling at the end of their usefulness, in order to keep the need for new, raw materials to a minimum, citing Vegetius' ideal of military self-sufficiency. Bishop proposed that the large quantities of materials deposited in pits and ditches, on abandonment and demolition of sites such as Newstead, are indicative of deliberate retention of scrap for potential reuse, rather than accidental loss (*ibid.*).

Bishop also suggested that objects may remain in use for long periods (as evidenced by signs of wear and combat damage, subsequent repairs and inscribed names of multiple owners), offering a notional 'twenty man-years period' for the lifetime of a piece of equipment in times of peace. However, it should be remembered that this notional lifetime would be greatly reduced under combat situations, and would also be relative to the type of equipment under discussion. For example, more resilient parts of the panoply (such as helmets, plate armour, etc.), would need less repair and remain in use through more owners and for longer periods (possibly considerably more than this notional twenty years) than would items made of more perishable materials (such as shoes or shields, made from leather and wood).

Bishop (1985, 15) also considered the possible regional differences in armour/equipment production across the Empire, proposing that distinctive features could be identified in the work of individual craftsmen operating with specific legions (as seen, for example, in the Upper German style of decoration of belt plates and scabbard fittings dating from the Tiberio-Claudian period), although some exchange of ideas may have occurred between legions during joint campaigns. He also proposed that, although the 'legionary' *fabrica* system operated in the West and along the frontier zones, a different system (the Greek-style *polis* system), could be seen in the Mediterranean zone and in the East, whereby individual city states were able to organise their citizenry to produce large quantities of equipment at short notice, in order to rapidly equip large armies. This 'mass production' he believed to be responsible for the poorer quality of the Imperial-Italic helmets produced by these workshops (Bishop, 1985, 16).

During the centuries immediately following, the organisation of arms and armour production is unclear, although it would appear that as frontiers became less volatile, and as there was a movement from armies of campaign towards standing armies, an increasing level of manufacture may have passed back to the private sector. This may have commenced with the provision of short-life equipment such as leather goods, but later on may be reflected in other 'heavier' industries, such as iron production and metalworking. For example, there is a suggestion from manufacturing sites such as Templeborough of an abandoning in later periods of the military presence (or a reduction to a minimum garrison staffing), with an apparent civilian continuance of industrial activity moving back inside the fort itself.

Towards the later stages of the Empire, the production of military equipment took a cyclic change, away from private enterprise to a controlled, organised system, this time under direct state control rather than by the military. This transition was discussed at length by James (1988, 259–331). In his discussion of the arms manufacturing sites of the later Empire, James relied mostly on the names of state *fabricae* listed in the *Notitia Dignitatum* (along with other military and government installations under the control of their relevant *Magistri*). Dating to the fifth century, this appears in two versions: the *Notitia Dignitatum Occidentalis* dealing with the Western Empire, and the *Notitia Dignitatum Orientalis* dealing with the East. James identified an organised network of *fabricae*, twenty in the Western Empire, fifteen in the East (along the Rhine and Danube frontiers, and evenly spread around the Eastern provinces, although with some areas, notably Britain, Egypt and the south-western provinces, where no *fabricae* appear to exist), which he categorised into those for general armour manufacture and those for the manufacture of specific/specialised equipment (1988, 261).

These categories of *fabricae*, according to James (1988, 261), are:

Specialist Equipment
Arcuaria – bows; *Sagittaria* – arrows; *Ballistaria* – artillery; *Hastaria* – spears; *Spatharia* – swords; *Scutaria* – shields; *Armamenta* – for marine fittings, but could mean arsenal, armoury or weapon store.

*General Equipment (*Armorum, Clibanaria, Loricaria*)*
Armorum – James suggested these as general workshops for any part of the panoply (helmet, body armour, weapons), except missiles, and possibly shields (as references are also found to *scutaria et armorum*, where shields were made at separate locations). Also possibly used for sword production in the east, where there are no *fabricae spathariae* identified.
Clibanaria – mostly found in the East (where most of *catafractarii* and *clibanarii* were located), which James interpreted to suggest heavy cavalry armour production.
Loricaria – only found in the West. James did not support the suggestion that these are for leather defences, but considered it a Western term for body armour, with swords coming from *fabricae spathariae*.

Those which he categorised as for general production he identified as being located in pairs in each of the Western dioceses, along with a single *scutaria* for shield production, although with no such pattern visible in the East, where there was no linear frontier. The more specialised *fabricae* then appear to have been irregularly placed, dependant on the needs of the relevant specialist units. For example, missile and archery equipment production was all located in the West. This James related to archery being an Eastern tradition, where archers would have made their own bows and ammunitions, with additional equipment possibly produced as a 'tax in kind' for export to other areas. In the West, however, where archery was not a local tradition, these had to be supplied, with the *fabrica* at Ticinum being centrally located to best import component parts and to distribute the end product (James, 1988, 264).

James discussed the locating of these *fabricae* in strategic positions along the frontiers, and in an organised distribution in the Eastern provinces, contrasting their absence in regions such as Britain and Egypt, which were no longer by that time of comparable military significance. He suggests that the majority of these *fabricae* are a phenomenon of Diocletian's building programme and reorganisation of the provinces. The army had become less self-sufficient after a period of civil wars, foreign invasions and political upheavals, making it more dependent on civilian workshops. Inflation in the third century AD had collapsed the coinage (and, along with it, the private market), leading to an increased use of 'taxes in kind', with the civilian armourer's almost exclusive outlet for their goods now being the army. A state nationalisation of armour production then became the next logical step, with its manpower (*fabricenses*) of well-paid free men, but tied for life to their trade by legislation (Theodosius II, AD 438, *Novellae*, 6), with sons following their fathers into their profession, but with additional recruitment from veterans and some volunteers. These artisans would have held a similar status to the militia, with the same privileges, exemptions and rights to draw financial support from the military tax, the *annonia militaris*, organised with a military-style command structure into a corporate body similar to the civilian guilds. James (1988, 276) then used his list of thirty-five known *fabricae* of the fifth century AD, compiled from the combined Western and Eastern editions of the *Notitia Dignitatum*, along with an estimation of 400 to 500 men being active at each site, to propose a total of 7,000 to 17,500 men being involved in armour production at that time.

James acknowledged that not all *fabricae* were established at this time, but argued that this was the time when the organised network of paired *fabricae* appears to have been initiated, and that many may have preceded this time, some possibly originating from earlier legionary-based *fabricae* (although this he viewed as 'nominal'). This suggests a differentiation between the early and later *fabricae* as two separate entities, albeit that the latter may have derived from the former, which James saw as the 'legionary' and the 'imperial' respectively. He cites the reduced quality of equipment at that time, and the abrupt change to the simplified, functional, bipartite and multi-pieced helmets, with armourers being directed to work to government quotas of a specific quantity and quality at a minimum cost (1988, 271).

By the third century AD, these later *fabricae* were no longer based at military locations, but in urban sites, where major cities could supply a ready workforce, ideally in areas where communities of armourers were traditionally found (often in mining areas, with advanced pre-Roman metalworking and arms production traditions). While proximity to raw materials was an important factor to location, James (1988, 267) considered that this was only contributory to the other factors of manpower, personal supply and distribution, where 'taxes in kind' could provide food, materials, and bullion, and the roads and navigable waterways network provided transport for raw materials and distribution of finished products.

Although the *fabricae* of this period were on the periphery of the armour manufacture discussed in this study, evidence for their organisational structure, location and manpower are of relevance to the earlier periods as they show a developmental progression, in both the arms industry itself and in the equipment produced by it, helping to explain some of the subsequent changes in quality, design and ethnic influences seen on the artefactual remains. The lists also demonstrate the use of general-function and specialist *fabricae*, the latter dedicated to the production of different types of equipment, linked to distinct units of specialist troops, which suggests that a similar segregation of production may have been the case in earlier periods, which may aid with the identification of such earlier period sites in the future.

Developmental changes can therefore be seen as production moving cyclically, from small-scale private civilian workshops to a large-scale organised military operation, with a gradual gravitation back towards private enterprise, and once more into a planned, large-scale, state-controlled operation. As the 'control' and level of production fluctuated, so did the level of quality and workmanship of the finished products, which implies different methods of manufacture, and which may then be evident in the archaeological record (in building design, site location and layout, tools used and waste materials produced). This also may have implications for the consumption of raw materials, the rate of repair/replacement and the use to which the equipment is put (with considerations such as the resilience of the panoply in comparison against lightness of use and ease/cost of replacement as a short-life commodity).

APPENDIX III

METAL

EVIDENCE FOR METALWORKING

Metalworking was no new innovation of the Roman period, with cold-worked nuggets of naturally occurring soft metals such as copper and gold dating back to the early Bronze Age. Later, in addition to the exploitation of the more precious but less practical metals, the hardening properties of natural impurities in copper can be seen being manipulated in a deliberate alloying of metals, possibly as a result of observation over time of the use of sulphide ores high in arsenic content, with hardened copper objects being produced from before the third millennium BC, and tin bronzes appearing in central Europe from around 1800 BC (Champion *et al.*, 1984, 198–213). Initially, bronze objects were small and mostly produced by use of simple casting methods, although as casting techniques became more sophisticated, allowing secondary casting on to preformed objects, with the introduction of the improved tin-bronze, sheet bronzes began to be used for larger objects, such as food vessels, shields and armour (Champion *et al.*, 1984, 215–84).

The bronze produced was not used exclusively close to the ore's point of origin, with trade in bar ingots from the second millennium and recycling of scrap metal to established industrial sites evidenced by numerous shipwrecks carrying cargoes of scrap along the coastal routes from Spain to France and Britain, who appear to be foremost during the later Bronze Age for both quantity and quality of bronze working, being credited with the innovation of the development of copper-tin-lead alloys from the tenth century BC. For example, finds of two bronze Etruscan Negau-style helmets (dating to the fifth and sixth centuries BC) were found from the Les Sorres shipwreck site (dating to the second century BC). Although in remarkably good condition, these were not in contemporary styles and did exhibit evidence of wear, suggesting that they must have been of considerable age at the time of the wreck, their presence being interpreted as part of a cargo destined for recycling (Izquierdo & Solias Aris, 2000, 1–11). The addition of 7–10 per cent lead to alloys of copper and tin produces a slightly softer compound, but one that pours more easily, with fewer casting failures, therefore increasing productivity.

From the tenth century BC a new metal, iron, began to appear. This was more difficult to produce, requiring a higher level of technology, but with its greater strength and hardness it began to replace the use of bronze for tools, weapons and armour (Champion *et al.*, 1984, 226). The Romans then built on these long-standing traditions with the introduction of new and innovative techniques to increase production and improve the quality of the metal, particularly and not entirely coincidentally at times of expansion and radical change within the structure of its military, in answer to a need for large quantities of mass-produced armour at short notice.

Although some use was made of the less practical, decorative metals such as gold and silver, for highest-status ceremonial officer equipment (which armour was less likely to ever see serious heavy combat), the majority of military equipment was made from iron or copper alloy, and for this reason, further discussion shall focus mainly on these two metals.

Mining and preliminary processing for both iron and copper were not completely dissimilar, although, as stated, iron requires higher temperatures and more technologically sophisticated furnaces. Primary processing of ores was probably carried out close to where it had been extracted (as suggested in contracts, such as '*Lex Metallum Vispascense*', one of two bronze tablets found on slag heaps at Vipasca, Aljustrel in Portugal; Travis, 2008), and then transported to secondary processing sites (probably in industrial complexes) using road, river and coastal systems. Apart from substantial deposits of iron ore in Britain (possibly a major factor influencing the Roman expansion into this country), the Romans also mined iron in many other provinces (such as Gaul, Spain, Italy, Elba, Sardinia, Sicily, central Europe, Noricum, Illyria, Macedonia, Asia Minor and Africa; Apollonius of Rhodes, *Argonautica* 2.1001–1007; Healy 1978, 64–5; Davies, 1935, 67, 76, 86, 152–3, 165–73). Ore was extracted mostly using 'opencast' methods ('bell pitting' of deposits close to the surface, and quarrying of outcrops from between agricultural field terracing), and the collection of nodules and pebbles from riverbeds, but with the possibility of some deeper mining from 'adits', as seen at Lydney Park (Tylecote, 1986, 155).

Evidence of iron or bronze working may take the form of smelting furnaces, although it is necessary to be mindful of the similarities to those used in each (in the possible presence of fayalite slag produced, or the presence of coal or charcoal fuel, common to both processes). Secondary processing may be more easily identified, with remains of casting hearths, crucibles, casting splashes, trimmed-off casting sprues (from filling funnels or 'breathing vents' in the mould), or flash (surplus metal from around joins in the mould). However, as the level of technology required for copper/bronze casting is relatively low, not all activity may necessarily have taken place within distinct and bespoke workshop *fabricae*, and casting could be carried out almost anywhere that a small, temporary hearth could be fashioned in a hollow in the ground. Although this would of course leave a trace archaeologically, if this location were not within a known civilian or military site, its discovery would be purely down to chance.

The bronze- or copper-casting hearth would probably have been fuelled using charcoal, coal being unlikely to have been used due to possible contamination from any sulphur present. As copper melts quite readily, at temperatures around 1000°C, this can be easily achieved using charcoal (which gives an intense but relatively short-life burn), the combustion aided by use of bellows. Further, the charcoal being a 'clean' fuel, with few chemical impurities, it is possible to gauge the readiness of the copper mix from the colour of the flame, which changes to a green colour when molten, at which point the mix may be augmented by the addition of other minerals to improve its properties.

If sheet metal has been used, it may be possible to find offcuts, part-formed objects or wasters, or, if objects have been lathe-spun, there may be distinct areas of copper alloy dust or small pieces of metal trimmed from the objects being shaped, indicating the location of lathes, as at Exeter (Bidwell, 1997, 90).

With the melting down of old copper alloy articles for recycling, the definition blurs between copper-tin (bronze) and copper-zinc (brass, or *oricalchum*), with some artefacts including a mixture of both. While it is possible that the resultant mixture in some objects is purely accidental, there is a possibility that the Roman craftsman was able to gauge the properties of the metal he was working with, to produce a mixture which best suited the artefact he intended to produce.

This view is supported by the results of examinations carried out by Bishop at the University of Sheffield on copper alloy artefacts from both Buxton Museum and from Longthorpe, near Peterborough, to analyse their composition using atomic absorption spectroscopy (Bishop, 1989a, 11–13; 1989b, 20–22). Among the samples analysed, there were examples of objects which had been cast and others which had been produced from flat plate, and although most appeared to be formed of the traditional Roman *oricalchum* (mainly copper and zinc), the levels of other inclusions varied, the cast objects also containing amounts of tin and lead.

TOOLS

Tools used during the Roman period were much the same as had been used in the fifth and fourth centuries BC, and indeed had been broadly similar from then until modern times, their function still remaining unchanged and so, correspondingly, their shape and appearance. The metalworker then and now would make use of the same basic toolset: a range of hammers (small or heavy, flat-headed or round-headed, similar to a modern cross-peen), tongs (to hold the hot iron), punches and drifts (to make holes in the metal), fullers (to make a piece of metal thinner), flatters (to even out the thickness after use of the fuller), swages (to mould a flat-sectioned bar into a round-section), sets (a heavy 'chisel' used to cut hot bar or sheet metal), anvil and bellows.

METALLURGICAL ANALYSIS

Iron as a metal (ferrite) is never usually found in pure form as it almost always has small quantities of impurities present, such as phosphorus, silicon, manganese, oxygen or nitrogen. Iron (wrought iron) is more correctly called 'low-carbon steel' if containing less than 0.5 per cent carbon, or 'medium carbon' and 'high carbon' steels if containing 0.5 per cent to 1.5 per cent carbon, and cast iron can contain up to 5 per cent carbon (cast iron, or crucible steel can be seen in use in India from the third century BC, and its origins are traditionally considered to lie in Asia, with the Romans acquiring knowledge of its production through trade contacts with India and China by around fifth to sixth centuries AD). Wrought iron cannot be hardened by heat treatment, but can be converted to steel by 'carburization', heating and maintaining at a temperature of over 900°C for several hours, while keeping the metal covered by carbon (coal or charcoal fuel), forcing it to slowly absorb further carbon into its structure (see Table 11).

Steel, however, is generally a deliberate alloy of iron with a greater percentage of carbon and other metals which can be hardened and tempered, for example modern 'mild steel' (only 0.25 per cent carbon, but also contains manganese) and 'stainless steel' (alloyed with nickel and chromium, and a small percentage of molybdenum). When heated and rapidly cooled, these deliberately added impurities increase the strength and hardness of the metal, but reduce the flexibility (see Table 12). Some 'mild' or 'natural' steels in antiquity were produced as a result of working ores containing manganese. Some deliberate steels were also produced from the early Iron Age, but these usually contained less than 1.5 per cent carbon. One example of a steel punch has been found however from a fourth century AD Roman context, at Heeten in the Netherlands, with an extremely high carbon content of 2 per cent, which the excavators feel may cause reconsideration of the previous view of a uniquely Near Eastern or Asian origin for this level of technology (Godfrey & van Nie, 2004). Most iron and steel was deliberately produced by the 'direct' or 'bloomery process', with the 'indirect' or 'blast furnace' processes, used for cast iron and crucible steels, generally being considered to be modern methods.

A metallographic examination was carried out in 2002 by Fulford, Sim and Doig, of polished sections from a range of Roman armour fragments, dating to the first to third centuries AD, from locations across Europe including Britain (from *lorica*, scale armour, mail and shield bosses), with the aim to determine if possible the composition, purity and hardness of metal used, the extent of use of steel, and to attempt to suggest methods of production, by measuring the thickness and mean hardness of the sample, and microscopically examining it to view the grain structure and estimated level of slag inclusions (Fulford *et al.*, 2004, 197–220).

It was found, on samples that had not mineralised too completely to permit examination, that the majority (70 per cent of the forty-three pieces sampled) were less than 1 mm thick, with almost all (with a few notable exceptions) measuring less than 2 mm in thickness. Most of the mail samples were less than 1.1 mm diameter, with only two samples exceeding 1.2 mm (Fulford *et al.*, 2004, 201).

It was also found that 80 per cent of the samples tested were formed from composite sheets of metal, with multiple layers (usually two or three sheets, but occasionally up to four layers), some of which (20 per cent, or seven samples in total) possibly being folded single sheets, but many (including all helmet and shield bosses) being formed from sheets of different metals, taking deliberate advantage of their different tensile properties. On examination of the grain structure in these samples, the interfaces between the grains on many were straight, suggesting that the metal had been thinned with an overall even pressure, an effect which Fulford *et al.* propose could have been produced by the use of hot rolling, or large area trip hammers, the use of which (water powered) has been suggested at a late Roman mill at Ickham, Kent (Fulford *et al.*, 2004, 201; Lewis, 1997, 111).

From the appearance of the grain structures it was possible to identify on examination those samples which were of martensitic quenched steel and others which were almost pure iron (ferrite), the grain shapes also indicating hot or cold working. Elongated grains, for example, would have formed when the metal was cold worked, the grains compressing and stretching as the metal was thinned. Where equiaxed grains were noted, this either indicated hot working or annealing, or may just represent elongated grains being viewed end-on, from a transverse position on an end edge (Fulford *et al.*, 2004, 211).

It was found that all helmets had elongated grain structures, suggesting cold working, without later annealing. This is as would have been anticipated considering the time and skilled labour involved in producing a helmet bowl, and the inherent difficulties in performing this task using hot metal. Annealing the metal after shaping would have softened the bowl unacceptably (with annealed iron usually being around 90 to 100 Hv in hardness). However, quite the opposite turned out to be the case, as it was discovered that all helmets and shield bosses sampled had been produced from multiple layers, using harder and stronger fine-grained metal on the outer surface to withstand blows, and softer, coarse-grained metal on the inner surface to absorb impacts (helmets being harder than bosses, the former being above 210 Hv, the latter below this), indicating the superior knowledge and skill of the Roman armourer (Fulford *et al.*, 2004, 211). In contrast, it was found that most *lorica segmentata* components consisted of mixed-grain metal, some particularly large and coarse-grained, indicating a lower level of working of the metal, again as would be anticipated, flat sheet requiring less working than the more complicated shaped helmets and bowls.

Among the forty-three samples examined by Fulford *et al.*, a number were found to have been of steel, including *lorica* and scale from Carlisle and Vindolanda, a shield boss from London, and several examples of mail from Thorsbjerg (Upper Germany) and Stuttgart (Fulford *et al.*, 2004, 206). All of the steel samples had equiaxed grain structures, indicating heating after forging to above 723°C, to become austenite, followed by either air cooling, to ferrite and lamellar pearlite (as seen on the Carlisle scale, although as in this case only the outer surface was seen to be of pearlite, it has been suggested that this may indicate use of carburization), or water quenching to martensite (three of the five samples of mail from Stuttgart being martensite, suggesting that they had been quenched in this way, producing a hardness rating of between 125 and 275 Hv; Fulford *et al.*, 2004, 206).

Fulford viewed the anomalies of the examples of the steel mail from Stuttgart as being possible evidence of regional variation in manufacture. This is also supported by examination of the level of slag inclusions and slag stringers in the samples, indicating the level of purity of the metal. Although remarking on the purity of all samples (with less than 4 per cent slag in over two-thirds of the samples), he noted that those from Denmark and Germany were particularly pure (at least 0.5 per cent), indicating the high level and sophistication of the technology in use (Fulford *et al.*, 2004, 206).

This level of purity of Roman ferrous metal, and absence of high levels of slag stringers, was further remarked on by Sim in his discussion of the examination of the Carlisle armour fragments and his unsuccessful attempted duplication of similar-quality metal (Sim, 2005). However, all of his experimental samples had been produced exclusively with the use of charcoal as fuel, without consideration of alternative fossil fuels, such as low-sulphur coal, the use of which he had been unaware of in the Roman period (Sim, pers. comm., October 2005), but which would have made these levels of purity achievable. It is therefore possible that this high quality of Roman ferrous material could indirectly strengthen the argument for greater use of coal in the manufacture of iron in the Roman period (Travis, 2008).

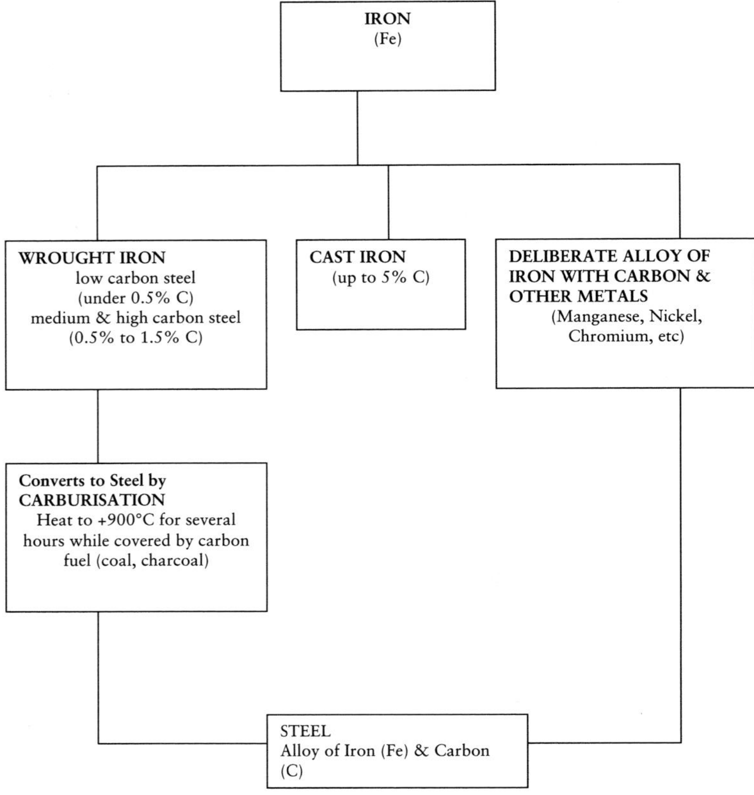

Table 11. Formation of steel.

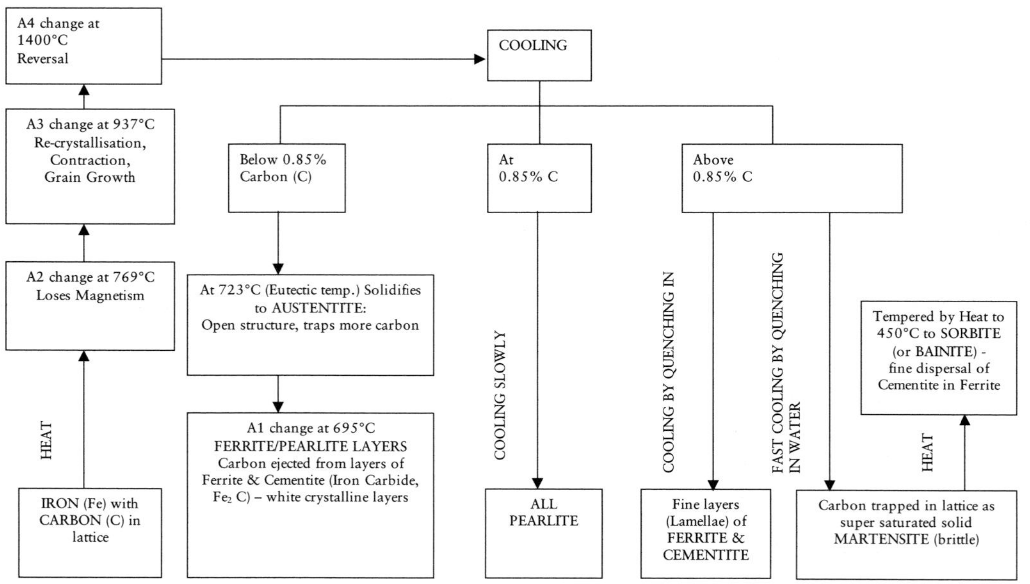

Table 12. The effects of cooling on iron.

APPENDIX IV

LIST OF KNOWN HELMETS

Continental	HRR system	Find location	(Br) (Ir)	Date	Additional info (inc. curent location, if known)
La Tène	Mont. Type A	Cigarralejo	Br	c375-350 BC	Durnberg-Bockweiler type (Celtic). No knob or cheekpieces. At Mula.
La Tène	Mont. Type A	Flüren (D)	Br		In Rheinisches Landesmuseum, Bonn (D)
La Tène	Mont. Type A	Trier-Olewig (D).	Br		Original in private collection (Trier, D). Reconstruction: Rheinisches Landesmuseum Trier (D),
Montefortino	Mont. Type ?B?	Pozo Moro	Br	3rd BC to early 2nd BC	Iberian mercenary, Punic wars
Montefortino	Mont. Type A	Alarcos	Br	mid 2nd BC	Mus. Ciudad Real
Montefortino	Mont. Type A	Almaciles	Br	mid 1st BC	Mus Murcia
Montefortino	Mont. Type A	unknown location	Br	4-3rd BC	British Museum
Montefortino	Mont. Type A	unknown location	Br	4-3rd BC	British Museum
Montefortino	Mont. Type A	unknown location	Br	4-3rd BC	Museo Nazionale di Antichita, Parma
Montefortino	Mont. Type A/B	Alto Chacon	Br	c2nd BC	Mus Teruel
Montefortino	Mont. Type A/B	Ampurias	Br	4th & 3rd BC	Museo de Ampurias
Montefortino	Mont. Type A/B	Baza	Br		
Montefortino	Mont. Type A/B	Cabecico del Tesoro	Br	c225-175 BC Punic wars	Mus Murcia
Montefortino	Mont. Type A/B	Cabecico del Tesoro	Br	3rd-2nd BC Punic wars	Mus Murcia
Montefortino	Mont. Type A/B	Castellones de Ceal	Br	c3rd BC	Jaen
Montefortino	Mont. Type A/B	Castellones de Ceal	Br	5th-3rd BC	Man. Caja
Montefortino	Mont. Type A/B	Collado Jardines	Br		
Montefortino	Mont. Type A/B	Fosos de Bayona	Br	2nd BC, but poss Sertorian	Only knob remains. In Mus. Cuenca.
Montefortino	Mont. Type A/B	Fosos de Bayona	Br	2nd BC, but poss Sertorian	Only knob remains
Montefortino	Mont. Type A/B	Galera	Br	3rd-2nd BC Punic wars	Man. Caja
Montefortino	Mont. Type A/B	Galera	Br	3rd-2nd BC Punic wars	Man. Caja
Montefortino	Mont. Type A/B	Galera	Br	3rd-2nd BC Punic wars	
Montefortino	Mont. Type A/B	Galera	Br	3rd-2nd BC Punic wars	
Montefortino	Mont. Type A/B	Galera	Br	3rd-2nd BC Punic wars	
Montefortino	Mont. Type A/B	Galera	Br	3rd-2nd BC Punic wars	Fundacion Rodriguez Acosta
Montefortino	Mont. Type A/B	Hoya de S. Ana	Br	3rd-2nd BC Punic wars	Albacete
Montefortino	Mont. Type A/B	Hoya de S. Ana	Br	3rd-2nd BC Punic wars	Albacete
Montefortino	Mont. Type A/B	La Azucarera	Br	c220-70 BC	lost
Montefortino	Mont. Type A/B	La Caridad	Br	c70BC	Teruel
Montefortino	Mont. Type A/B	La Pedrera	Br		Mus Lerida
Montefortino	Mont. Type A/B	La Serreta de Alcoy N	Br		Mus Alcoi
Montefortino	Mont. Type A/B	Las Corts	Br	2nd or early 1st BC	Museo de Ampurias
Montefortino	Mont. Type A/B	Loreto Apruntino	Br		Loreto Apruntino?

Conintental	HRR system	Find location	(Br) (Ir)	Date	Additional info (inc. curent location, if known)
Montefortino	Mont. Type A/B	Osca	Br		
Montefortino	Mont. Type A/B	Pago de Gorrita	Br		Museo Valladolid
Montefortino	Mont. Type A/B	Piedras Barbadas	Br		Col Particular J. Gregori, 2nd Punic war disembarkation anchorage
Montefortino	Mont. Type A/B	Piedras Barbadas	Br		Museo de Benicarlo
Montefortino	Mont. Type A/B	Toya	Br	3rd-2nd BC Punic wars	Man Col Roman Pulido
Montefortino	Mont. Type A/B	Toya	Br	3rd-2nd BC Punic wars	Mus. Cabre Calaceite?
Montefortino	Mont. Type A/B	Villaricos	Br	3rd-2nd BC Punic wars	Man. Caja
Montefortino	Mont. Type A/B	Villaricos	Br	3rd-2nd BC Punic wars	Man. Caja
Montefortino	Mont. Type A/B	Villaricos	Br	3rd-2nd BC Punic wars	Man. Caja
Montefortino	Mont. Type A/B	Villaricos	Br	3rd-2nd BC Punic wars	Man. Caja
Montefortino	Mont. Type A/B	Villaricos	Br	3rd-2nd BC Punic wars	Man. Caja?
Montefortino	Mont. Type A/B	S. Juan Aznalfarache	Br		Col Particular J. Gregori
Montefortino	Mont. Type B	Castellones de Ceal	Br	3rd-2nd BC Punic wars	Jaen
Montefortino	Mont. Type B	Cola de Zama	Br		Albacete
Montefortino	Mont. Type B	Hoya de S. Ana	Br	3rd-2nd BC Punic wars	Albacete
Montefortino	Mont. Type B	Las Corts	Br	2nd or early 1st BC	Museo de Ampurias
Montefortino	Mont. Type B	Las Corts	Br	2nd or early 1st BC	Museo de Ampurias
Montefortino	Mont. Type B	Piedras Barbadas	Br		Museo de Benicarlo
Montefortino	Mont. Type B	unknown location	Br	late 3rd to 2nd BC	British Museum
Montefortino	Mont. Type B	unknown location	Br	late 3rd to 2nd BC	Museo Stibbert, Florence
Montefortino	Mont. Type B	Villaricos	Br	3rd-2nd BC Punic wars	Man. Caja?
Montefortino	Mont. Type C	Castellani	Br	1st BC to 1st AD	Ashmolean Mus.
Montefortino	Mont. Type C	Fliegenhohle, near Dane, St Kanzian	Br	1st BC to 1st AD	Kunsthistorische Mus. Vienna
Montefortino	Mont. Type C	Galera	Br	3rd-2nd BC Punic wars	Univ Barcelona
Montefortino	Mont. Type C	Millingen (NL).	Br	1st BC to 1st AD	Partially tinned. In Rijksmuseum G.M. Kam, now Museum het Valkhof, Nijmegen (NL)
Montefortino	Mont. Type C	Quintana Redonda	Br	early 2nd-early 1st BC	Sertorian Civil wars c80 BC. At Real Academia de la Historia
Montefortino	Mont. Type C	unknown location	Br	1st BC to 1st AD	Meyrick Collection, Brit Mus.
Montefortino	Mont. Type D	Nijmegen/Pannerden (NL)	Br	late 1st BC to early 1st AD	partially tinned. Knob has addnl tube for crest. Paddock claims "spun". In Rijksmuseum G.M. Kam, now Museum het Valkhof, Nijmegen (NL)
Montefortino	Mont. Type D	unknown location	Br	late 1st BC to early 1st AD	Museo Gregoriano, Vatican
Montefortino	Mont. Type E	Rhine, at Mainz	Br	1st half of 1st AD	Mittelrheinisches Landemuseum, Mainz
Montefortino	Mont. Type F	Cremona-Pizzihettone (River Po)	Br	?AD 69	
Montefortino	Mont. Ital. Var	Can Miralles	Br	c225-175 BC	2nd Punic wars or Roman Rebellion 195BC. In Mus Mataro

Continental	HRR system	Find location	(Br) (Ir)	Date	Additional info (inc. curent location, if known)
Montefortino	Mont. Variant	Briteiros	Br	Pre Augustan 2nd 1/2 1st BC	Galatian local prod based on Mont. & Buggenum
Montefortino	Mont. Variant	Caldelas de Tuy	Br	Pre Augustan 2nd 1/2 1st BC	Galatian local prod based on Mont. & Buggenum. At Museo Diocesan de Tuy
Montefortino	Mont.Varia nt	Castelo de Neiva	Br	Augustan 2nd 1/2 1st BC	Galatian local prod based on Mont. & Buggenum. At Museo de Conimbriga
Montefortino	Mont. Variant B/C	Castelo de Neiva	Br	Augustan 2nd 1/2 1st BC	Galatian local prod based on Mont. & Buggenum. At Museo de Conimbriga
Montefortino	Mont. Variant B/C	Lanhoso	Br	Pre Augustan 2nd 1/2 1st BC	Galatian local prod based on Mont. & Buggenum.
Montefortino	Mont. Type n/k	Canosa (I),	Br		Museo Archaeologico, Firenze (I)
Montefortino	Mont. Type n/k	La Osera I-II	Br		Man. Caja
Montefortino	Mont. Type n/k	Montenerodomo	Br	1st C BC	Montenerodomo?
Montefortino	Mont. Type n/k	Olfen, near Haltern (D).	Br		Landesmuseum für Vor- und Frühgeschichte, Münster (D), Now in Westfälisches Römermuseum Haltern (D) or in Westfälisches Museum für Archäologie, Herne (D) ?,
Montefortino	Mont. Type n/k	Rieti, Forum Novum (I).	Br		Staatliche Antikensammlung München (D)
Montefortino	Mont. Type n/k	Unknown location (Italy?).	Br		Axel Guttmann Collection
Montefortino	Mont. Type n/k	Unknown location (Italy?).	Br		Axel Guttmann Collection
Montefortino	Mont. Type n/k	Unknown location (Italy?).	Br		Axel Guttmann Collection
Montefortino	Mont. Type n/k	Unknown location (Italy?).	Br		Axel Guttmann Collection
Montefortino	Mont. Type n/k	Unknown location (Italy?).	Br		Axel Guttmann Collection
Montefortino	Mont. Type n/k	Unknown location (Italy?).	Br		Axel Guttmann Collection
Montefortino	Mont. Type n/k	Unknown location (Italy?).	Br		Axel Guttmann Collection
Montefortino	Mont. Type n/k	Unknown location (Mid-Italy?).	Br		Montefortino-Talamone. In Axel Guttmann Collection
Montefortino	Mont. Type n/k	Unknown location.	Br		Montefortino-Hagenau transitional. In Axel Guttmann Collection
Montefortino	Mont. Type n/k	Unknown location.	Br		Axel Guttmann Collection
Montefortino	Mont. Type n/k	Unknown location.	Br		Axel Guttmann Collection
Montefortino	Mont. Type n/k	Unknown location.	Br		Axel Guttmann Collection
Montefortino	Mont. Type n/k	Unknown location.	Br		Axel Guttmann Collection
Montefortino	Mont. Type n/k	Unknown location.	Br		Axel Guttmann Collection
Montefortino	Mont. Type n/k	Unknown location.	Br		Axel Guttmann Collection
Montefortino	Mont. Type n/k	Unknown location.	Br		Axel Guttmann Collection
Montefortino	Mont. Type n/k	Unknown location.	Br		Axel Guttmann Collection
Montefortino	Mont. Type n/k	Unknown location.	Br		Axel Guttmann Collection
Montefortino	Mont. Type n/k	Unknown location.	Br		Axel Guttmann Collection

Continental	HRR system	Find location	(Br) (Ir)	Date	Additional info (inc. curent location, if known)
Buggenum	Mont. Type ?C/D	Piquete de la Atalaya	Br	mid 1st BC	Zaragoza
Buggenum	Mont. Type C	Alcaracejos	Br	mid 1st BC	Desconolido
Buggenum	Mont. Type C	Aljezur	Br	mid 1st BC	Mus Reg de Lagos
Buggenum	Mont. Type C	Buggenum, Limburg, NL	Br	c 12 BC	Gemeentelijk Museum, Roermond
Buggenum	Mont. Type C	Lacimurga	Br	mid 1st BC Caesarian	Caesarian. Col Particular J. Gregori
Buggenum	Mont. Type C	Wardt-Lüttingen, near Xanten (D).	Br	1st BC to 1st AD	Niederrheinisches Museum Duisburg (D)
Buggenum	Mont. Type C/D	Mesas do Castelinho	Br	mid 1st BC Caesarian	
Buggenum	Mont. Type D	Vaiamonde	Br	mid 1st BC Caesarian	Mus Etnol Alentejo
Montefortino	Coolus Type B	Düsseldorf (D).	Br	late 1st BC to early 1st AD	Rheinisches Landesmuseum, Bonn (D)
Mannheim	Coolus Type A	Tongres, Limburg	Br	3rd to 1st BC	Musee Royaux d'Art et d'Histoire, Brussels
Mannheim	Coolus Type A	Vadenay, Suippes, Marne	Br	3rd to 1st BC	Musee des Antiquites Nationales, St Germain-en-Laye
Mannheim	Coolus Type C	Podsusjeda	Br	late 1st BC to early 1st AD	Zagreb Museum
Mannheim	Coolus Type C	Schaan, Liechtenstein	Br	late 1st BC to early 1st AD	
Mannheim	Coolus Type C	Schaan, Liechtenstein	Br	late 1st BC to early 1st AD	copy, location of original unknown. In Romisch-Germanisches Zentralmuseum, Mainz
Mannheim	Coolus	Straubing (D).	Br		
Hagenau	Mont. Type E	Nijmegen (NL)	Br	1st half of 1st AD	Paddock claims "spun". In Rijksmuseum G.M. Kam, now Museum het Valkhof, Nijmegen (NL)
Hagenau	Mont. Type E	Nijmegen (NL).	Br	1st half of 1st AD	Rijksmuseum G.M. Kam, now Museum het Valkhof, Nijmegen (NL)
Hagenau	Coolus Type D	Haltern (D).	Br	1st half of 1st AD	Landesmuseum für Vor- und Frühgeschichte, Münster (D)
Hagenau	Coolus Type D	Hönnepel (D).	Br	1st half of 1st AD	Rheinisches Landesmuseum, Bonn (D)
Hagenau	Coolus Type D	Nijmegen (NL) (The Waal)	Br	1st half of 1st AD	Tinned. In Rijksmuseum van Oudheden, Leiden (NL)
Hagenau	Coolus Type D	Wardt-Lüttingen (D).	Br	1st half of 1st AD	Rheinisches Landesmuseum, Bonn (D)
Hagenau	Coolus Type D	Wissel (D).	Br	1st half 1st AD	Rheinisches Landesmuseum, Bonn (D)
Hagenau	Coolus Type E	Berkhamstead	Br	1st half of 1st AD	Paddock claims "spun". In British Museum
Hagenau	Coolus Type E	Cologne	Br	1st half of 1st AD	Rheinisches Landesmuseum, Bonn (D)
Hagenau	Coolus Type E	Lobith/Nijmegen (NL) or Rees (D).	Br	1st half of 1st AD	Rijksmuseum G.M. Kam, now Museum het Valkhof, Nijmegen (NL)
Hagenau	Coolus Type E	Mitrovice	Br	1st half of 1st AD	Zagreb Museum
Hagenau	Coolus Type E	St Albans	Br	1st half of 1st AD	Verulamium Museum
Hagenau	Coolus Type E	Texel (NL) (Tescel - beach)	Br	1st half of 1st AD	Rijksmuseum van Oudheden, Leiden (NL)
Hagenau	Coolus Type E	Thames, London (the Walbrook)	Br	1st half of 1st AD	Paddock claims "spun". In British Museum
Hagenau	Coolus Type E	The Salva, Rugvica	Br	1st half of 1st AD	Paddock claims "spun". In Zagreb Museum
Hagenau	Coolus Type E	unknown location	Br	1st half of 1st AD	Narodni Museum, Belgrade
Hagenau	Coolus Type E	Xanten (D). (Rhine)	Br	1st half of 1st AD	Rijksmuseum van Oudheden, Leiden (NL)
Hagenau	Coolus Type F	Bosham harbour	Br	1st half of 1st AD	Paddock claims "spun". In Sussex Arch Soc Museum, Lewes

Continental	HRR system	Find location	(Br) (Ir)	Date	Additional info (inc. curent location, if known)
Hagenau	Coolus Type G	Burlafingen (D).(The Donau)	Br	3rd 1/4 1st AD	Prähistorische Staatssammlung, now Archäologische Staatssammlung, München (D),
Hagenau	Coolus Type G	Drusenheim, near Hagenau	Br	3rd 1/4 1st AD	Paddock claims "spun". In Hagenau Museum
Hagenau	Coolus Type G	Nijmegen (NL) (The Waal)	Br	3rd 1/4 1st AD	Paddock claims "spun". In Rijksmuseum van Oudheden, Leiden (NL)
Hagenau	Coolus Type I	Rhine, at Köln-Mühlheim (D).	Br	mid-3/4 1st AD	Rheinisches Landesmuseum, Bonn (D)
Hagenau	Coolus	Alem (NL).	Br		Privately owned Dr. S. M. van Ommeren, Elst (NL).
Hagenau	Coolus	Haltern (D).	Br		Römisch-Germanisches Museum, Haltern (D)
Hagenau	Coolus	Köln (D).	Br		Rheinisches Landesmuseum, Bonn (D)
Hagenau	Coolus	Neuss (D)	Br		tinned.From legionary barracks. Paddock claims "spun". In Clemens-Sels-Museum, Neuss (D)
Hagenau	Coolus	Xanten (D) (?).	Br		Regionalmuseum Xanten (D), Property of Altertumsverein Xanten.
Weisenau	Coolus Type C	Oberaden	Ir	late 1st BC to early 1st AD	Was Dortmund, destroyed WWII
Weisenau	Coolus Type H	Nidda, near Heddernheim (D)	Br	mid-3/4 1st AD	Port/Weisenau transitional. In Museum für Vor- und Frühgeschichte, Frankfurt am Main (D).
Weisenau	Agen/ Port	Alesia	Ir	mid 1st BC	Musee des Antiquites Nationales, St Germain-en-Laye
Weisenau	Agen/ Port	Giubiasco, Ticino, Kanton Tessin	Ir	mid 1st BC	Schweiz Landesmuseum, Zurick
Weisenau	Agen/ Port	Plateau de l'Ermitage, Agen, Lot-et-Garonne (well)	Ir	mid 1st BC	Musee d'Agen
Weisenau	Agen/ Port	Port bei Nidau	Ir	mid 1st BC	Schweiz Landesmuseum, Zurick
Weisenau	Agen/ Port	River Thiele	Ir	mid 1st BC	Historisches Mus. Bern
Weisenau	Agen/ Port	Vie Cioutat, near Mejannes-les-Ales, Gard	Ir	mid 1st BC	Musee Archaeologique de Nimes
Hagenau	Aux. Infantry Type A	Flüren (D)	Br	1st C AD	Rheinisches Landesmuseum, Bonn (D)
Weisenau	Aux. Infantry Type B	Rhine, at Mainz	Br	1st C AD	Mittelrheinisches Landemuseum, Mainz
Weisenau	Imp. Gallic	Kakheti, Eastern Georgia	Br	End 1st BC or early 1st AD	E Georgia
Weisenau	Imp. Gallic Type A	Nijmegen (NL).	Ir	late 1st BC to early 1st AD	Rijksmuseum G.M. Kam, now Museum het Valkhof, Nijmegen (NL)
Weisenau	Imp. Gallic Type A?	Unknown location	Brass		Rivets filled with red substance. 'Eyebrows' pointing downward. In Axel Guttmann Collection
Weisenau	Imp. Gallic Type B	The Kupa, near Sissek	Ir	1st 1/4 1st AD	Formerly in J. Salzer Collection, Vienna
Weisenau	Imp. Gallic Type C	River Kupa	Ir	1st 1/4 1st AD	Archaeological Museum Zagreb
Weisenau	Imp. Gallic Type D	Rhine, Weisenau	Ir	2nd 1/4 1st AD	Mittelrheinisches Landemuseum, Mainz
Weisenau	Imp. Gallic Type E	Idria, near Baca (grave field)	Ir	2nd 1/4 1st AD	Prähistorische sammlung, Vienna
Weisenau	Imp. Gallic Type E	Valkenburg (NL) (fort)	Ir	2nd 1/4 1st AD	Instituut voor Prae en Protohistorie, Amsterdam

Continental	HRR system	Find location	(Br) (Ir)	Date	Additional info (inc. curent location, if known)
Weisenau	Imp. Gallic Type F	Besancon	Ir	2nd 1/4 1st AD	Besancon Museum
Weisenau	Imp. Gallic Type F	Sisak, Yugoslavia	Ir	2nd 1/4 1st AD	Archaeological Museum Zagreb
Weisenau	Imp. Gallic Type F	unknown location	Ir	2nd 1/4 1st AD	Romisch-Germanisches Zentralmuseum, Mainz
Weisenau	Imp. Gallic Type G	Rhine, at Mainz	Ir	3rd 1/4 1st AD	Worms Museum
Weisenau	Imp. Gallic Type H	Lech, near Augsburg	Ir	3rd 1/4 1st AD	Maximilian Museum, Augsburg
Weisenau	Imp. Gallic Type I	Rhine, at Mainz	Ir	3rd to last 1/4 1st AD	Germanisches Nationalmuseum, Nürnberg (D)
Weisenau	Imp. Gallic Type J	Brigetio, Hungary	Ir	1st 1/4 2nd AD	National Museum of Wales
Weisenau	Imp. Gallic Type K	Wiesbaden (fort)	Ir	1st 1/4 2nd AD	Stadtisches Museum, Wiesbaden
Weisenau	Imp. Gallic	Haltern (D).	Ir		copper-plated. Landesmuseum für Vor- und Frühgeschichte, Münster (D)
Weisenau	Imp. Italic Type A	Herculaneum	Br	1st half of 1st AD	Museo Nazionale, Napoli (I).
Weisenau	Imp. Ital. Type A	Herculaneum	Br	1st half 1st AD	Museo Nazionale, Napoli (I).
Weisenau	Imp. Ital. Type B	Klakanje, Yugoslavia	Ir	2nd 1/4 1st AD	Archaeological Museum Zagreb
Weisenau	Imp. Ital. Type C	Cremona (River Po)	Br	3rd 1/4 1st AD	Museo Cremona (Museo Civico Ala Ponzone?) (I).
Weisenau	Imp. Ital. Type C	Cremona, River Po	Br	AD69	Museo Stibbert, Florence
Weisenau	Imp. Ital. Type C	Kiel	Br	3rd 1/4 1st AD	Romisch-Germanisches Zentralmuseum, Mainz
Weisenau	Imp. Ital. Type D	Rhine, at Mainz	Ir	2nd half 1st AD	Worms museum
Weisenau	Imp. Ital. Type E	Hofheim (fort)	Ir	late 1st AD	Landesarchaologe von Hessen
Weisenau	Imp. Ital. Type F	Rhine, at Mainz	Ir	2nd 1/2 1st AD	Destroyed WWII. Was in Mittelrheinisches Landemuseum, Mainz
Weisenau	Imp. Ital. Type F/G	Theilenhofen (D)	Ir		Prähistorische Staatssammlung, now Archäologische Staatssammlung, München (D),
Weisenau	Imp. Ital. Type G	Hebron, Israel (cave)	Ir	1st half 2nd AD	Israel Museum, Jerusalem
Weisenau	Imp. Ital. Type H	Hessan	Ir	late 2nd to early 3rd AD	Museum für Vor- und Frühgeschichte, Frankfurt am Main (D).
Weisenau		Aquincum/Budapest (HU).	Br		Budapest Museum (HU) (?).
Weisenau		Balkans (unproven)	Brass		copper rivets, fragmentary iron hinges. Five inscriptions. In Axel Guttmann Collection
Weisenau		Mainz. (D)	Br		Germanisches Nationalmuseum, Nürnberg (D)
Weisenau		Niedermörmter (D).	Br		Rheinisches Landesmuseum, Bonn (D)
Weisenau		Northern England (GB) (unproven)	Brass		Axel Guttmann Collection
Weisenau		Unknown location.	Br		tinned. Brass rivets with lead core.
Weisenau		Unknown location.	Br		tinned.
Weisenau		Unknown location.	Ir		brass applications. In Axel Guttmann Collection
Niedermörmter	Imp. Italic Type H	Balkans.	Ir		brass applications (Two small 'mice'). In Axel Guttmann Collection

Continental	HRR system	Find location	(Br) (Ir)	Date	Additional info (inc. curent location, if known)
Niedermörmter	Imp. Italic Type H	Niedermörmter, near Xanten (D)	Br	late 2nd to early 3rd AD	Rheinisches Landesmuseum, Bonn (D)
Weisenau	Aux. Infantry Type C	unknown location	Br	2nd C AD	Weisenau/ Niederbieber. In Museo Archaeologico Florence
Eastern/ Levantine	Aux. Infantry Type D	Dakovo, Bosna, Yugoslavia	Br	2nd C AD	Conical. Browband embossed with Victory, Jupiter, Mars. In Archaeological Museum Zagreb
Niederbieber	Aux. Cavalry Type C	River Sava, at Brod	Br	early 2nd AD	Archaeological Museum Zagreb
Niederbieber	Aux. Cavalry Type D	Niederbieber-Segendorf (D)	Ir	2nd 1/4 2nd AD	bronze applications. In Fürstlich Wied'sche Sammlung, Neuwied (D)
Niederbieber	Aux. Cavalry Type E	Friedburg (D)	Br	2nd C AD	Destroyed WWII. Was in Damstadt,
Niederbieber	Aux. Cavalry Type E	Heddernheim (D)	Ir	2nd C AD	bronze-plated. In Museum für Vor- und Frühgeschichte, Frankfurt am Main (D).
Niederbieber	Aux. Cavalry Type E	Mercey (from the Saone) (F)	Ir	2nd C AD	Musee des Antiquites Nationales, St Germain-en-Laye
Niederbieber	Aux. Cavalry Type F	Amerongen (NL)	Br	2nd C AD	Rijksmuseum van Oudheden, Leiden (NL)
Niederbieber	Aux. Cavalry Type F	Dura Europos	Ir	2nd C AD	Yale
Niederbieber	Aux. Cavalry Type F	Hönnepel (D)	Br	2nd C AD	Privately owned
Niederbieber	Aux. Cavalry	Unknown location	Br		Large sword (?) hit mark at back side. Cheek guards missing. Privately owned
Niederbieber	Aux. Cavalry	Unknown location	Br or Brass.		Axel Guttmann Collection
Cavalry parade	Aux. Cavalry Type A	Newstead (UK)	Ir	cAD98-100	Mus of Antiquities, Edinburgh
Cavalry parade	Aux. Cavalry Type A	Northwich (UK)	Ir	1st C AD	Salt Museum, Northwich
Cavalry parade	Aux. Cavalry Type B	Witcham (UK)	Ir	1st C AD	bronze brow & casing. Large bosses. In British Museum
Cavalry parade	Aux. Cavalry Type G	Nijmegen (NL)	Ir	2nd half 2nd AD	Weiler type. Bronze applications. Rijksmuseum van Oudheden, Leiden (NL)
Cavalry parade	Aux. Cavalry Type H	Bodegraven, (NL).	Br	late 2nd to early 3rd AD	Rijksmuseum van Oudheden, Leiden (NL)
Cavalry parade	Aux. Cavalry Type H	Heddernheim (D)	Ir	late 2nd to early 3rd AD	bronze fittings. In Museum für Vor- und Frühgeschichte, Frankfurt am Main (D).
Cavalry parade	Aux. Cavalry Type H	Nijmegen (NL)	Ir	late 2nd to early 3rd AD	bronze applications. Rijksmuseum van Oudheden, Leiden (NL)
Cavalry parade	Aux. Cavalry Type H	Nijmegen (NL).	Br	late 2nd to early 3rd AD	Fragments of fittings/applications (front, neck, earguards). Rijksmuseum van Oudheden, Leiden (NL)
Cavalry parade	Aux. Cavalry	Amerongen (NL)	Br		Fragment of forehead fitting/application. Tinned. Rijksmuseum van Oudheden, Leiden (NL)
Cavalry parade	Aux. Cavalry	Bulgaria (BG)	Brass		Fragmentary back with crest. Tinning removed. Axel Guttmann Collection
Cavalry parade	Aux. Cavalry	Koblenz-Bubenheim (D)	Ir		bronze-plated. Partially tinned and silver plated. Mittelrhein-Museum, Koblenz (D)

Continental	HRR system	Find location	(Br) (Ir)	Date	Additional info (inc. curent location, if known)
Cavalry parade	Aux. Cavalry	Nijmegen (NL).	Br		Fragment of fittings/applications (forehead and left earguard) partially tinned. Instituut voor Oude Geschiedenis en Archeologie, R. K. Universiteit Nijmegen (NL)
Cavalry parade	Aux. Cavalry	Nijmegen (NL).	Br		Fragments of forehead and neck guard. Rijksmuseum G.M. Kam, now Museum het Valkhof, Nijmegen (NL)
Cavalry parade	Aux. Cavalry	Nijmegen (NL).	Br		Fragment of forehead fitting/application. Rijksmuseum van Oudheden, Leiden (NL)
Cavalry parade	Aux. Cavalry	Thorsberg/Nydam bog (DK)	Br		Snake motifs around back. Some weapon (?) hit marks at front. Archäologisches Landesmuseum Schleswig (D)
Cavalry parade	Aux. Cavalry	Unknown location			Pfrondorf type. Dug out with shield boss. Axel Guttmann Collection
Cavalry parade	Aux. Cavalry	Unknown location.	Ir		Weiler/Koblenz-Bubenheim. Brass-plated, tinned.
Cavalry parade	Aux. Cavalry	Unknown location.	Brass		Fragment. Remains of tinning. Columns, Mars and eagles. Axel Guttmann Collection
Cavalry parade	Aux. Cavalry	Unknown location.	Brass		Fragment of forehead guard. Remains of tinning. Hunting scene.
Cavalry parade	Aux. Cavalry	Xanten (D).	Ir		silver-plated. Rheinisches Landesmuseum, Bonn (D)
Cavalry parade	Officer	Autun	Br	1st C AD	Corinthian. large peak. Gilt. Embossed leaves. Musee Rolin, Autun
Face helmets	Cav. Sports Type A	Semandria	Br	1st C BC	helmet + mask. Archaeological Museum Belgrade
Face helmets	Cav. Sports Type B	Newstead (UK)	Br	late 1st C AD	no mask. Mus of Antiquities, Edinburgh
Face helmets	Cav. Sports Type B	Nicopolis	Br	late 1st C AD	no mask. Kunsthistorisches Museum, Vienna
Face helmets	Cav. Sports Type B	Ribchester (UK)	Br	late 1st C AD	helmet + mask. British Museum
Face helmets	Cav. Sports Type C	Aintab,Syria	Br	late 1st to 3rdAD	mask. British Museum
Face helmets	Cav. Sports Type C	Echzell Kreis Budingen (Hessen)	Ir	2nd to 3rd AD	mask. Location not known
Face helmets	Cav. Sports Type C	Hirchova	Br	2nd to 3rd AD	mask. Nat Museum of Antiquities, Bucharest
Face helmets	Cav. Sports Type C	Newstead (UK)	Ir	late 1st to 3rdAD	helmet + mask. Mus of Antiquities, Edinburgh
Face helmets	Cav. Sports Type C	Straubing (D)	Br	late 1st to 3rdAD	no mask. Straubing Museum
Face helmets	Cav. Sports Type C	Straubing (D)	Br	late 2nd to 3rd AD	4 masks. Straubing Museum
Face helmets	Cav. Sports Type C	Ubbergen (NL).	Ir	2nd to 3rd AD	Remains of silver plating. Rijksmuseum G.M. Kam, now Museum het Valkhof, Nijmegen (NL), property of Gemeente Nijmegen.
Face helmets	Cav. Sports Type C	Unknown location	Br	late 1st to 3rdAD	mask with moustache. Archaeological Museum Belgrade
Face helmets	Cav. Sports Type D	Antinupolis	Br	2nd C AD	no mask. Archaeological Museum, Berlin
Face helmets	Cav. Sports Type D	Chassenard	Ir & Br	AD 37-41	mask. Found with mail fragment. Musee des Antiquites Nationales, St Germain-en-Laye

Continental	HRR system	Find location	(Br) (Ir)	Date	Additional info (inc. curent location, if known)
Face helmets	Cav. Sports Type D	Emesa, Syria	Ir	early 1st AD	helmet + mask. Eastern style. Musee Nationale de Damas
Face helmets	Cav. Sports Type D	Kalkriese (D).	Ir	early 1st AD	Mask. Remains of silver plating. Museum Kalkriese (D)
Face helmets	Cav. Sports Type D	Mainz	Ir	2nd C AD	mask. Kunsthistorisches Museum, Vienna
Face helmets	Cav. Sports Type D	Nijmegen (NL).	Ir & Br	2nd C AD	tinned. Mask. Rijksmuseum van Oudheden, Leiden (NL)
Face helmets	Cav. Sports Type D	Nijmegen (NL).	Ir & Br	early 2nd AD	tinned. Rijksmuseum G.M. Kam, now Museum het Valkhof, Nijmegen (NL)
Face helmets	Cav. Sports Type D	Rome	Br	2nd C AD	mask. National Mus Copenhagen
Face helmets	Cav. Sports Type D	Tel Oum Hauran	Br	2nd 1/2 2nd AD	helmet + mask. Moustached. Musee Nationale de Damas
Face helmets	Cav. Sports Type D	Vechten (NL).	Ir & Br	2nd C AD	mask. Rijksmuseum van Oudheden, Leiden (NL)
Face helmets	Cav. Sports Type D	Vize, Thrace	Br	before AD 45	tinned. Simulated cheekpieces on mask. Archaeological Museum, Istanbul
Face helmets	Cav. Sports Type E	Crosby Garrett	Br	late 1st to mid 3rd AD	mask. Female
Face helmets	Cav. Sports Type E	Grafenhausen/Dietlingn	Br	2nd to 3rd AD	mask. Female. High peak of hair. Landesmuseum, Stuttgart
Face helmets	Cav. Sports Type E	Newstead (UK)	Br	late 1st to 2nd AD	mask. Mus of Antiquities, Edinburgh
Face helmets	Cav. Sports Type E	Nola, Italy	Br	late 1st to 2nd AD	mask. Female. British Museum
Face helmets	Cav. Sports Type E	River Olt, Romania	Br	2nd to 3rd AD	mask. Female. Kunsthistorisches Museum, Vienna
Face helmets	Cav. Sports Type E	Straubing (D)	Br	2nd to 3rd AD	2 masks. Female. High peak of hair. Straubing Museum
Face helmets	Cav. Sports Type F	Mainz, Stadtpark	Br	2nd C AD	2 masks. Mittelrheinisches Landemuseum, Mainz
Face helmets	Cav. Sports Type F	Ostrov, Romania	Br	2nd C AD	fragmentary.triple crested. no mask. In Romania?
Face helmets	Cav. Sports Type F	Pfrondorf	Br	late 2nd AD	helmet + mask. Landesmuseum, Stuttgart
Face helmets	Cav. Sports Type G	Brigetio, Hungary	Br	late 2nd to 3rd AD	no mask. Hungarian National Museum, Budapest
Face helmets	Cav. Sports Type G	Eisernes Thor (on Donau)	Br	late 2nd to 3rd AD	no mask. Hungarian National Museum, Budapest
Face helmets	Cav. Sports Type G	Heddernheim (D)	Br	late 2nd to 3rd AD	no mask. Museum für Vor- und Frühgeschichte, Frankfurt am Main (D).
Face helmets	Cav. Sports Type H	Aschberg	Br	3rd C AD	fragments. Dillingen Museum
Face helmets	Cav. Sports Type H	Norfolk, River Wensum (UK)	Br	3rd C AD	no mask. Norwich Museum

Continental	HRR system	Find location	(Br) (Ir)	Date	Additional info (inc. curent location, if known)
Face helmets	Cav. Sports Type H	Norfolk, River Wensum (UK)	Br	3rd C AD	Mask. Norwich Museum
Face helmets	Cav. Sports Type H	Rodez	Br	3rd C AD	Mask. Musee Fenaille, Rodez
Face helmets	Cav. Sports Type I	Chalon, River Saone	Br	3rd C AD	no mask. In Musee des Antiquites Nationales, St Germain-en-Laye
Face helmets	Cav. Sports Type I	Guisborough, Yorkshire (UK)	Br	3rd C AD	no mask. In British Museum
Face helmets	Cav. Sports Type I	Hallaton	Br	3rd C AD	no mask
Face helmets	Cav. Sports Type I	Tel Oum Hauran	Br	2nd C AD	no mask. Crushed. In Musee Nationale de Damas
Face helmets	Cav. Sports Type I	Theilenhofen (D)	Br	2nd half of 2nd C AD	no mask. Weißenburg-Gunzenhausen Prähistorische Staatssammlung, München
Face helmets	Cav. Sports Type J	Ostrov, Romania	Br	2nd 1/4 2nd AD	Tall. Like Phrygian cap. In Romania?
Face helmets	Cav. Sports	Eastern Danube region (estimated).	Ir & Brass		Axel Guttmann Collection
Face helmets	Cav. Sports	Eastern Danube Region.	Br or Brass		Resca type. Fragment. In Axel Guttmann Collection
Face helmets	Cav. Sports	Hellingen (LU).	Br		Musee National d'Art et d'Histoire Luxembourg
Face helmets	Cav. Sports	Thorsberg/Nydam bog (DK).	Silver		Crown/ ‚spangen' cap. In Archäologisches Landesmuseum Schleswig (D)
Face helmets	Cav. Sports	Thorsberg/Nydam bog (DK).	Silver		Reworked by ancient German craftsmen. In Archäologisches Landesmuseum Schleswig (D)
Face helmets	Cav. Sports	Unknown location. (possibly Bulgaria).	Ir		Very similar to AG 449. In Axel Guttmann Collection
Late Roman ridge helmets		Augsburg (D).	Ir	4th C AD	Heavy' Berkasovo-type. silver and gold-plated. Germanisches Nationalmuseum Nürnberg (D), / Prähistorische Staatssammlung (K).
Late Roman ridge helmets		Deurne (NL).	Ir	4th C AD	'Heavy' Berkasovo-type. 4 part bowl. silver and gold-plated. Rijksmuseum van Oudheden, Leiden (NL)
Late Roman ridge helmets		Burgh Castle	Ir	4th C AD	Heavy Berkasovo-type. 4 part bowl
Late Roman ridge helmets		Conçesti	Ir	4th C AD	Heavy Berkasovo-type. 4 part bowl
Late Roman ridge helmets		Berkasovo (1)	Ir	4th C AD	Heavy Berkasovo-type. 4 part bowl
Late Roman ridge helmets		Berkasovo (2)	Ir	4th C AD	Heavy Berkasovo-type. bipartite bowl
Late Roman ridge helmets		Budapest	Ir	4th C AD	Heavy Berkasovo-type. bipartite bowl
Late Roman ridge helmets		Intercisa (1)	Ir	4th C AD	Simple' Intercisa-type. Bipartite bowl. With crest
Late Roman ridge helmets		Intercisa (2)	Ir	4th C AD	Simple Intercisa-type. Bipartite bowl
Late Roman ridge helmets		Intercisa (3)	Ir	4th C AD	Simple Intercisa-type. Bipartite bowl
Late Roman ridge helmets		Intercisa (4)	Ir	4th C AD	Simple Intercisa-type. Bipartite bowl
Late Roman ridge helmets		Trier	Ir	4th C AD	Simple Intercisa-type. Bipartite bowl
Late Roman ridge helmets		Augst	Ir	4th C AD	Simple Intercisa-type. Bipartite bowl
Late Roman ridge helmets		Worms	Ir	4th C AD	Simple Intercisa-type. Bipartite bowl

Continental	HRR system	Find location	(Br) (Ir)	Date	Additional info (inc. curent location, if known)
Late Roman ridge helmets		Augsberg-Pfersee (1)	Ir	4th C AD	Simple Intercisa-type. Bipartite bowl. With nasal guard. Traces of silver sheathing
Late Roman ridge helmets		Augsberg-Pfersee (2)	Ir	4th C AD	Simple Intercisa-type. Bipartite bowl. With nasal guard. Traces of silver sheathing
Late Roman ridge helmets		Richborough (1)	Ir	4th C AD	Simple Intercisa-type. Bipartite bowl. Fragmentary
Late Roman ridge helmets		Richborough (2)	Ir	4th C AD	Simple Intercisa-type. Bipartite bowl. Fragmentary
Late Roman ridge helmets		Richborough (3)	Ir	4th C AD	Simple Intercisa-type. Bipartite bowl. Fragmentary
Late Roman ridge helmets		Richborough (4)	Ir	4th C AD	Simple Intercisa-type. Bipartite bowl. Fragmentary
Late Roman spangenhelm		Der-el-Medineh, Egypt	Ir	mid 3rd AD	Radial construction: 6 plate & 6 ribs. Berkasovo-type cheek pieces. Nasal guard.
Late Roman spangenhelm		Egypt	Ir	mid 3rd AD	Radial construction: 4 plate & 4 wide ribs. Narrow cheek pieces. No neck or nasal guard. Rijksmuseum van Oudheden, Leiden (NL)

BIBLIOGRAPHY

ANCIENT SOURCES

Ammianus Marcellinus, *Histories*, trans. J. C. Rolfe, 3 vols (Loeb Classic Library, 1935–40).

Anonymous, *De rebus bellicis*, trans. E. A. Thompson (Oxford, 1952).

Anonymous, *Notitia Dignitatum*, ed. O. Seeck (Berlin, 1876).

Anonymous, *Scriptores Historiae Augustae*, trans. A. Birley, as *Lives of the Later Caesars* (Penguin Classics, 1976).

Apollonius of Rhodes, *Argonautica*, trans. R. C. Seaton (Loeb Classic Library, 1912).

Aristotle, *On Marvellous Things Heard*, trans. W. S. Hett (Loeb Classic Library, 1936).

Arrian, *Ars tactica*, trans. P. A. Brunt (Loeb Classic Library, 1976–83).

Cassius Dio, *Roman History*, trans. I. Scott-Kilvert, as *The Roman History: the Reign of Augustus* (Penguin Classics, 1988).

Cicero, *pro Rabirio Perduellionis Reo 20*, trans. H. G. Hodge (Loeb Classic Library).

Cicero, *pro Sestio, in Vatinium B. Orations*, trans. R. Gardner (Loeb Classic Library no. 309, 1958).

Diodorus Siculus, *Library of History, Books III–VIII* trans. C. H. Oldfather (Loeb Classic Library, Volumes 303 and 340, 1935).

Dionysius of Halicarnassus, *Roman Antiquities* (from Rich, J. 2007. 'Warfare and the Army in Early Rome', *A Companion to the Roman Army*, ed. P. Erdkamp, Oxford).

Heliodorus, *Aethiopica*, trans. I. Bekker (1855).

Hyginus, *Fabulae de munitionibus castrorum*, trans. P. K. Marshall (Leipzig, 1993).

Josephus, *bellum Iudaicum*, trans. H. St J. Thackerey, R. Marcus, A Wikgren & L. H. Feldman, as *The Jewish War* (Loeb Classic Library, 1926–65).

Julius Caesar, *Bellum Civile*, trans. J. F. Mitchell, as *The Civil War* (Penguin Classics, 1967).

Julius Caesar, *Bellum Gallium* (Gallic Wars), trans. S. A. Handford, as *The Conquest of Gaul* (Penguin Classics, 1976).

Livy, *Books I–V*, trans. A. de Selincourt, as *The Early History of Rome from its foundation* (Penguin Classics, 1969).

Livy, *Books VI–X*, trans. B. Radice, as *Rome and Italy* (Penguin Classics, 1982).

Livy, *Books XXI–XXX*, trans. A. de Selincourt, as *The War with Hannibal* (Penguin Classics, 1972).

Livy, *Books XXXI–XLV*, trans. H. Bettenson, as *Rome and the Mediterranean* (Penguin Classics, 1976).

Maurice, *Strategikon: Handbook of Byzantine Military strategy*, trans. G. T. Dennis (University of Pennsylvania Press, 1984).

Pausanias, *Books I–X*, trans. W. H. Jones & H. A. Ormerod, 4 vols (Loeb Classic Library, 1918–35).

Pliny the Elder, *Natural History*, trans. H. Rackham and others, 10 vols (Loeb Classic Library, 1938–67).

Plutarch, *Camillus*, Vol. II, trans. B. Perrin (Loeb Classic Library, 1914).

Plutarch, *Coriolanus, F. Maximus, Marcellus, Cato the elder, T & G Gracchus, Sertorius, Brutus, M. Anthony*, trans. I. Scott-Kilvert, as *Makers of Rome* (Penguin Classics, 1965).

Plutarch, *Marius, Sulla, Crassus, Pompey, Caesar, Cicero*, trans. R. Warner, as *Fall of the Roman Republic* (Penguin Classics, 1972).

Polybius, *Histories*, trans. I. Scott-Kilvert, as *The Rise of the Roman Empire* (Penguin Classics, 1979).
Sallust, *Bellum Iugurthinum & Catilinae Coniuratio*, trans. S. A. Handford, as *Jugurthine War, Conspiracy of Catilene* (Penguin Classics, 1970).
Tarruntenus Paternus, *Digesta: Corpus Iuris Civilis* (ed. T. Mommsen, vol. 1, Berlin, 1872).
Tacitus, *Annales*, trans. M. Grant, as *The Annals of Imperial Rome* (Penguin Classics, 1973).
Historiae, trans. K. Wellesley, as *The Histories* (Penguin Classics, 1972).
Theophrastus, *De Lapidibus*, ed. D. E. Gichholy (Loeb Classic Library, 1965).
Valerius Maximus, *Books I–V*, vol. I, trans. D. R. Shackleton (Loeb Classic Library, 2000).
Valerius Maximus, *Books VI-IX*, vol. II, trans. J. Henderson (Loeb Classic Library, 2000).
Vegetius, *epitoma rei militaris*, trans. N. P. Milner, as *Epitome of Military Science (*Liverpool University Press, 1993).
Xenophon. *Hell.*, 'Hellenica', 2; 4; and 6.
Xenophon. *Lac. Pol.*, 'Lacedemoneion Politeia', 11.5–10.
Xenophon. *Mem.*, 'Memorabilia', 3.12.

MODERN SOURCES

Addyman, P. V., Pearson, N. & D. Tweddle, 1982. 'The Coppergate Helmet', *Antiquity*, I. VI, pp. 189–94.
Anglim, S., Jestice, P. G., Rice, S., Rusch, S. M. & J. Serrati, 2002. *Fighting Techniques of the Ancient World*, Kent.
Bidwell, P. 2001. 'A probable Roman shipwreck on the Herd Sand at South Shields', *The Arbeia Journal Volume 6–7 1997–98*, South Shields.
Bidwell, P. 1997. *Roman Forts in Britain*, English Heritage, London.
Birley, A. R. 2007. 'Making Emperors. Imperial Instrument or Independent Force?', *A Companion to the Roman Army*, ed. P. Erdkamp, Oxford, pp. 379–94.
Birley, R. 1977. *Vindolanda, A Roman Frontier Post on Hadrian's Wall*, London.
Bishop, M. C. 1985. *Proceedings of the First Roman Military Equipment Conference*, ed. M. C. Bishop, BAR International Series, Oxford.
Bishop, M. C. 1989a. 'Belt fittings in Buxton Museum', *Arma*, Vol. 1.1.
Bishop, M. C. & J. C. N Coulston, 1993. *Roman Military Equipment from the Punic Wars to the fall of Rome.* London.
Bishop, M. C. & J. C. N. Coulston, 2006. *Roman Military Equipment from the Punic Wars to the Fall of Rome*, 2nd Edition, Oxford.
Braat, W. C. *et al.* 1973. Der Fund von Deurne, Holland', in Klumbach, *Spätrömische Gardehelme*, pp. 51–83.
Broadhead, W. 2007. 'Colonization, Land Distribution, & Veteran Settlement', *A Companion to the Roman Army*, ed. P. Erdkamp, Oxford, pp. 148–163.
Bruce-Mitford, R. L. S. 1978. 'The Sutton Hoo Ship Burial', *Arms Armour and Regalia*, Volume 2, London, pp. 138–231.
Bunz, K. & W. Spickermann, 2006. KALKRIESE, Die Örtlichkeit der Varusschlacht, Ein studentisches Projekt an der Universität Osnabrück, http://www.geschichte.uni-osnabrueck.de/projekt, 5.12.2006.
Burns, M. 2003. *The Homogenisation of Military Equipment under the Roman Republic*, Institute of Archaeology, University College London, in 'Romanization?', Digressus Supplement 1, pp. 60–85, http://www.digressus.org.
Cagniart, P. 2007. 'The Late Republican Army', *A Companion to the Roman Army*, ed. P. Erdkamp, Oxford, pp. 80–95
Campbell, B. 2000. *The Roman Army 31BC – AD337, a source book*, London.
Cary, M. & H. Scullard, 1979. *A History of Rome*, 3rd edition, London.
Cerutti, S. M. & Richardson, L. 1989, 'The Retiarius Tunicatus of Suetonius, Juvenal, and Petronius' *American Journal of Philology*, 110, 589–594.
Champion, T. & C. Gamble, S. Shennon, A. Whittle, 1984. *Prehistoric Europe*, London.
Cichorius, C. 1896. *Die Reliefs der Traianssäule*, vol. ii (1896), vol. iii (1900), Berlin.

Connolly, P. 1975. *The Roman Army*, London.
Connolly, P. 1977. *The Greek Armies*, London.
Connolly, P. 1978. *Hannibal & the enemies of Rome*, London.
Connolly, P. 1981. *Greece & Rome at war*, London.
Connolly, P. 2000. 'The reconstruction and use of Roman weaponry in the second century BC', *Journal of Roman Military Equipment Studies (Re-enactment as Research), Proceedings of the Twelfth International Roman Military Equipment Conference, South Shields, 1999*, Vol. 11, Armatura Press, pp. 43–46.
Cottrell, L. 1992. *Hannibal Enemy of Rome*, New York.
Couissin, P. 1926. *Les Armes Romaines*, Paris.
Coulston, J. C. N. 1995. 'Sculpture of an armoured figure at Alba Iulia, Romania', *Arma*, Vol. 7, pp. 13–17.
Curle, J. 1911. *Newstead: 'A Roman Frontier Post and its People'*, Glasgow
Davies, O. 1935. *Roman mines in Europe*, Oxford.
Davies, P. J. E. 1997. 'The Politics of Perpetuation: Trajan's Column and the Art of Commemoration', *American Journal of Archaeology*, Vol. 101, pp. 41–65.
Dittmann, K. H. 1940. 'Ein Eiserne Spangenhelm in Kairo', *Germania*, XXIV, pp. 54–58.
Ebert, M. 1909. 'Ein Spangenhelm aus Ägypten', *Prähistorische Zeitschrift*, I, pp. 163–170.
Fagan, B. 2004. *The Seventy Great Inventions of the Ancient World*, London.
Feugère, M. 2002. *Weapons of the Romans*, Stroud.
Fields, N. 2011. *Early Roman Warrior 753–321 BC*, Warrior 156, Osprey, Oxford.
Forsythe, G. 2007. 'The Army & Centuriate Organization in Early Rome', *A Companion to the Roman Army*, ed. P. Erdkamp, Oxford, pp. 24–42.
Franzius, G. 1995. 'Die Römische Funde Aus Kalkriese 1987–95', *Proceedings of the International Roman Military Equipment Conference*, JRMES, Vol. 6, pp. 69–88.
Fulford, M. & D. Sim, A. Doig, 2004. 'The production of Roman ferrous armour: a metallographic survey of material from Britain, Denmark, Germany, and its implications', *Journal of Roman Archaeology*, Vol. 17, pp. 197–220.
Futrell, A. 1997, *Blood in the Arena: The Spectacle of Roman Power*, Texas, 34.
Gilliver, C. M. 2007. 'The Augustan Reform & the Structure of the Imperial Army', *A Companion to the Roman Army*, ed. P. Erdkamp, Oxford, pp. 180–200.
Godfrey E. & M. van Nie, 2004. 'Germanic ultrahigh carbon steel punch of the Late Roman-Iron Age', *Journal of Archaeological Science*, Vol. 31, Issue 8, pp. 1117–1125.
Goldsworthy, A. 2003. *The Complete Roman Army*, London.
Hanson, W. S. & C. M. Daniels, J. N. Dore, J. P. Gillam, 1979. 'The Agricolan Supply Base at Red House, Corbridge', *Archaeologia Aeliana*, 5th Series, Vol. VII, Society of Antiquaries, Newcastle upon Tyne.
Healy, J. F. 1978. *Mining and metallurgy in the Greek and Roman world*. London.
Hill, J. D, 2012. 'Finishing a 3D, 2000 year old Roman jigsaw puzzle: the Hallaton helmet unveiled', British Museum Blog,
(http://blog.britishmuseum.org/2012/01/10/finishing-a-3d-2000–year-old-roman-jigsaw-puzzle-the-hallaton-helmet-unveiled/', January 10 2012 – 3.27pm.
Hoyos, D. 2007. 'The Age of Overseas Expansion', *A Companion to the Roman Army*, ed. P. Erdkamp, Oxford, pp. 63–79.
Iriarte, A. 1996. 'Reconstructing the iron core of the Deurne Helmet', *Journal of Roman Military Equipment Studies*, JRMES Vol. 7, pp. 51–57.
Izquierdo, P. & J. M. Solias Aris, 2000. *Two Bronze helmets of Etruscan typology from a Roman wreck*, Nordic Underwater Archaeology.
Jacobelli, L. 2003. *Gladiators at Pompeii*, trans. M. Becker, Los Angeles.
James, S. 1986. 'Evidence from Dura Europos for the origins of Late Roman helmets', *Syria*, Tome 63, fascicule 1–2, pp. 107–134.
James, S. 1988. The *fabricae*: state arms factories of the Later Roman Empire, *Military Equipment and the Identity of Roman Soldiers, Proceedings of 4th Roman Military Equipment Conference* (ROMEC), ed. J. C. Coulston, BAR International Series 394, Oxford, pp. 257–331.
James, S. 2004. *Excavations at Dura Europos 1928–1937, Final Report VII*, British Museum Press.

Jazdzewska, M. 1986. 'A Roman Legionary Helmet found in Poland', *Gladius*, XVII, pp. 57–62.

Johnson, J. S. 1980. 'A Late Roman Ridge Helmet from Burgh Castle', *Britannia* XI, pp. 303–312.

Junkelmann, M. 1986. *Die Legionen des Augustus. Der römische Soldat im archäologischen Experiment*, Mainz.

Junkelmann, M. 1999. 'Roman Helmets in the Axel Guttmann Collection, Berlin', *Proceedings of the Eleventh International Roman Military Equipment Conference, Mainz, 1998*, JRMES Vol. 10.

Junkelmann, M. 2000. *Römische Helme*, Band VIII, Axel Guttmann Collection, Mainz.

Junkelmann, M. 2000a. 'Familia Gladiatoria: 'The Heroes of the Amphitheatre'', *The Power of Spectacle in Ancient Rome: Gladiators and Caesars*, ed. E. Köhne & C. Ewigleben, London, 59–63.

Junkelmann, M. 2000b. *Das Spiel mit dem Tod. So kämpften Roms Gladiatoren.* Mainz.

Junkelmann, M. 2000c. 'Gladiatorial and military equipment and fighting technique: a comparison', *Journal for Roman Military Equipment Studies* (JRMES) II, pp. 113–117.

Keppie, L. 1998. *The Making of the Roman Army from Republic to Empire*, London.

Kimmig, W. 1940. 'Ein Keltenschild aus Agypten', *Germania* 24, pp. 106–111.

Klumbach, H. 1973. *Spätrömische Gardehelme.* Munich.

Klumbach, H. 1974. *Römische Helme aus Niedergermanien.* Rheinland, Cologne.

Köhne, E. & Ewigleben, C. 2000, *The Power of Spectacle in Ancient Rome: Gladiators and Caesars*, London.

Künzl, E. 1997. Waffendekor in Hellenismus', *Journal for Roman Military Equipment Studies*, JRMES Vol. 8, pp. 68–82.

Lancaster, L. 1998. 'Building Trajan's Markets', *American Journal of Archaeology*, Vol. 102, pp. 283–308.

Lancaster, L. 1999. 'Building Trajan's Column', *American Journal of Archaeology*, Vol. 103, pp. 419 – 439.

Le Bohec, Y. 2001. *The Imperial Roman Army*, London.

Le Glay, M. & J. L. Voisin, Y. Le Bohec, 2005. *A History of Rome*, 3rd Edition, trans. A. Nevill, additional material by D. Cherry & D. G. Kyle, Oxford.

Lepper, F. & S. Frere, 1988. *Trajan's Column. A New Edition of the Cichorius Plates*, Gloucester.

Lewis, M. J. T. 1997. *Millstone and hammer: the origins of water power*, London, p. 111.

Lucie-Smith, E. 1971. *A Concise History of French Painting*, London.

Luttwark, E. 1999. *The Grand Strategy of the Roman Empire: from the 1st century AD to the third*, London.

Lyne, M. 1994. 'Late Roman helmet fragments from Richborough', *Journal of Roman Military Equipment Studies*, JRMES Vol. 5, pp 97–105.

May, T. 1922. *The Roman Forts at Templeborough near Rotherham.* Rotherham.

Mihaljević, M. & Dizdar, M. 2007, 'Late La Tène Bronze Helmet from the River Sava near Stara Gradiška', *VAMZ*, 3.s, XL pp. 117–146.

Negin, A. E. 1998. 'Sarmatian Cataphracts as prototypes for Roman Equites Cataphractarii', *Journal for Roman Military Equipment Studies* (JRMES) 9, pp. 71–74.

Paddock, J. 1985. 'Some changes in the manufacture and supply of Roman Bronze helmets under the Late Republic and Early Empire', *The Production & Distribution of Roman Military Equipment, Proceedings of 2nd Roman Military Equipment Conference* (ROMEC), ed. M. C. Bishop, BAR International Series 275, Oxford.

Paterson, T. 2007. 'Glue used by the Romans has stuck around for 2,000 years', *The Independent*, http://news.independent.co.uk/europe/article3226417.ece, 08/12/07.

Quesada Sanz, F. 1997. 'Montefortino-type and related helmets in the Iberian Peninsula', *Journal of Roman Military Equipment Studies* 8, pp. 151–166.

Rawlings, L. 2007. 'Army & Battle during the conquest of Italy (350–264 BC)', *A Companion to the Roman Army*, ed. P. Erdkamp, Oxford, pp. 45–62.

Rich, J. 2007. 'Warfare and the Army in Early Rome', *A Companion to the Roman Army*, ed. P. Erdkamp, Oxford, pp. 7–23.

Richmond, I. A. 1967. 'Adamklissi', *Papers of the British School at Rome*, Vol. XXXV, pp. 34–35.

Richmond, I. A. 1982. *Trajan's Army on Trajan's Column*, London.

Rosenstein, N. 2007. 'Military Command, Political Power & the Republican Elite', *A Companion to the Roman Army*, ed. P. Erdkamp, Oxford, pp. 132–147.
Rossi, L. 1971. *Trajan's Column and the Dacian Wars*, trans. JMC Toynbee, New York.
Russell-Robinson, H. 1975. *The Armour of Imperial Rome*, London.
Schoppa, H. 1961. *Die Funde aus dem Vicus des Steinkastells Hofheim*. Wiesbaden.
Scullard, H. H. 1970. *From the Gracchi to Nero, A History of Rome from 133BC to AD68*, London.
Sim, D. 2005. Presentation at the Carlisle Millennium Conference.
Southern, P. 1988. 'The Numeri of the Roman Imperial Army', *Britannia*, Vol 10, pp. 81–140.
Southern, P. & Dixon, K. R. 1996. *The Late Roman Army*, London, pp 91–96.
Stary, P. F. 1979. 'Keltische Waffen auf der Apennin-Halbinsel', *Germania* 57, pp. 90–110.
Stephenson, I. P. 1999. *Roman Infantry Equipment – The Later Empire*, Stroud.
Stephenson I. P. & K. R. Dixon, 2003. *Roman Cavalry Equipment*, Stroud.
Stiebel, G. D. & J. Magness, 2007. 'The Military Equipment from Masada', *Masada VIII The Yigael Yadin Excavations 1963–1965 Final Reports*, Jerusalem, pp 1–94.
Thomas, M. 2001. 'Roman Military Headgear',
www.hmforum/articles/mikethomas/romanheadgear/romanheadgear.htm, 02/02/01
Thomas, M. 2003. *Lorica Segmentata* Vol. II, JRMES, Armatura Press.
Travis, J. R. 2008. *Coal in Roman Britain*, Bar British Series 468.
Tweddle, D. 1984. *The Coppergate Helmet*, York.
Tylecote, R. F. 1986. *The prehistory of metallurgy in the British Isles*, The Institute of Metals. London.
Van Wees, 2004. (from Rich, J. 2007. 'Warfare and the Army in Early Rome', *A Companion to the Roman Army*, ed. P. Erdkamp, Oxford).
Völling, T. 1997. 'Römische Militaria in Griechenland: ein uberblick', *Journal of Roman Military Equipment Studies*, JRMES Vol. 8, 1997, pp. 91–103.
Warry, J. 1980. *Warfare in the Classical World*, London.
Webster, G. 1998. *The Roman Imperial Army of the first and second centuries AD*, 3rd Edition, London.
Willems, W. J. H. 1992. 'Roman Face Masks from the Kops Plateau, Nijmegen, The Netherlands', *Journal of Roman Military Equipment Studies*, JRMES Vol. 3, pp 57–66.
Wisdom, S. 2001. *Gladiators 100BC-AD200*, Osprey Warrior, 39, Oxford.
Wood, M. 1981. *In Search of the Dark Ages*, London.
Woolley, L. 1976. *The Great Archaeologists*, ed. E. Bacon, Illustrated London News, London.
Worrell, S. *et al.* 2011, 'The Crosby Garret Roman Helmet', *British Archaeology*, Jan/Feb 2011, York, 20–27.
Zotti, N. 2006. *La Situla della Certosa*, www.warfare.it/tattiche/situla_certosa.html, 10/12/06.

INDEX